History-Fiction Interface
in
Indian English Novel

History-Fiction Interface in Indian English Novel

Mulk Raj Anand

Nayantara Sahgal

Salman Rushdie

Shashi Tharoor

O.V. Vijayan

T. N. DHAR

PRESTIGE

Published by
Prestige Books
3/28, East Patel Nagar
New Delhi 110 008

1999

ISBN: 81-7551-059-5

Photo Typesetting by
Pivot Computers
Delhi 110 006
Ph. 3981867

Printed at
Dhawan Industries Offset
New Delhi 110 028

Contents

Preface

From among the various literary forms, the novel's connection with history has been the closest; it has steadily grown over time in its range and complexity. In the West, in its early phase, the novel established its base by imitating history; in its middle phase, that is when it consolidated its position as a powerful and popular genre, it made massive use of history by incorporating within the fictional frame a large number of actual social, political, and cultural events and happenings; in its most recent phase, that is after it survived a crisis of existence in the early decades of the present century, it has not only kept up with the practices of the nineteenth century, but also interrogated and problematized the discourse of history. This constant enhancement in the nature and scope of the novelist's engagement with history had its effect on the historians too. From the novelists, they learnt over time to widen the range and scope of their subject matter, to choose appropriate modes of presentation, and the need to cultivate an effective style of writing.

The active involvement of the novelist with history drew the attention of various men of learning—philosophers, historians, and different kinds of academic critics—from time to time, to formulate the connection between the novel and history in some kind of a theoretical frame. Its early result was the popularization of the generic category of the historical novel which, in course of time, came to be used as a critical category to explain and evaluate the history-fiction connection in very specific terms. Although it has gone through several expansions from Manzoni to Turner, it has never proved adequate for understanding and assessing the whole range of the novelist's fascinating engagement with history, which has acquired more complex edges during the last several decades. Because of this, most of our modern-day critics have chosen to study the history-novel connection within the theoretical frames of postmodernism and post-colonialism. The latter has particularly been used for studying the use of history by the novelists of the erstwhile colonies.

Moving away from these inhibiting and limiting categories, the present study examines the history-fiction connection within a more open framework. It concentrates on the actual practice of the Indian English novelists, and focusses on how they deal with the social, political, and cultural past of their country, the kind of self-consciousness which informs their use of such details, their choice of narrative procedures, their modes of characterization, as also their overall fictional style. The choice of novelists—Anand, Sahgal, Rushdie, Tharoor, and Vijayan—has been governed more by considerations of illustrating the variety in the novelists' use of history than by personal preference.

A substantial part of this work was completed at the Indian Institute of Advanced Study, Shimla. I am thankful to the Institute for awarding me a Fellowship and to then-Director Prof. J S Grewal for his kindness and consideration during the course of my stay there.

The early drafts of this work were read and commented upon by several people from different disciplines. I have greatly benefited from their criticisms and advice; some responses were so diverse and conflicting that I had to do a bit of tightrope walking to hold them in balance. I am grateful to Romila Thapar, Nirmal Singh, Karuna Goswamy, Badri Raina and Ajit Bhattacharjea for their extremely valuable comments on the first two chapters of the book, which deal with theoretical, methodological, and historical issues related to history-fiction interface, and to R K Kaul, Jaidev, and N K Jain for their careful reading of the entire manuscript. C K Raju cheerfully looked after the preparation of the manuscript for the publisher, for which I am thankful to him.

The work was done during some of the most stressful years of my life, when I had to live away from my home in Srinagar, Kashmir. I am thankful to a large number of friends and relatives who kept me going, particularly to my wife Usha Kiran and my children Vasudha and Vikram for their unstinted support.

Chapter I

Towards an Understanding of History-Fiction Nexus

> Man, in a word, has no nature; what he has is…history. Expressed differently: what nature is to things, history, *res gestea*, is to man.
>
> Jose Ortega y Gasset (217)

Both as a record of actual social life and a discipline which describes and analyzes events and characters which figure in it, history has become increasingly unstable and problematic.[1] Debates on its ontological and epistemological status have reached a fevered pitch. Even professional historians and philosophers of history no longer vouch for history and history-writing with the kind of assurance with which they did until not too long ago. In spite of this, it still remains true that man's very being is intimately connected with history. Even though the mode of representing and understanding it has become problematic in recent times, his knowledge of himself and the world he inhabits continues to be largely shaped and very often conditioned by his understanding of what it was like in the past.[2]

On account of the deep-rooted connection between man and his past, almost all disciplines of knowledge which developed during the course of human evolution have had a close link with history. This eventually prompted the writing of histories of all branches of knowledge in the nineteenth century, for providing a mechanism for consolidating and controlling whatever man had learnt over time. History's connection with literature too is fairly well-known (See Bremner). From among the various literary forms, the novel's connection with history has been the closest and had most far-reaching cultural consequences.[3] There has been evidence of this as early as when the novel was in the process of acquiring a distinct identity of its own. The growing connection between the two had a mutual bearing on their changing shape and content, which shall be dealt with in some detail in Chapter II. Here I would only like to state that the novelist's active involvement with history stimulated the use and popularization of the generic category of the 'historical novel'; in course of time, it also gained currency as a critical category, for explaining and evaluating history-fiction connection in very specific terms.

There already exist quite a number of interpretations and studies of the 'historical novel.'[4] Some have proved quite influential, so much so that the term is still being used as a critical and evaluative category. However, as a term which describes, analyzes, and evaluates the connection between history and fiction, it has never had a consistent meaning; in fact, its meaning and scope has changed with every new user. Because of this, it has been used somewhat vaguely and imprecisely.[5] This has led to critical confusion, and novelists have felt shy of using it in connection with their work.[6] I shall briefly examine some selected expositions of the term which have been put forth by critics from time to time to point out how adequate or otherwise they can be for understanding and evaluating the whole range of history-fiction interface from the past to the present. This will be followed by a short analysis of its use by contemporary Indian English critics, for explaining the Indian English novelists' interest in and use of history.

Written around the middle of the nineteenth century in Italian, Allesandro Manzoni's essay on the historical novel is one of the earliest attempts at expounding and commenting on the assumptions underlying the nature and scope of history-fiction connection. Manzoni did not consider the term a happy one, because he thought that by its very definition, historical novel represented a false genre and failed to satisfy the basic expectations of its readers. Being a mix of "things that occurred and things that have been invented, two different objects of two different, fully contrary, sorts of belief" (70), such novels did not help the readers to distinguish between the factual and the invented. Since these novels combined promiscuously invented actions and people with the actual events and people of a particular time and place, Manzoni held that they were neither informed with a sense of purpose nor could they be valuable.

Though Manzoni is unequivocal in stating that the term 'historical novel' is inappropriate and its use both unfortunate and misleading, the reasons given by him are not quite relevant in the context of the present thinking on the connection between history and fiction. His appeal is to expectations which may have been weighty during his time, but are not relevant now: the boundary between history and fiction is no longer water-tight or fixed. I concede that the use of the term for describing and assessing the novelist's interest in history is not helpful;[7]—in fact, that is the main argument of my discussion—but my reasons are different. Nor can we support Manzoni's inference that the novelist's use of history is purposeless. This is true neither of the novelists of the past nor of the present; neither in the West, nor in the Third World. However, Manzoni did alert us to the possibility that as a generic category 'historical novel' can be confusing. It can promote expectations and encourage critical practices which are limiting and inhibiting.

Georg Lukacs's *The Historical Novel* was first published in the late thirties. In the preface to the English edition of 1960, Lukacs wrote that his book was a part of his larger concern, of making "a theoretical examination of the interaction between the historical spirit and the great genres of literature which portray the totality of history" in the context of "bourgeois literature" (13). He, thus, clarifies at the very start that his conception of this novel is located within a specifically-postulated relationship between artistic forms and socio-historical transformations. Since he sees this relationship in a state of continuous change, he documents changes in the fortune of this novel too "to show how the historical novel in its origin, development, rise and decline follows inevitably upon the great social transformations of modern times" (17). This gives his study the orientation of a historical essay which traces the rise and fall of the phenomenon of the 'historical novel.'

Since the keyword in Lukacs's formulations is "theoretical," it is necessary that we pay attention to his theoretical stance on history and its representation. He believes that a historical novel can come to life only in a specific social and ideological setting; history itself is seen as a kind of mass experience, which offers "concrete possibilities for men to comprehend their own existence as something historically conditioned, for them to see in history something which deeply affects their daily lives and immediately concerns them" (24). This experience has links with social transformations and people's awareness of their relationship with national and world history. Lukacs visualizes the life of humanity as a historical process in the Hegelian sense, and a true historical novel as one which comes into its own by virtue of portraying artistically the rising tide of awareness of man's location in time, conditioned by social and economic development. For this a historical novelist does not need "the re-telling of great historical events," but concentrate on "the poetic awakening of the people who figured in those events. What matters is that we should reexperience the social and human motives which led men to think, feel and act just as they did in historical reality" (42).

Although for many of us the interest of the novelist in history begins right from the time novels came to be written, for Lukacs, because of his very specific understanding of the historical process, it is exemplified in the work of Walter Scott; the novelists who preceded him could not individuate their characters on the basis of the "historical peculiarity of their age." By combining the "laws of epic poetry" with "creative principles of the great English writers of the eighteenth century," Scott produced what Lukacs calls a true historical novel, which "demonstrate[s] by artistic means that historical circumstances and characters existed in precisely such and such a way" (43). His novels, therefore, succeed in "reflecting historical reality adequately, without either romantically monumentalizing the important figures of history or dragging them down to the level of private, psychological trivia" (47).

Lukacs's praise for Scott's method is directly connected with his specific theoretical position on history and its representation which combines the insights of Hegel and Marx. At one point, he states it plainly: "What in Morgan, Marx and Engels was worked out and proved with theoretical and historical clarity, lives, moves and has its being poetically in the best historical novels of Scott" (56). On account of his successful delineation of the most significant aspects of the historical process, Lukacs justifies and praises even those aspects of Scott's fiction, which have been censured by critics, especially his choice of mediocre, prosaic heroes as central figures of his narratives (Craig 198-99). Lukacs also condones factual errors in his novels, because he thinks that for "historical faithfulness" it "matters little whether individual details, individual facts are historically correct or not" (59).

It is quite understandable that with a pre-determined model of historical process and its representation, only some novelists could fit into the Luckacsian schema. Without questioning its twin bases, I shall restrict myself to pointing out its shortcomings as a workable concept. Its main limitation is that it fails to accommodate all those novels which are concerned with history in a significant way, because they do not fulfill the conditions which Lukacs considers essential for historical novels. He himself admits that he had to leave several European novels of the seventeenth and eighteenth centuries from his account because he thought them historical only in their choice of theme or their costumery. At the same time, he did not hesitate to include the works of lesser writers, merely because they met the requirements of his theoretical standpoint. Since he considered a true historical novel as one which "provided a concrete prehistory of the present [and] portrayed the evolution of the people through the crisis of the past up to the present" (296), he found that it virtually disappeared after the upheavals of 1848. After that time, there was no prehistory to the present, which meant that the historian proceeded "from the belief that the fundamental structure of the past is economically and ideologically the same as that of the present." Because of this, he thinks that even Flaubert and Maupassant, whose links with history have been commented upon by several critics,[8] could hardly be called historical novelists. In fact, in their hands "it degenerate[d] into a collection of episodes. There is no connection between the exclusively private individual experiences of characters and historical events. The characters cease to be really historical; the historical events become external and exotic, a merely decorative backdrop" (206).

I concede there is a great deal of merit in Lukacs's estimation of Scott who, as I shall point out in my next chapter, occupies an important place in the evolution of history-fiction nexus. Lukacs also provides insight into the evolving relationship between the rise of artistic genres and changes in social and economic milieu. But his concept of the 'historical novel,' though invoked by critics even now, is restrictive, mainly because of self-imposed exclusions. By setting up *a priori* criteria, he disregards a great mass of novels which are seriously involved with history. In fact, when

Lukacs speaks of the decline of the historical novel after 1848, he implicitly admits that the genre is no more than a historical phenomenon. If we consider historical novel as a genre peculiar only to a certain period, which was amenable to its growth, then we automatically delimit its usefulness as a critical category.[9] Nevertheless, it remains true that the Lukacsian spirit and sense of history is evident in many Indian and non-Indian novels. But one does not need to postulate it in terms of ideological pre-conditions, nor would it be realistic to insist that this is the only way in which the novelist can deal with history.

A more comprehensive exposition of the term has been provided by Avrom Fleishman, who brings within its fold a large number of British novelists of the nineteenth century, including the ones Lukacs excluded. Guided mostly by what he considers popular practice and acceptability, he specifies a number of conditions that a historical novel should satisfy. First, it should be "set in the past—beyond an arbitrary number of years, say 40-60 (two generations)"; second, its "plot must include a number of 'historical' events, particularly those in the public sphere (war, politics, economic change, etc.)" (3); and third, it must at least have one historically 'real' person in it. Considering that novelists usually situate their fiction in a recognizable, even historically-identifiable, background, which means weaving into it realistic details in respect of places, peoples, and events, the last condition assumes vital significance. Perhaps conscious of the privileged position he bestows on it, Fleishman clinches his discussion with a terse, final statement: "When life is seen in the context of history, we have a novel; when the novel's characters live in the same world with historical persons, we have a historical novel" (4). The inclusion of a historical person, therefore, acquires key importance in maintaining novel's specific links with history.

Fleishman also discusses some theoretical issues related to the points of convergence between fiction and history by invoking the names of Collingwood, Gallie, and Dilthey. He concludes his discussion by stating that genuine historical fiction is a product of the "historical imagination" which is synthetic in nature: "it unifies disparates, creating an order from the vertiginous kaleidoscope of temporal experience" (14). Fleishman's theory, like Manzoni's, works within the framework of "what fiction shares with history or what fiction claims for itself." This, as I shall try to demonstrate later, is neither feasible nor fruitful for examining the novelist's concern with history.

Although Fleishman's theory of the historical novel is comprehensive and somewhat more open than the two already discussed, it too suffers from several limitations. It does not give adequate importance to the fact that it is no longer possible to think of history in very rigid terms. That is why his definition has been characterized as one "which confuses as much as it clarifies" (Turner 334). Besides, he does not foresee the difficulties involved in stressing the presence of a historically 'real' person in historical novels. Can one think of a fixed picture/image of such a person? What has the novelist to do with him? Has he to be guided by a historian in this? If yes, what kind of a historian, one might ask. These questions are not adequately answered by Fleishman. Besides, by overemphasizing this condition he puts a serious and unwarranted limitation on the novelist's use of history. The present study includes several novels in which there are no 'real' persons from the history of India.

Almost on the lines of Fleishman, F J Tickner gives his definition of the historical novel by stating that it "must conform to fact by a reasonable show of historical accuracy. The actual personages who appear in its pages must resemble, more or less closely, the real persons of history; the fictitious characters must behave, more or less, as if they had been living at the time" (x). Tickner's concept combines elements from Fleishman and Lukacs. His stress on the inclusion of real historical persons, happenings, and events in historical novels links him with the former; that the fictitious people should resemble the ones who lived at a particular time in history invokes the spirit of the latter. When compared with their definitions, however, Tickner's is vague and loosely phrased; expressions like "a reasonable show of accuracy" and to "resemble more or less closely" are too imprecise for any expository definition. Besides, as a norm for identifying such novels, his statement that "the fictitious must behave more or less, as if they had been living at that time" is not only ambiguous, but also misleading. Tickner also finds such novels negative, for he considers them limited and circumscribed forms of fiction.

The general assumption behind Tickner's definition is that there is a fixed view of the past, of the people and events of a particular time, to which historical novels should conform as far as possible. We know it for certain that after the decline of positivistic historiography, there has been a drastic change in the conception and recreation of historical past. In fact, the idea of a uniform, generalized, and generally-accepted view of the past, so essential to Tickner's view, is not held even by professional historians. To suggest that the novelist must depend upon and respect versions of the past given by historians also amounts to putting a severe limitation on his possible uses of history. We can cite examples of several novelists from the West and the Third World who wrote novels about history because of their dissatisfaction with the efforts of the historians.

Compared with the concepts already discussed, the one given by Harry Henderson, specifically in the context of the American novel, shows greater awareness of the complex ways in which history can be studied in relation to the novel. He criticizes the theories of Ernest Leisey and David Levin on this mainly because they are rooted in their faith in scientific historiography, which has wrongly led them to state that the job of a historical novelist is to fictionalize what has already been known through the scientific method (11). The art of the historical novelist, according to them, lay entirely in his "treatment" of "real" history. Henderson rightly points out that this is not acceptable, because it is based on a controversial assumption and poses several practical difficulties. It may happen that in assessing the success or otherwise of a historical novel, we may confront a situation in which the "real" of a historian collides with the "real" of the novelist. As such, the very conception of a historical novel which rests on the assumption that it has to present artistically only the pre-determined "accurate" picture of the past is not adequate. It also fails to do justice to the truth-value of such novels.

Since a total reliance on the procedure of comparing such novels with the work of historians can lead to problems, Henderson suggests that for their understanding and evaluation, we should adopt a pragmatic and flexible approach, of complementing the "historistic" method with the "philosophic" one. Though this frees such novels from the oppressive binding of a fixcd historical content, the philosophic method raises complications of another kind. For he relates it to the structures of "interlocking constellations of assumptions about history and society" which have a very specific American context (13). This may not prove useful for novels which come from other cultures. Nevertheless, Henderson rightly emphasizes the need for going beyond the traditional ways of looking at the novelist's concern with history. He also accepts the legitimacy of the novelist's version of the past.

To overcome the inadequacies of earlier conceptualizations and the methodological problems they give rise to, Joseph Turner has advanced a new theory of the historical novel. Its main feature is that it does not conceive of this novel as a single, monolithic category. Conceding that the novelist's involvement with history can be for different reasons, which can result in novels of different shapes, he suggests that it is better that we think of several kinds of historical novels. Instead of attempting what the earlier conceptualizations did in varying degrees, that is work out parallels between 'history' in fiction and history proper, he provides for three categories of the historical novel within two boundaries: "one between historical novels and other fiction, one between historical novels and narrative history" (336). These are the documented historical novel, the disguised historical novel, and the invented historical novel.

The documented historical novel is the most usually known form of this novel, which incorporates actual events and people in it. The disguised one does not do so, but provides sufficient evidence of the novelist's interest in the past. It stands somewhere between documented history and conventional fiction, such as *All the King's Men*: "Neither drawn directly from recorded history nor composed as an outright fiction, Warren's disguised historical novel situates itself half-way between documented and invented history" (338). This novel deals with history through a camouflage, which can take diverse forms. The disguise too can vary; it can either be too transparent or too obscure. In the invented historical novel, characters and events are imaginary, but "the novel's setting and the author's relationship to it" (340) become the important factors for making it into a historical novel and also for distinguishing it from other types. The characters and setting are so far removed from the author's immediate experience that their handling by a novelist necessitates what Turner calls the exercise of a distinctively historical imagination and involves grappling with problems related to historical interpretation: "Generally speaking, then, unless they have a complex narrative structure, invented historical novels remain distinct from other fiction only by placing the action far enough into the past as to claim for themselves the status of a historical reconstruction" (340).

This brief description of the categories of the historical novel given by Turner is meant to show that it is a problematic category and can create several difficulties for the readers of such novels. Turner, of course, suggests that the way out could be to expand its scope, by paying attention to the formal, structural, and contextual aspects of historical representation. But even this may not help. Turner himself admits that the enlarged schema proposed by him cannot accommodate all the possible forms of the novelist's use of history; he even visualizes its collapse in the face of the current use of history by the novelists the world over. Besides, Turner's schema does not directly confront the question of historical imagination and the novelist's freedom to use the so-called historical materials.

Perhaps because of his awareness of the shortcomings of his schema, Turner, towards the end of his discussion, proposes an alternative model, in which historical novelists are divided into three categories, on the basis of Hegel's three classes of historical consciousness: original, reflective, and philosophical. The writers in the original mode are the ones whose "principal concern is to create a compelling picture of the past—history *in itself*." In the reflective mode, he includes those novels in which "the chasm between past and present is recognized only to be bridged—history *in and for itself*." For the writers of the philosophical mode "the primary concern becomes how, or if, history itself is possible—history *in and for*, but primarily *about itself*" (354). These are value-loaded terms. Turner's personal preference is for the novels of the last category. Even after elaborating this new schema, Turner, once again, admits that it is inadequate for understanding wholly the use of history by the novelists, particularly of the nineteenth century. Therefore, he suggests that "other discriminations, along somewhat different lines, would need to be made" (355). Since history-fiction nexus has assumed a more complicated character in recent times than what it was like in the nineteenth century, Turner's honest confession underlines the need for re-thinking and a new approach to deal with it.

II

Almost all the critics in India are agreed that the novel in India came into its own under the impact of the novel in the West, particularly of Britain. In fact, the novel's engagement with history was at the very root of its development. To present a truthful picture of life in their novels, the novelists located human actions in a recognizable geographical and historical space and a comprehensible time-frame. This paved the way for a more serious and purposeful engagement of the novelist with history in the nineteenth century. It was this novel which had a major influence on the novelists in India, first on the ones who wrote in regional languages and, later, on the ones who wrote in English.[10]

This particular circumstance compounded with another significant development, which added an urgent and significant dimension to Indian novelists' involvement with history: their awareness of the colonial situation and the social and political ferment it generated in the country.[11] This stimulated their interest in its past, which they tried either to recreate or reinterpret for different purposes in their novels: to make their countrymen understand how it was different from what they had been taught about it by the British; to glorify it for purposes of instilling a sense of pride in them; to valorize it for galvanizing people to fight their tyrannical masters. Many novelists wrote novels about social and political developments with varying degrees of commitment.

The response of Indian critics to such novels has, by and large, been to analyze the 'historical' content of such novels by doing precisely what Henderson disapproved of as a valid critical practice: that is, comparing it with what they thought had actually happened in history. In the context of the present-day views about history, historiography, and historical representation, which provide for several valid versions of the past of any kind, such a procedure appears naive and simplistic. Such critics assume that the past is something already known, and has congealed into a fixed shape; if the novelists want to write novels about it, all they need to do is to incorporate it into their work faithfully. If they fail to do so, they are bad artists. This not only promotes sloppy criticism, but also sets fallacious standards for judging the artistic merit of such novels.[12] Besides, it sets an arbitrary limit on the novelist's concern with the past. I have already suggested that besides representing it through the mode of fiction, a novelist can use history for various other purposes. I shall analyze briefly some critical evaluations of Indian novelists' concern with history, in which the critics have applied historical novel as a critical concept. It needs to be stated here that, unlike the Western critics, the Indian critics have not expounded the term in depth. They have invariably used it as an established critical concept, without paying attention to its problematic character.

In his study of the rise of the Indian novel in English, Ramamurti has an exclusive chapter on "Historical Novels," in which he discusses the novelists who published their novels before 1930. The generalised statement with which he opens his discussion provides a clue to his theoretical base: "The historical novel, as we understand it in terms of the novels of Scott, Balzac, Pushkin, Manzoni, Anatole France and Romain Rolland, is yet to make its appearance in Indian-English, though a few historical romances and novels with a historical background have been produced by those who wrote before 1930" (227). Ramamurti considers Bankim Chandra Chatterjee, Romesh Chunder Dutt and Jogender Singh representatives of this trend.

In line with his main thesis, which he contradicts too often in his discussion, Ramamurti writes that Bankim's *Durgesha Nandini* is no more than a romance, because the novelist weaves the story of the romantic love of Jagat Singh for Tilotama and Ayesha on the basis of a single historical fact. As such, the novel "gives us no picture of the sweep and magnificence of the times crowded with historical events nor does it make any attempt to vitalize the past" (231). But shortly afterwards, he picks another detail from it to assert that it symbolizes the policy of Akbar for winning the support of the Rajputs, which makes it an "interesting study in historical fiction" (232). Ramamurti praises Dutt's portrayal of the character and personality of Akbar in *The Slave Girl of Agra*, because it is in conformity with "history and tradition." Elaborating on this, he writes: "The romance and glamour which surround the personality of Akbar and his court are, in fact, historically true and most of the events which take place in the court and the palace are based on historical facts. To this extent, *The Slave Girl of Agra* is a good historical novel" (235). For the same reasons, Ramamurti considers Jogender Singh's *Nur Jehan* a successful historical novel:

> In an historical novel of smaller dimensions all that we can look for are historical veracity and consistency and Jogender Singh's novel has both. There is in the characters of both Jahangir and Nur Jehan a consistency which is not only in keeping with historical truth but also explains that historical truth. They may not be very "living" but they are true and convincing portrayals (254).

Ramamurti's analysis poses several difficulties, most of which arise from his incapacity to pay attention to the problems connected with historical reconstruction. He uses terms like historical truth and historical facts rather loosely, and is not aware of the contradictions in his position. Although he begins by stating that Indian novelists wrote only historical romances, he goes on to show that they are effective historical novels too. Instead of studying the implications of the novelist's use of a supposedly historical fact or a detail and its function in the fictional frame of the novel, he only judges them by comparing the facts and details in them with some written version of what it was like in the past. I have already stated that making such comparisons does not help in understanding the novelist's involvement with the past, because there is no single fixed or received version about the past, on which the novelist may rely. Let me illustrate Ramamurti's simplistic procedure to make my point. For establishing the truthfulness of Jogender Singh's presentation of Nur Jehan, he compares the novelist's version with the one in the history of R C Majumdar. Because he finds that the two are similar, he considers *Nur Jehan* a successful historical novel. He accepts Majumdar's version as the true, final, and authoritative one. We are told by some contemporary historians that the accuracy of Majumdar's historical accounts is suspect.[13] In the wake of such controversies, which could crop up with regard to all past accounts, because there are and can be several versions of every happening, each as authoritative as the other, Ramamurti could at best make a neutral, descriptive statement, that the novelist's conception of Nur Jehan resembles that of Majumdar's (which would, in effect, not add up to saying anything significant) and not make it the basis of an evaluative judgment on the novel. Ramamurti's stance also assumes a very limited use of history by a novelist, such as incorporating an actual scene or a character from the past. This, we have already seen, is not true. The novelist has used history for other purposes too, for evaluating it and its representations critically. Reappraisals have become so common and necessary in contemporary times that one does not need to emphasize their relevance.

Uma Parameswaran's essay on Manohar Malgonkar's fiction is another example of the evaluation of a historical novelist. She compares Malgonkar with Scott, because, like him, he has written several volumes of straightforward history and novels about historical events and people. Soon after, she adds that like Scott he has also recreated history successfully not through "historical figures or events but through types who are moulded by historical circumstances but are at the same time individualistic enough to be round characters. Like Scott, Malgonkar has reanimated a portion of the country's past" (331). A little later, she makes a larger claim for Malgonkar: that he provides us history through his novels which is better than the history written by professional historians, though she does not name any particular historian whom he has bettered. That this is no more than a generalized statement which is partly rooted in the Lukacsian understanding of Scott is clear from the operative part of her statement, that "in *The Devil's Wind*, *The Princes*, and *A Bend in the Ganges* he has compiled a history of the fifteen decades between 1800 and 1950 that is more authentic than most history books, because it examines the social and psychological motivations of people who made history" (331).

Parameswaran's statement on Malgonkar's achievement implicitly assumes that there are two ways of recreating or representing history: either through the events which really happened or by exploring the psyche of the people involved in the making of history. Malgonkar's choice of the second procedure is in a way a partial acceptance of Lukacs's description of Scott's approach to history: that of portraying the awakening of people who figured in the making of history. It also comes close to what Shelby Foote calls the novelist's view of history, which assumes that though historians and novelists both seek the truth about the past, their methods are different: "The historian attempts this by communicating facts, whereas the novelist would communicate sensation. The one stresses action, the other reaction" (440). This may be a proper strategy for some writers, but may not be acceptable to those who use history for purposes other than that of communicating sensation. Besides it is rooted in a fallacy that 'facts' exist independently of a historian's perception of them, that they have an *a priori* existence, and the historian's job is just to incorporate them in his account; the novelist is not interested in them, because his priorities lie elsewhere: to unravel the psyche behind the concrete happenings of history. Present-day historians, let alone the novelists, would not accept the division which is at the heart of this distinction.

Parameswaran, however, does not stop at stating that as a novelist, Malgonkar is better than a historian. She makes him into a historian proper, who, through his characters, "has written his interpretation of recent Indian history" (332). It is not my intention to examine the validity of her views. My intention is only to point out that Parameswaran makes several statements about Malgonkar as a historical novelist, which are qualitatively different from each other in their levels of signification; but she does not seem to be aware of the differences. Malgonkar's position as a novelist merges too often into that of a historian proper, although she asserts that he is better than a historian. Confronted with several other features of his fiction, which are far removed from his interest in history, she defends him by stating that he is primarily a novelist. For example, she explains away his "James Bond touch in matters of suspense and sex" as something "acceptable in the context of the genre" (335). The main problem with her analysis is her methodological inconsistency. She implicitly defines and redefines the scope of the historical novel to accommodate the variety she finds in Malgonkar's treatment of the past, without realizing the contradictions she builds into her use of the term and her assessment of the novelist. This problem is also there in her short book on Rushdie, in which she pays little attention to the problematic nature of history and historiography.[14]

A more recent example is Krishna Rao's essay on two recent novels of Nayantara Sahgal: *Plans for Departure* and *Mistaken Identity* (Rao 91, 117-23). I shall not discuss the content of his discussion of the two novels, only analyze the basis on which he links history and fiction in them. His basic assumption is that "a fiction of history is at once realistic and interpretative. It is, in addition, evaluative of the segment of historical reality as projected by the novelist whose techniques of writing fiction enable him or her to discover his or her vision or world-view" (117). Apart from the vagueness of the statement, Rao fails to adhere to it. Had he done so, then *Mistaken Identity* should not have figured in his discussion. He himself disqualifies it as a fiction of history, though he hardly realizes it, when he writes that it is "a comedy in the manner of Indian folk tales and the Arabian Nights. The element of phantasy and parody seem to have compounded to produce the comic effect..." (120).

In his discussion of the elements he considers essential for his conceptualization of the term historical fiction, Rao quotes statement after statement, from T S Eliot, Henry James, and Bernard Bergonzi, spreading, in the process, wider and wider the net of inexactitude. For example, at one point, he writes that "for recreating and illuminating an event or events of the past a novelist takes recourse to, what Bergonzi calls 'conscious realism' in demonstrating the function of history in fiction" (117). Instead of expounding 'conscious realism' and explaining what the function of history in fiction precisely is, he gives a quotation from James, commenting on the representational character of the novel, which it shares with history. As if there was not enough confusion already, Rao yet again attempts a definition of historical consciousness, by mixing a large chunk of Taine with a pinch of Indian philosophy: "Historical consciousness may be described...[as] one's awareness of not only the confluence of the moment, the milieu and the individual but also the sensibility that enables one to abstract meaning out of the *maya* of human existence" (118). Rao is neither conscious of the various contradictory positions he has taken, nor is he aware of the implications of *maya* in any discussion on history.

This brief discussion of the various uses of the term historical novel by the critics of the West and its application by our critics for analyzing the Indian English novel demonstrates that its use has been riddled with problems. Although the concepts of Manzoni, Lukacs, Henderson, Fleishman, and Turner have helped in illustrating the various ways in which the novelists have used history from time to time, no single concept is free from serious limitations. These, as I have tried to show, arise largely from assumptions with regard to the novelists' use of history, which may partially be located in history itself. Besides, all of them have tried to circumscribe the efforts of the novelist within certain prescriptive norms. Because of this, none of these conceptualizations can do justice to the complex variety which one finds in the history-fiction interface at present. Their inadequacy is also related to the unique nature of the novel as an art form.

Right from the time the novel emerged as a literary form, it has changed constantly, which makes it what Bakhtin calls a plastic and uncompleted genre. In fact, he considers it not just another literary genre, but a kind of force, which he calls "novelness." As "the only developing genre," it "reflects more deeply, more essentially, more sensitively and rapidly, reality itself in the process of its unfolding" (7). Its connection with reality is one of open-mindedness, which implies that it cannot be framed in any concrete, fixed form. Because of this, Bakhtin distinguishes between the novel and epic, especially in their treatment of the past. Unlike the novel, the epic is a completed genre; it views past as something which is closed, that is "walled off from all subsequent times by an impenetrable boundary," because of which "it is impossible to change, to rethink, to re-evaluate anything in it" (17). The novel deals with the past differently; it takes it out of its closeness, by re-thinking and re-evaluating it. Even when it deals with remote past, it observes "no epic distance, and contemporary reality provides the point of view" (23). The past and the present are thus brought into a new relationship, which promotes a new awareness of the past. In this process, the novel too keeps on changing in its shape. That is why the history of the novel is a history of its continual transformations, in which new possibilities of change are worked out between the individual and his world. The novel also increasingly assimilates more and more of historical time and space and even actual historical persons. This is what it has been doing over centuries and what it would probably continue doing in future as well.

Thus we see that novel's extraordinary powers of inclusion, which also account for its resilience, vigour, and popularity, are partly reflected in the changes in the nature and quality of the novelist's engagement with history. Largely because of this, no schematic categories of the historical novel, even when they were redefined from time to time, could fully accommodate them.[15] This makes it necessary that we adopt a more open and practical mode for examining the various ways in which the novelist uses, incorporates, reconstructs, or reinterprets the past.[16] In other words, we admit the possibility that the novelist can and does use history in multiple ways and for various effects. The older conceptions of the historical novel virtually presuppose that the novel deals with the past almost like an epic: that it incorporates it as a pre-formed thing, and treats it almost with reverence. If a novelist does not do so, then he is not a good historical novelist. This, as I have already stated, cannot be accepted. The novelist can do whatever he likes with the past. What is important about it is to study the kind of self-consciousness he brings to his effort, the different strategies he employs to realize his ends, and the manner in which all these impinge on the shape and style of his novels. These can provide a more meaningful framework for understanding the history-fiction interface. The approach may or may not lead to new definitions (which, in any case, have created problems rather than solved them); it will certainly prove a more viable and fruitful exercise for evaluating the novelist's importance in a society in which both novel and history come to life and derive sustenance from each other.

I have already mentioned in passing that the most common tendency among the Indian critics has been to see the history-fiction nexus in terms of the similarities between the 'history' contained in the fictional frame of novels and the history proper produced by professional historians. It is largely true, and I shall point this out in my own analysis of novels, that they do incorporate specific historical details in them, but it would be both unfair and uncritical to assume that the novelists do it merely for the sake of duplicating what is already known.[17] On the contrary, what one can easily find, even by a cursory reading of novels, is that in the hands of novelists the past takes different shapes and for different reasons.[18] History can be romanticized, sensationalised, interrogated, and problematized. The novelist may critique it, satirize it, play with it, even trivialize it. All these different purposes can not only have far-reaching implications for his fiction, but also determine his arrangement of events and characters, his choice of the modes of presentation and narrative strategies.[19] Besides, his whole enterprise will have consequences for society and its cultural politics.

It is fairly understandable that the novelist's engagement with history may or may not be of the same kind as that of a historian, but this does not in any way lessen its significance. Considering that novels can be often more readable and accessible, their engagement with history can neither be considered an eccentric whimsicality (even if it may appear so) nor be dismissed as an insignificant triviality.[20] One has also to remember that this use has been promoted by tradition and the changing cultural climate of times. If it is more conspicuous in recent times, it is because of far-reaching changes in our thinking on history and historiography, which has become revisionary and dialogical. It is not merely because new facts are discovered from time to time, but also because the existing ones are reinterpreted differently and given a new signification. The modes of history-writing have changed radically and the boundaries between history and fiction are no longer as tight as they were thought to be during the ascendancy of scientific and objective historiography.

Since the novelist's involvement with history is at the centre of this study, it is in order that we must clarify what history investigates. In the course of its growth as a discipline which deals with human past, there has been a steady and continuous change in its scope and character. With the passage of time more and more areas of human experience were brought within its frame. It is not without significance that for stretching the subject matter of their histories, the historians of the eighteenth and nineteenth centuries learnt a great deal from the novelists of the times, which I shall demonstrate in Chapter II. The interesting thing is that they continue to learn from them even now.

Although during the past several decades, historians and philosophers of history have devoted most of their energies to the discussion of questions relating to the characteristics of historical reconstruction, historical imagination, and narratology, questions pertaining to the enhancement of the content of history have figured no less prominently. In fact, in the actual writing of history, they have had a significant role. Two such major influences have been the growth of Marxist historiography and the steady increase in the prestige of the Annales school. Whatever one may think of the ideological core at the heart of Marxist view of history, or of its totalizing tendency, it had a strong influence on history-writing, by leading the historians on to areas of social, political and economic experience which the historians had either not considered worthy of attention or considered only of minor importance.[21] The Marxists stressed that history was not to be seen merely as a sequence of happenings in time, but also in a less diachronic sense, as consisting of the struggle between social classes, paying special attention to modes of production and the development of social formations.

In the hands of the Annales school, history became a larger entity, attaining another kind of totalization. In the words of Stoianovich, it is a paradigm which "constitutes an inquiry into how one of the systems of a society functions or how a whole collectivity functions in terms of its multiple, temporal, spatial, human, social, economic, cultural, and even mental dimensions" (quoted in Hunt 2). These expansions go much beyond the possibilities suggested for history by E H Carr in the early sixties, when he said "the more sociological history becomes, and the more historical sociology becomes, the better for both."

In the wake of the totalizing approaches to history, which are not confined to the ones I have already mentioned and could be the product of specific cultural situations where history is used as a resource for legitimizing power structures or ideologies, several unconventional historians like Foucault have pleaded that the historical discourse should open out not only to accommodate areas and voices which have been consistently neglected by the historians, but also to the ones which have been marginalized by totalities.[22] It is this spirit which has led some historians to state that the subject-matter of history should become immensely wide-ranging, and embrace areas from familiar and common to the strange and the esoteric, from "constitutions to forgery, from magic to menstruation." Commenting on the stretching of the historical canvas, which is already a part of the history-writing practice of our times, Juliet Gardiner writes that the phenomenon is

> largely a result of the educational, social and political experience of those writing and reading history. It is in this spirit that the contours of the past have been remapped; existing questions have been reformulated; known facts have been reinterrogated; what was once considered marginal has been woven into the centrality of historical enquiry and historical research has been recognized as a more profound exercise than simply filling the gaps (75).

This stretching of the subject-matter of historical investigation in itself opens up new possibilities for examining the novelist's concern with history, for even before the historians could catch up with these new areas of social and cultural past of societies, because of their traditional and conservative moorings, the novelists dealt with them in full measure. For long stretches of time in the past, historians remained heavily preoccupied with political events and happenings, which in the estimation of Braudel constitute only the foam or dust of history. Novels also score over traditional histories in another interesting way: they can and do translate a lot of historical knowledge, which is "non-novelistic knowledge into the language of the novel." More importantly, they also provide "the illustration of a historical situation, the description of a society at a given moment, a novelized historiography" (Kundera 36). This is one of the most valuable aspects of the novelist's connection with history.

By drawing attention to this unique feature of the novel, I do not, however, want to suggest that this is the most relevant or useful involvement of the novelist with history. I have already pointed out that he can do several things with it. Seen specifically in the context of the situation in our country, where history writing for a long period of time was conservative, and hide-bound, and has now become increasingly controversial, especially during the last three or four decades, the novelist's use of the historical past assumes greater significance. Take, for example, what a contemporary historian has to write about the most momentous period in our history, which witnessed popular ferment against the British and the growth of nationalism. Most of the recreations of this period, he writes, have largely been done through a very narrow angle of the "activities, ideals, or factional manoeuvres of leaders," which make the recreations highly tendentious and unreliable. They also leave out of reckoning large areas of societal formations, groups, communities, and other institutional structures. In fact, the most vital area of social history "unfortunately still remains a very neglected subject in India" (Sarkar 9). In such a scenario, an investigation into the efforts of our novelists who have taken keen interest in our past can certainly prove significant and useful. The assumption here is that they may illuminate areas of social and cultural experience which have not received the attention of historians.

The approach that I have outlined for this investigation also frees us from the constricting limitation of studying the novelist's concern with history in terms of a past which is somewhat removed from the present, say by about thirty or forty years, the kind of arbitrary limit which has been postulated by Fleishman in his conceptualization of the historical novel. When the novelist Margaret Laurence stated that "all fiction is written about the past" (15), she meant to suggest that the novelist's concern with the past did not tie him to any chronologically-determined depth. The writer is not bound by any periodized view of time, which the historian may find convenient or even necessary. Privileged with a greater degree of freedom, the novelist can have a more flexible view of the degrees of pastness. It may vary between events or happenings which have just passed or a period which stretches to the limits of one's memory. Some novelists may take it beyond the point where memory fades, and some may delve into the remote past.[23] The novelist may not postulate them as tight categories; he may jump barriers to make his point. In fact, by doing so, he may even free himself from the sequential patterns of linearity which a large majority of historians tend to observe with a high degree of meticulous consistency, because they consider it essential. In this arrangement the novelist is also freed from another constriction which Fleishman considers one of the essential features of a novel which deals with history, that is, to incorporate at least one major historical figure into its fictional space.

It would be useful here to outline the scope of the present study, as an explanation and an elucidation of our novelists' concern with history. The chapter that immediately follows this attempts a conspectus of the history-fiction overlap in the West, from the earliest times to the present. Almost like a historical essay, it plots and interprets the significant intersections of history and fiction with a twofold purpose: to illustrate how the two developed separate identities through a continuous process of mutual relationship, and to provide examples of how variously the novel affected history and how also it accommodated history within its frame because of the exigencies of cultural pressure. This would be especially valuable for providing a kind of illustrative morphology for identifying and understanding similar interpenetrations in the Indian English novel. This is also because we know that in its early phase of development, the novel in India was influenced by the nineteenth century British novel, especially of Scott and the later Victorian novelists.

The second part of this chapter consists of a brief section on the use of history by our novelists before the 1920s, including the ones who wrote in various Indian languages. It also pays attention to the complications arising out of our thinking on history and historiography, largely because of the multicultural character of our society, the effect of British colonialism on our thinking and attitudes, and the problems the country had to face before and after independence. In short, it dwells on various historiographic traditions and practices, their contestations and their impingement on history-writing in India for a better understanding of the novelist's engagement with history. It would not be an exaggeration to say that the problems connected with the writing of history in India are of a more complex nature than they are in the West. Their cultural fallout too is more problematic here than in those societies in which the levels of cultural heterogeneity are not so pronounced.

Since the main thrust of the study is to explore the variety of possible ways in which novelists use history with consequences for their art and their times, I have restricted myself to a selected few. Almost all of them are the ones who have not been discussed as historical novelists, except in an occasional essay, by which I imply that their involvement with and use of history has not been sufficiently noticed or assessed. This, of course, excludes Rushdie, whose concern with history has been noticed. Some novelists included in this study have been labelled novelists with political consciousness.

From among those who started writing in the pre-independence era of our country, I have chosen Mulk Raj Anand. Though he has been writing for over five decades now, his most influential work was published before 1947. In my reckoning, he is the best example of a novelist who virtually bends his novels to the needs of history; they largely derive their purpose and shape from it. His novels provide his understanding of the British rule in India and the modes of resistance which people built to fight it. He brings in specific historical details in them to recreate the ways in which people faced up to their situation. More importantly, he dramatizes the dialectical tension between the divine and the humanistic modes of historical change. This makes his engagement with history rich and rewarding.

Although, of late, Nayantara Sahgal has written novels in which she deals with issues related to historical reconstructions more self-consciously, in her earlier novels too she deftly combines personal and public history by intertwining the past of individual lives with India's historical past. In the process she has produced a variety of disguised history of post-independence India, with accent on the aspirations and traumas of its people, arising largely out of the discrepancies between the pre-and post-independence times. Her novels deal with issues of considerable import—social, political, and cultural—with discrimination and intelligence. She generally avoids weaving her narratives in a concretely-developed time-frame, but provides sufficient hints about the historical period about which she is writing. This disguise, through which she refrains from making direct references to important people and events of those periods, is used by her as a strategy for analyzing and commenting on them with a greater degree of dispassionateness. She is a fine example of a novelist who subjects historical trends and their relation to value-structures to a careful scrutiny.

In tune with new developments in the interface of history and fiction in the West, especially in the culture of postmodernism, Salman Rushdie has injected a new dimension into our novelists' encounter with history. Like most of his Western counterparts, he problematizes historical discourse by employing the historiographic metafictional mode. But his involvement with history, strictly speaking, cannot be adequately comprehended in Western terms alone. It is because in spite of his complicated relationship with both India and Pakistan, he evinces a sense of a strong cultural base, which is largely Indian or, to use a more neutral term, subcontinental. His cultural moorings, however tenuous they might seem, lend his enterprise an additional element of complexity which one does not find in the West and which has not therefore been sufficiently noticed.

To bring the novelist's involvement with history to its full circle, as it were, the final chapter demonstrates how the novelists deal with history by using narrative modes which are essentially non-mimetic: such as comedy, satire, allegory. The assumption here is that, unlike the historian, the novelist is not bound to deal with history only by producing realistic narratives, where the very mode of presentation can create the illusion of history, but can plough history back into fiction through the backdoor. He does it through different schemas and constructs: he filters it through the dense cover of comedy; represents it through the rational construct of an allegory; critiques it through the satirical speculum. The novelist is free to use them singly or in varied mixtures. This chapter analyzes two novels: Shashi Tharoor's *The Great Indian Novel* and O V Vijayan's *The Saga of Dharmapuri.*

Notes

1 Throughout this study, I have used the word history in these two senses; this has the sanction of social scientists and philosophers. John Dewey, for example, writes that history means "that which happened in the past" as well as "the intellectual reconstruction of these happenings at a subsequent time" (169). See also Morroe Berger (163).

2 I would like to clarify that the present study steers clear of several extremist views, which are inimical to history and its epistemic value. With specific reference to capitalistic society, Joseph Episto writes: "... there is very little need for historians to survey the past in order that we may be able to know ourselves better. At best in the popular culture of capitalist society there is an interest, not in actual history, nor in vivid history with its poignant reminder of suffering and injustice, but in a fictional history of a generalized and usually romanticized historical past, as presented in a historical novel. In such

circumstances it is no wonder that historians increasingly came to question the social standing of their enterprise " (36).

The second view is of Roland Barthes. He states that history has no power to describe the past; it only induces in us an illusion that it actually describes past reality, an illusion adopted from fiction. In his words: "It is clear that the attenuation (if not disappearance) of narrative in contemporary historians, who deal in structures rather than chronologies, implies much more than a change of school; it represents in fact a fundamental ideological transformation: historical narrative is dying: from now on the touchstone of history is not so much reality as intelligibility" (155).

Though the postmodernist position provides for revisionary history, some positions within it postulate the disappearance of a sense of history. Fredric Jameson, for example, states that postmodernism marks a loss of depth—visual as well as interpretative, "a new kind of conceptualization which no longer involves *philosophical* notions of depth, that is various hermeneutics in which one interprets an appearance in terms of some underlying reality, which these philosophies then uncode. Finally, historicity and historical depth, which used to be called historical consciousness or the sense of the past, are abolished. In short, objects fall into the world and become decoration again; visual depth and systems of interpretation fade away; and something peculiar happens to historical time" (Ross 4).

3 The connection between history and novel forms the basis of my next chapter. For a general discussion, see Laurence Lerner (12-94); Morroe Berger (162-85); Dominick LaCapra (1985, 115-34); David Carroll (88-160); and Lionel Grossman (228-50).

4 A wide range of views on the historical novel has been documented by Bernbaum. He illustrates how its estimations have varied because of the critics' understanding of how history and novel could be related. The views included are of William Hazlitt, Sainte-Beuve, J S Mill and Leslie Stephen (424-441). For an interesting and informative supplement to this, which provides a random sampling of contemporary views of novelists and historians on historical novels, see "My Favorite Historical Novel" (84-107).

5 I shall discuss several such imprecise definitions. Here I quote the one used about Bankim Chander: "A novel which has a historical setting may not be reliable as a source of accurate historical information, but it can have a place in literature as a novel, and there seems no harm in calling it a historical novel" (66).

6 One recent example, in which the novelist Valerie Miner speaks about it in relation to her novel *All Good Women* (1987): "I guess I have a hard time calling it a historical novel as a lot of historical novels are rather silly, and sort of gloss over history." See "Historical Fiction and Fictional History: An Interview with Valerie Miner," *Meanjin,* 46, 4 (December 1987), 551.

7 In a fairly recent study, Ralph J Crane writes: "As a genre, the historical novel is as loose and baggy as Henry James's monsters of fiction." He mentions several novels which do not "conform to definitions of the historical novel," but deal with India's history (10).

8 In a perceptive study, Anne Green states that the significant point about Flaubert's use of history is that "it owes less to the debate about the role of history in fiction than it does to shifts in the much more serious contemporary debate about the theory of historiography" (16).

9 Lukacs, like Maigron, makes historical novel into a period piece. For Maigron it was a "genre peculiar to the Romantic period, a form developed to give expression to a passionate concern with national history and delight in the picturesque, and which faded once these preoccupations had gone." See Green (1).

10 Meenakshi Mukherjee has pointed out how the European and British novel of the time modified and ultimately changed the narrative forms commonly used by Indian writers in the nineteenth century (3-18).

11 The fillip that the writing of fiction received in the country because of the rise of national awakening has been widely noted and commented upon. These have been systematically catalogued by K S Ramamurti (11-15). For details on this, see K R Srinivasa Iyenger (271-94).

12 This widespread tendency has been the main stimulus for undertaking this study. See my "The Use of the Historical Method by Indian English Critics: An Evaluation," *The Literary Criterion* (71-83).

13 Doubts about the authenticity of Majumdar's accounts have been stated in Sumit Sarkar (455-56). I would, however, like to clarify that the remarks of Sarkar are about Majumdar's reconstructions of the nationalist movement.

14 See my review of her "The Perforated Sheet: Essays on Salman Rushdie's Art," *The Journal of Indian Writing in English,* 14, 2 (July 1991), 24-25.

15 The problem of relating history and fiction has always hinged upon the similarities and differences between the two, which have constantly varied. The points of convergence between the two have been seen in narrative, figurative, and rhetorical terms, but emphasizing or

blurring their similarities and dissimilarities is also a political act. For interesting details on this, see Roger Seamon (197-218).

16 As imitations and representations of reality, novels enjoy a unique status. The historians have often made use of techniques of representation which were first used by the novelists. For specific details on this, see Elazar Weinryb (139-58).

17 Most of these shapes have been documented in the next chapter. I have not illustrated all the uses of history that I have catalogued here; some of these are quite well known.

18 A competent example of demonstrating how a writer's involvement with history can have consequences for the fictional strategies he employs is Judie Newman's *Saul Bellow and History*. A more compact analysis and defence of Newman's position, which is to "establish that the historical content of his work does enter the novels functionally, organizing their structure, rather than, in Tanner's view, in quotation marks," is available in her essay "Bellow's Sixth Sense: The Sense of History" (1992, 12).

19 Most of these positions have been dealt with at length in the subsequent chapter. For their crisp account in the context of the representational school, in which Hayden White has collapsed the idea of history and the idea of the text, see Richard Lehan (533-53).

20 Since history has been used by novelists differently, some literary critics have described it as an idiosyncratic tendency, because of which they produce factitious and synthetic histories. See Daniel Aaron (231-41) and Cushing Strout (428-43).

21 The Marxian views on history with all their variations are documented lucidly and with discriminating attention, but with different projections, in Helmut Fleischer and Gregor McLennan. My statement is a rephrased version of Jameson, which he made specifically in the context of the Marxian method of literary and cultural interpretation (1981, 74-75).

22 For Foucault's views on these structurings and their implications, see Mark Poster (105). For his influence on the growth of general histories as opposed to total history, see Patricia O'Brien, "Michel Foucault's History of Culture," *The New Cultural History* (33-34).

23 For a discussion on the degrees of pastness and their significance in historical reconstructions, see Bikhu Parekh (13-18).

Chapter II

History-Fiction Conspectus in Time

While outlining my approach for understanding the nature, variety, and cultural implications of the history-fiction nexus in the previous chapter, I stated that sometime after the middle of the present century in the West, there was an upsurge in the complexity and sophistication of the novelist's use of and engagement with history. This reflects a part of the evolving connection between the two, which goes back several centuries. It has varied from time to time because of changes in thinking on history and its modes of representation and also in the purpose and function of literature in general and of the novel in particular. These shifting perspectives have their roots also in the advances in philosophical thinking and the actual practice of writing history and fiction.[1]

As an older civilization than the West, India had a highly-evolved philosophical tradition, which encompassed diverse areas of knowledge, such as aesthetics, metaphysics, ethics, and numerous other complicated speculative systems, but it could not generate and sustain the kind of debate over issues concerning the relation between history and the arts (including fiction), that we witness in the West. This is, however, not to imply that thinking on them was totally non-existent; terms like *itihasa* and *kavya* do figure in the ancient Sanskrit for history and literature/poetry. But this is about all. Some believe that there must have been some thinking on the issues related to them, but it has not survived. Others, however, maintain that, on account of their distinctive outlook on life, ancient Indians neither attached the kind of importance to history that it got in the West nor did they understand it the way it was understood there.[2] Any further possibilities of development in this direction were thwarted by the country's chequered history. Constant invasions from the outside and the rise of several new faiths and religions from within brought periodic changes in its cultural style. This did not prove conducive for debates on issues relating to the nature and purpose of history, which could lead to a unidirectional development with evolutionary possibilities. On the contrary, it encouraged the growth of differing historiographies, with distinct cultural markers.

This process was further complicated by the consolidation of the British power in India. Through their interest in the country's social and cultural past, the British aroused the interest of Indians in finding 'their' past; in course of time, this exercise changed the differing historiographies into contesting ones, with a sharply accentuated tone and tenor. Through a carefully planned policy, which combined coercion with subtle inducement, the British also privileged the Western modes of historiography over the ones already available in the country. In the wake of momentous developments in the political and cultural climate of Europe and the erstwhile Socialist world, our historians also employed diverse other ways of recreating the country's past. It has led to a situation in which historiography is in a "kind of permanent civil war" (Devahuti 1979, xviii).

In two sections, this chapter examines the whole range of differences seen between history and fiction over time and their changing relationship in the West and in our country, the implications these had for the writing of history and fiction, and their consequences for the novelist's understanding of history and its use in his novels.

Section I

The Western Paradigm

It is fairly well-known that in the West, history, like literature, had a mythical origin. In his monumental work on history, Arnold Toynbee writes that "History, like the drama and the novel, grew out of mythology, a primitive form of apprehension and expression in which—as in fairy tales listened to by children or in dreams dreamt by sophisticated adults—the line between fact and fiction is left undrawn" (44). The statement not merely points to the common origins of history and the novel, it also implies that in their initial stages, the two had a common subject matter as well. Early history abounds in details about myths and gods and goddesses. Even after the divine figures disappeared from historical accounts and human beings took their place, the mode of establishing historical reality relied largely on beliefs, assertions and statements which had the sanction of tradition. They had the force of authority, merely because they had descended down the generations. Judging from what history came to stand for in the nineteenth century, Collingwood describes such attempts as examples of "theocratic history" or "quasi history" (15-16). Early forms of prose writings too consisted of narratives in which the lives of human beings often got intertwined with the miraculous lives and actions of divine and supernatural beings.

Even after historical and literary works acquired distinguishing features, they continued to make use of each other's materials. Basing himself on contemporary practice, Aristotle permitted the use of historical events and happenings for creating poetic fictions. The poet, he wrote, is "just as much a poet even if the material of his poetry comprises actual events, since there is no reason why *some* historical events should not be in conformity with probability, and it is with respect to probability that the poet can make his poetry from them" (Haliwell 41). This use continued for several centuries after Aristotle. In the sixteenth century, Scaliger remarked that "History, sometimes delineated only in semblance, sometimes idealized, and always with changed aspect, is made the basis of poetry" (qtd. in Kreiger 339).

During the Greek era, the line between fact and fiction was not always clear in historical writings or in literary creations. Toynbee regards Homer's *Iliad* a unique blend of history and fiction. Similarly, though the work of Herodotus and Thucydides is credited by Collingwood with several essential features of historical works, he specifically states that Herodotus did not have to say much on the most vital quality of evidence (19). As we move from the Greeks to the Romans, we can discern fitful changes in the direction of history-writing, but no concerted effort at evolving an approach towards a properly worked out factual presentation. Historians have ascribed it to the anti-historical attitude of both the Greeks and the Romans, because they believed in substantialist metaphysics, which "implies a theory of knowledge according to which only what is unchanging is knowable. But what is unchanging is not historical. What is historical is the transitory event" (42). The historical, therefore, did not figure in their priorities.

Christianity altered this perspective on history, but introduced into it the element of Providence, which proved a deterrent for the growth of a critically-conscious view of history. For it held that change was the result of divine forces and not of human actions. Its faith in the redeeming power of Christianity also led to the growth of a periodized view of history, in which past was divided into two broad divisions purely for religious reasons. It also endorsed a teleological view of history which was rooted in faith.

Renaissance changed this situation. The element of divine will dropped from the histories of the time, yielding place to the primacy of human actions. Even when the historians wrote about religion, it was understood as a social force or as an institutional arrangement. The realization that the proper study of past meant the past produced by human action in which divine intervention had no role marked a significant change in the conception of history as a body of writing, but advances in the actual writing of history were not of the same order, because of methodological inadequacies, reflected in the thinking of people like Bacon and Descartes. Vico was, in a way, the first historian to put history on a scientific basis. He stated that the fabric of history was the product of man's creation, and therefore knowable. The writers, like the Greek and Roman ones before them, continued to show considerable interest in history. Shakespeare's plays are an influential example of the manner in which history was used by a writer not merely as a source of material for writing plays, but also for providing insight into the history and politics of his times.

For the purpose of examining how history and the novel interacted with each other from time to time, the eighteenth century is of crucial importance. This was when the novel came into being as a distinct form of prose fiction and critical thinking on the appropriate content and form of history struck a firm base. If the novelists wrote comprehensively about its nature and function, historians, too, thought of history as a special form of thought, different from science and theology (Collingwood 5); historians like Hume and Gibbon created a new form of history-writing in the eighteenth century. Both novelists and historians worked to give a distinct shape to their respective disciplines. Fielding called his novels 'histories' because he wanted the readers to distinguish his work from the existing narrative form of the romances. The historians too laboured to distinguish their work from various forms of quasi-legend and antiquarian history. The result of their effort was that "the factual world of historical interpretation and the fictive world of the novel gradually achieved more distinct identities" (Braudy 4-5).

Among several developments which took place around this time, one which had serious implications for the future of both history and the novel was that the novelists and historians chose to learn from each other. In this process, the two acquired many structural affinities. In virtually all his novels, Fielding suspended his narrative to formulate and expound his theory of the novel to convince the readers that the world of his novels was no different from the 'real' world. This he reinforced by calling them 'histories,' a practice followed by the novelists even now. This helped him dispel what Hillis Miller calls the "implications of gratuitousness, of baseless creativity and lie, involved in the word 'fiction.' At the same time he affirms for his novel that verisimilitude, that solid basis in pre-existing fact, which is associated with the idea of history" (457). Fielding thus wrote novels under the protective cover of history.

While the novelists took sustenance from history, the historians too showed keenness to benefit from the experiments of the novelists. In order to make history relevant for common people, they moved away from the dull and effete antiquarianism of their predecessors, and employed new methods and styles from the novelists. For example, to make history interesting and relevant, they learnt from them to bring new kinds of social details within the corpus of their writings; they also worked hard to take "the greatest pains with their style, so that they could be widely read" (Hale 24). Braudy points out that this consideration weighed so heavily with them that for historians like Hume and Gibbon "literary method and a literary sensibility were more important than research" (11). Hale too remarks that in their eagerness and enthusiasm to present a wholesome picture of society, the historians grew impatient with "exact scholarship, especially the criticism of sources, and with detail" (24). The result of this borrowing from each other's methods was that historians and novelists moved closer in their objectives and procedures, and worked to "present a plausible world, complete in itself, yet directly relevant to the reader's actual life; both usually asserted that their worlds were based on verifiable facts; and both tended to define the 'truth' they sought in the language of general moral precepts" (Braudy 4).

It is important to point out here that although Fielding was a novelist, his novel-writing and the rules he carefully framed for it were partly the result of his conscious response to the historiography of his times. If he chose to call his prose compositions 'histories,' it is because he knew what histories were and should be like and how best they could be written. Like several historians of his day, such as Hume, Voltaire, and Montesquieu, Fielding emphasized that a true 'history' should contain details about people, their activities, and even their customs; it should also deal with the social formation of classes in a society and their effect on individual lives. He also held that it was not enough to define the scope and nature of the contents of a history; one also needed to find a suitable method for arranging social facts and details, so that they could lead to knowledge. In the hands of Fielding, novel-writing thus became a consistent attempt at working out these arrangements. Although he based his novels on social facts to create an effect of 'actuality,' he refrained from identifying truth with 'objectivity' or 'impersonality.' A detached contemplation of facts, he believed, led to superficiality and too public a view of things. He disapproved of Hume's method of history-writing, whose preoccupation with facts prevented him from creating an appropriate narrative voice. Hume feared that interpretation would result in distortion of facts. But because Fielding had already learnt that this was not true, he called historians who did not pay adequate attention to these aspects "topographers" and "chronographers."

Fielding's main purpose in his novels was to create an appropriate place for a narrator in the scheme of fact-oriented history. This was not possible without devising a proper and effective pattern for presenting his materials. Fielding understood the paradox involved in this, that "pattern by its nature falsifies. But we cannot collect knowledge in an infinitude of separate bundles; there must be means of ordering, however provisional" (Braudy 145). In other words, Fielding drew attention to what is now commonly recognized: that fictional elements are bound to enter into the creation of narrative histories. Fielding's efforts in this direction resulted in a near-perfect role for the narrator in *Tom Jones.* Braudy considers the narrator's voice in the novel the voice of a model historian "who constructs from the materials of observation, learning, and authority an appropriate causal pattern without necessity but with plausibility, and totally fitted to the varied world in which we must live" (180).

The best evidence of Fielding's wide-ranging interest in the form and content of history is that after having succeeded in understanding and achieving what was involved in the writing of history, he commented with perspicacity and confidence on the methods and achievements of past writers, who had either written history or showed interest in it. In *The Journal of a Voyage to Lisbon,* he remarks:

> ...I must confess I should have honoured and loved Homer more had he written a true history of his own times in humble prose, than all those noble poems that have so justly collected the praise of all ages; for, though I read these with more admiration and astonishment, I still read Herodotus, Thucydides, and Xenophon with more amusement and more satisfaction (185-86).

I have already mentioned that Fielding was critical of Hume because he found his historiography inadequate for a history which could impart knowledge; but Hume did work hard to write readable prose. Gibbon absorbed Fielding's influence in both respects, which can be seen at its best in the *Decline and Fall,* on its narrative organization and the manner in which it handles the interplay between the demands of "facts and the need for an imaginative order." Like Fielding, Gibbon understood that facts by themselves cannot help make history; they have to be apprehended by a historian. Fielding's influence on the conception and execution of Gibbon's work is brought out in its fulness in Braudy's assessment:

> The shape of history in the *Decline and Fall* is pre-eminently a construction, a literary work with aesthetic rather than systematic order and coherence. In the course of the *Decline and Fall* Gibbon's controlling presence becomes more and more palpable, ordering, assorting, varying, and qualifying. By its conclusion the *Decline and Fall* has become an enclosed object, to be contem-

> plated as much for its formal and detailed beauty as for its accurate transcription of what was (214).[3]

History-fiction connection in Britain acquired solidity and mass in the nineteenth century; novelists and historians influenced each other in new and meaningful ways. Building on the stable foundations provided by Fielding and his contemporaries, novelists gave up their pretence of writing novels in the guise of histories, and took to history openly and in a big way. Historians too benefited from the work of novelists, for thinking anew about the scope and purpose of history and cultivating the art of writing it. Walter Scott occupies a significant position in this new history-fiction overlap. He used historiographical methods to enrich the texture of his fiction, which, in turn, had an unprecedented influence on the historians of his time.[4]

For seeing this development in its proper perspective, it is necessary to pay attention to an important detail. In spite of the advances made by the eighteenth-century historians, their general attitude and outlook was not, strictly speaking, historical. They thought that large portions of the human past, most especially medieval times, were barbaric, and, therefore, not worthy of investigation. But Rousseau and Herder changed this thinking, which eventually paved the way for the flowering of Romanticism. Literary artists and historians both looked at the medieval times from a fresh perspective. This provided the right kind of setting for Scott's influential work, which put the history-fiction nexus on a firm footing.

Scott had a very strong antiquarian interest. Like a proficient man of letters of his times, he also commanded nearly half a dozen European languages. Starting out as a writer of historical works, which included a *History of Scotland,* he eventually used his scholarship and knowledge to write novels, which became popular as historical novels. These exerted a positive influence on the art of history-writing of his day. Scott used materials from actual past, covering a fairly wide range of time; these included actual events and people. Like many novelists of the present times, he invariably juxtaposed them with invented characters.[5] It has also been noticed that he blended "information from several periods into the portrait of one." If judged strictly on the basis of historical 'accuracy,' Scott is guilty of factual errors. In spite of this, it is also widely held, even by professional historians, that "the general fidelity to the spirit and manner of the times" in his novels was "backed by formidable mass of miscellaneous learning and downright scholarship" (Hale 37).

I have already pointed out in my previous chapter why Lukacs rated Scott highly as a historical novelist and considered him a model novelist even for those who did not have his kind of interest in history. What needs to be emphasized, however, is that Scott is important not just because his novels exemplify a specific attitude towards historical representation, which Lukacs valued, but because he was the first novelist to make massive use of specific details from the past. It has also to be remembered that his choice of these details reflects his own view and interpretation of history. Fleishman has called it a speculative view of history, a view in which the "picture of the past was a reconstruction of the major stages in the course of civilization, often without hard data, but deduced from generalizations about the forms of all social phenomena" (42). He also states that Scott's historical thinking is based on the views of a number of philosophers, which have been analyzed by him in detail. I do not comment or elaborate on them here. I only want to stress that Scott's reconstruction of the past is based on his own view of it, with which we may or may not agree. If Lukacs was charmed by the poetry of Scott's historical representation in which he could see what led men to think, feel, and act in reality, we have to remember that this "reality" is Scott's creation, and not just a replication of an already-known reality. Scott's practice is a concrete and specific example of what Fielding called the interpretation of historical reality. The fact that it suited Lukacs does not make it a model interpretation, which could be recommended for other novelists to follow.

In whatever way we may interpret Scott's achievement as a novelist who deals with history (and not as a historical novelist, because it can be a misleading category), the fact remains that he consolidated the novelist's links with history. Almost all the novelists who followed him maintained this connection either by writing novels in the form of realistic presentations of life or by incorporating historical materials in them with the conscious intention of responding to the historiographic moment of their times. I shall describe very briefly the views and actual practice of some novelists of the nineteenth century to illustrate these variations.

Though Henry James's fiction bears no direct involvement with actual historical figures or events of the kind we find in Scott, he accepted that the novelists had strong links with the historians: "It is impossible to imagine what a novelist takes himself to be unless he regards himself as an historian and his narrative as history.... It is only as an historian that he has the smallest *locus standi*. As a narrator of fictitious events he is nowhere" (59-60). George Eliot, who uses a great deal of history in her novels, stresses the connection between the two, by dwelling on the importance of "veracious imagination" in the writing of novels. In a notebook entry entitled "Historic Imagination," she writes:

> The exercise of a veracious imagination in historical picturing seems to be capable of a development that might help the judgment greatly with regard to present and future events. By veracious imagination, I mean the working out in detail of the various steps by which a political or social change was reached, using all extant evidence and supplying deficiencies by careful analogical creation. How triumphant opinions originally spread—how institutions arose—what were the conditions of great inventions, discoveries, or theoretic conceptions—what circumstances affecting individual lots are attendant on the decay of long-established systems—all these grand elements of history require the illumination of special imaginative treatment.[6]

This remarkable passage not only tells us about the novelists's complex engagement with history, but also details the specific ways in which he/she should give it a practical shape. The passage also analyzes the distinguishing features of the historical imagination: it helps the novelist to visualize interconnections between different events, as parts of the frame of a larger design, the web of historical reality. In other words, George Eliot reaffirms the theoretical premise of Fielding that past events have to be woven into a fabric; that is where imagination plays a crucial role in making history intelligible and illuminating.

Thackeray's involvement with the historiographic questions of his day is as important as that of Fielding. But here I confine myself to its most significant detail. He had very definite views on the theory and practice of history, and felt so strongly about them that he could not resist the temptation of contesting the views of Macaulay in his novels.[7] His views on history and historiographic method form a part of the texture of *The History of Henry Esmond*. He finds that the Muse of history in his day had become somewhat theatrical. She busied "herself with the affairs only of kings; waiting on them obsequiously and stately, as if she were but a mistress of court ceremonies, and had nothing to do with the registering of the affairs of the common people." He wants history to change its posture and take within its fold a larger area of human experience. For this, he suggests a new historiography: "I would have history familiar rather than heroic: and think that Mr. Hogarth and Mr. Fielding will give our children a much better idea of the manners of our present age in England, than the *Court Gazette* and the newspapers which we get thence" (3-4). Dickens and Hardy further consolidated the novelist's interest in history; their novels provide an unusual insight into the times in which they flourished.

This brief reference to the novelists who came after Scott and wrote about the points of commonality between novelists and historians was to show that even after him, novel-writing maintained its relation with history at levels of both form and content. But this is only one side of the story. On the other side, we find that Scott exerted a strong influence on the historians as well. This is because he used historical materials to recreate his view of the past. Imagination played a key role in this process of recreation (Fisher 98). The leading historians of his times expressed their indebtedness to him for making them aware of the power of imagination for evolving a new method of history-writing and also for drawing their attention to areas of human experience they had neglected. Carlyle admitted that Scott's "historical novels have taught all men this truth, which looks like a truism, yet was unknown to writers of history and others, till so taught: that the bygone ages of the world were actually filled by living men, not by protocols, state papers, controversies, and abstractions of men" (qtd. in Hale 36). Carlyle's words clearly state that Scott helped historians to effect a change in their priorities and in the scope of their work; he also made them aware that for producing a composite picture of the people who lived in the past, they needed to incorporate new social facts into their framework.

Another historian whom Scott influenced profoundly was Macaulay. He called Scott a model historian, to be emulated for his understanding of the historical process and its representation. In his essay "History" he writes:

> The perfect historian is he in whose work the character and spirit of an age is exhibited in miniature. He relates no facts, he attributes no expression to his characters, which is not authenticated by sufficient testimony. But by judicious selection, rejection, and arrangement, he gives to truth those attractions which have been usurped by fiction....Sir Walter Scott, in the same manner, has used those fragments of truth which historians have scornfully thrown behind them, in a manner which may well excite their envy. He has constructed out of their gleanings works which, even considered as histories, are scarcely less valuable than theirs. But a truly great historian would reclaim those materials which the novelist has appropriated. The history of the government, and the history of the people, would be exhibited in that mode in which alone they can be exhibited justly, in inseparable conjunction and intermixture.[8]

I have quoted Macaulay at length because, under the influence of Scott's thinking, he not only confirmed what had already been accepted about the relation between history and fiction, but also anticipated views which became current in the middle of the present century. Though he wrote about the importance of testimony in the making of historical works, he also gave extraordinary freedom to the historian to choose and even reject bits of testimony for making his account as interesting as that of a novelist. This in a way reaffirms and extends the principle of pattern given by Fielding and elaborated by George Eliot. It also anticipates the principle of historical reconstruction which was developed by Collingwood in the present century. Macaulay also confirms the idea of Carlyle that historians should reclaim from novelists the materials appropriated by them. He was, thus, indirectly suggesting that the novelist had already anticipated the historian in his better understanding of the proper subject matter of historical investigation.

Since Macaulay had pronounced literary leanings, it is quite understandable that Scott should influence him to such an extent. The interesting thing is that even Ranke, who had a strong influence on the development of scientific historiography, took notice of him, when he wrote that the "historical works of Sir Walter Scott, which are well known in all languages and to all nations, played a principal part in awakening my sympathy for the actions and passions of past ages" (Hale 36).

This brief reference to the views of novelists and historians was intended to demonstrate that during the eighteenth century and a large part of the nineteenth century, history and fiction shared a very substantial common ground. Historiography had a pronounced literary tilt; history-writing was regarded a literary art. This implied that "the imagination no less than the reason had to be engaged in any adequate representation of the truth; and this meant that the techniques of fiction-making were as necessary to the composition of a historical discourse as erudition might be" (White 1982, 123). But this situation did not last long.

Towards the close of the nineteenth century, the historiographic method, which had grown under the influence of Scott and the novelists who succeeded him, came under attack. Many historians felt that it had strengthened speculative elements in the writings of history, which had undermined its credibility as a discipline of knowledge. To trim history of its excesses, they advocated the alternative concept of scientific historiography. What actually happened in this was that in the process of correcting its speculative excess, the historians also defictionalized it. This promoted an altered, dichotomous relationship between history and the novel, in which history represented the real and novel the imaginary. A new emphasis on the importance of facts in the writing of history led to the growth of positivistic historiography, and the "ideal of historical literature became the monograph" (Collingwood 127). However, this reaction did not cause a complete break with the proven procedures of the history-writing of earlier times. The result was the simultaneous presence of two kinds of history: the serious and the popular, the kind of division the novel was also to experience in the early part of the present century. Here was a cultural moment of great significance: the beginnings of the elite versus the popular culture, which had serious implications for history and the arts in the years to come.

The first kind of history was the result of the new method of research and the creation of scholarship. The historian too changed from a private scholar or a public man of letters into a person who got identified with the universities. History became academicized and, as Hale puts it, "austere and unreadable." The results of this tendency were felt in greater intensity in the early years of the present century, when the reasons for such a change were felt severely: "the loss of faith by the historians in their own subject save as a training for the mind; the cult of research work on narrow subjects at the universities; and the isolation of a small group of 'serious readers' of history from the reading public at large" (Hale 56).

Under the positivistic impact, the writing of history was characterized by increasing use of quantitative methods and analytical rigour. The historians began to use statistical methods, and Clio the muse turned into cliometrics. However, alongside this, a fresh and renewed interest in history as narrative began to grow. Theoretical discussions on the fact-fiction overlap and sophisticated analyses of the relationship between fictive and historical imagination also received a spurt. The novel, too, survived a crisis of existence. After a brief spell of shying away from history, the novelists faced up to it with renewed vigour and vitality.

It was around the 1920s, right from Croce onwards, that the idea of history as a mode of reconstruction started gaining ground. This brought it closer to the idea of history as narrative, and narrative as a mode of knowledge. Though Collingwood did not refer specifically to history as narrative, he elaborated the idea of history as a process of recreation, wrote elaborately on the role of the historical imagination, and established that there was a close connection between the historical and the fictive imagination. He stressed that the historian reenacts the past in the context of his own knowledge; even while he recreates it, he also criticizes it, "forms his own judgment of its value, corrects whatever errors he can discern in it" (215).

For linking events and happenings, the historian uses his imagination, which Collingwood characterizes as being "structural." It implies that the "historian's picture of the past is the product of his own *a priori* imagination, that has to justify the sources used in its construction." This leads to one of his seminal formulations on how the historian builds the picture of the past:

> Freed from its dependence of fixed points supplied from without, the historian's picture of the past is thus in every detail an imaginary picture, and its necessity is at every point the necessity of the *a priori* imagination. Whatever goes into it, goes into it not because his imagination passively accepts it, but because it actively demands it (245).

At this point, the similarity between the historian and the novelist reaches its highest point. Collingwood elaborates it thus:

> Each of them makes it his business to construct a picture which is partly a narrative of events, partly a description of situations, exhibition of motives, analysis of characters. Each aims at making his picture a coherent whole, where every character and every situation is bound up with the rest....The novel and the history must both of them make sense; nothing is admissible in either except what is necessary, and the judge of this necessity is in both cases the imagination. Both the novel and the history are self-explanatory, self-justifying, the product of an autonomous or self-authorizing activity; and in both cases this activity is the *a priori* imagination (245-46).

Several significant points follow from this. First, the picture of the past the historian creates is his picture. This implies that its overall shape and its contours and details are ordered by him. His reasons, motivations, compulsions for making this picture may vary. Second, though he recreates his version of the past with the help of facts, he selects the ones that serve his needs. This point needs to be emphasized because later, when the very notion of 'fact' became problematic, the active involvement of the novelist with history changed its character. Collingwood, however, maintained that there was a significant point of difference between the historian and the novelist. The former had to build his picture with the things that had happened; the latter had no such obligation. His main aim was to create a coherent picture.

Another important thing that emerged from Collingwood's concept of historical reconstruction was that it set into motion a chain of thinking, which unravelled other dimensions of this new way of looking at history. For example, W H Walsh states that history proper is "a significant rather than a plain narrative of the past experience of human beings. The historian is not content to tell us merely what happened; he wishes to make us see why it happened, too. In other words, he aims... at a reconstruction of the past which is both intelligent and intelligible" (32). The idea of historical reconstruction, followed by history as narrative, and then history as an intelligible narrative—these were further elaborated by other philosophers of history, which have a bearing on the history-fiction relationship.[9]

In his exposition of the concept of history as narrative, W B Gallie states that the historian does not merely create a "coherent picture," but also a "followable narrative." According to him, this narrative, which embodies within it characters, situations, complications, etcetera, develops through a series of interim conclusions to a final conclusion. The very movement of people, incidents and happenings provides us the basis of following the story, so that it looks like a game which moves ahead according to the "teleologically guided form of attention." The most noticeable aspect of this is that though the conclusion looks acceptable to the reader or the audience, it is unpredictable. In both these respects, history resembles imaginative literature, because it "is as much a journey as an arrival, as much an approach as a result. Again, every genuine work of history is read in this way because its subject matter is felt to be worth following—through contingencies, accidents, setbacks, and all the multifarious details of its development" (67).

Louis O Mink refines this thinking further. He finds the second part of Gallie's formulation, that the reader finds the conclusion unpredictable, somewhat simplistic. For this could be true only of a naive reader, "*who does not know how the story ends*, and who is 'pulled along' by interest, sympathy, and curiosity" (112). Mink is right in what he says. We do not read stories only because we are curious to know how they are going to end. By emphasizing this we give undue importance to the element of mystery in the experience of reading, and the element of followability receives a setback. Mink states that "among both historians and critics...familiarity sometimes breeds respect" (112). What is important is not "following a story" but "having followed a story," that is, having understood it. Thus the main and also the most meaningful similarity between historians and other artists lies in creating the possibilities of this understanding.

To sharpen our perception of the affinities between the modes of understanding in history and fiction, which he relates to their processes of production, Mink distinguishes between three modes of understanding: the theoretical mode of natural sciences; the categoreal mode of philosophy; and the configurational mode common to both history and fiction. In the configurational mode, events are presented in a particular configuration as parts of a puzzle: a number of things are seen as elements in a single and concrete complex of relationships: "It is in this *configurational* mode that we see together the complex of imagery in a poem, or the combination of motives, pressures, promises, and principles which explain a Senator's vote, or the pattern of words, gestures and actions which constitute our understanding of the personality of a friend" (117). History and fiction thus teach us to follow and understand complex stories which provide answers to our questions.

Since historians and philosophers of history have shown a greater degree of open-mindedness to the absorption of influences from other disciplines, orientations towards historiography have also changed. In history as narrative which leads to knowledge, they also paid close attention to the role of language. This has led to the uncovering of other similarities between the structure and form of history and fiction. Hayden White, for example, has written copiously on the similarities between the aims and forms of historical and fictional discourses. In one of his essays, he states that the "technique or strategies that they use in the composition of their discourse can be shown to be substantially the same, however different they may appear on a purely surface, or dictional level of their texts" (1982, 121).

White believes that even in the heyday of fact-oriented historical writings, the historians wrote like the novelists, though they did not admit it. Some, as I have pointed out already, admitted their links with the novelists and even wrote about it. White also stresses a vital detail concerning the use of facts by historians, which had consequences for their writing of histories; they did not, he tells us, realize

> that the facts do not speak for themselves, but that the historian speaks for them, speaks on their behalf, and fashions the fragments of the past into a whole whose integrity is—in its representation—a purely discursive one. Novelists might be dealing with only imaginary events whereas historians are dealing with

> real ones, but the process of fusing events, whether imaginary or real, into a comprehensible totality capable of serving as the object of a representation is a poetic process (1982, 125).

Looked at closely, the passage is very similar to the one I quoted from Collingwood, especially with regard to the views on the historians's approach to the creation of his picture of the past and the affinity between historians and novelists. However, what distinguishes White from him is his rigorous analysis of the poetic process which makes these histories possible. This is perhaps the most impressive and for some the most controversial contribution of his to the debate on the history-fiction relationship, and constitutes the mainstay of *Metahistory*. It has also a strong bearing on the actual writing of history by professional historians.

According to White, the poetic process is the "deep structural content" or the "metahistorical" content of all history. It is characterized by the twin modes of emplotment and argument. Emplotment is the manner by "which a sequence of events fashioned into a story is gradually revealed to be a story of a particular kind" (1975, 7). Relying heavily on the comprehensively-schematic structural approach of Northrop Frye in *Anatomy of Criticism*, White uses his four pre-generic *mythoi* or plot-making to analyze the structure and the rhetorical strategies of the major works of history of the nineteenth century. The four modes of romance, comedy, tragedy, and satire dominated the imagination of the historians. In Michelet it is the romance; in Ranke comedy; in Tocqueville tragedy; and in Burckhardt satire. The historians also used three other devices: explanation by a formal argument at the end: formism, organicism, mechanism, and contextualism; the mode of ideological implication: anarchism, conservatism, radicalism, and liberalism; and stylistic tropes: metaphoric, metonymic, synecdochic, and ironic.

My main purpose in sketching the barest-possible outline of White's typology of the rhetorical combinations is to reinforce the evolving argument of this section that in the writing of history we have already reached a point in the West where we accept that because of methodological and stylistic choices, any set of facts can be variously described for creating different effects. Because of this, it is being increasingly believed that we cannot possibly think of a "single correct original description of anything—there can be many correct views, each requiring its own style of representation."

The historian's loss of faith in the idea of a scientific, objective conception of history, which ruled the academy for several decades, has also weakened his belief in a solid, pre-existing fact. All professional historians now accept that facts become historical only when historians invest them with significance in their narrative and analytical schemas. They also accept that history needs to be rewritten constantly, not after the gap of an age or a generation, but within the same generation, from one historian to the other: "It is indeed the wide and varied range of experience covered by all the days of all the historians that makes the rewriting of history—not in each generation but for each historian—at once necessary and inevitable" (Hexter 13). Gallie, however, pleads for the rewriting of history, because of the inadequacies of the historians; they have a tendency to oversimplify, "to see important historical conflicts in terms of black and white, as duels rather than three- or four-cornered fights" (117).

Considering that the novel is an evolving genre and that thinking on history and fiction provided a tempting situation for the novelist to incorporate more and more of history into his novels, the history-fiction connection has grown considerably in the present century, after it suffered a temporary setback because of the popularity of ahistorical formalism. In recent years, this connection has taken a new form because of some disconcerting features in the modes of history-writing. It has been seen that with the rise of the spirit of nationalism,[10] a great deal of power-politics has intruded into the writing of histories, which has provoked the novelists to write their own versions of history. For example, the colonial historians wrote the history of the colonized people in a manner that they could serve the interests of the colonial masters. This has produced little ironies of its own. In one of his very last addresses at the University of Oxford, Hugh Trevor-Roper, while speaking on the craft of the historian and the way he could function best, noted regretfully that "historians in general are great toadies of power" (381). According to one of the prominent African novelists, Ngugi, Trevor-Roper himself wrote highly unreliable things about Africa, when it was a colony of the British: "despite all the evidence of modern archaeological, historical, and anthropological scholarship [Roper] thinks that Africa had only darkness to exhibit before the colonial era" (42). This tendency among the historians persists, and has only changed its complexion. Because of their overt and covert affiliations with political establishments, and therefore their bad faith, the process and mechanism of reconstructing the past has got vitiated. This has touched grievous and alarming proportions in our country.

All the developments that I have sketched so far about history-writing and the kind of unease which the historians no longer fight shy of admitting have given an entirely new dimension to the novelist's old habit of using and interpreting history in his fiction. Earlier his involvement with it was largely because traditionally the genre had strong affinities with it. After that he built history into the very fabric of its being, so that novels became models for professional historians. But now, the novelist's use of history in fiction is more wilful, more self-conscious, more sophisticated, and invariably prompted by his desire to compete with the historian on his own terms. Many have done so in the West; some have done it with a greater degree of earnestness in erstwhile colonies. The motivations for doing so have varied because of variations in political and social conditions obtaining in these countries.

In advanced countries such as the United States, novelists have tried to present their own versions of the past of their country because they have been revolted by the political nature of the historical enterprise of the professional historians. They have openly criticized the versions of the historians as being distorted and branded their modes of presentation dull and boring. I quote the views of two leading American novelists on the nature of the historical construction and their reasons for writing histories through the novelistic mode. This is E L Doctorow in one of his interviews:

> All history is composed. A professional historian won't make the claims for objectivity of his discipline that the lay person may grant him.... We used to laugh at the way the Russians knocked people out of their encyclopaedias from one edition to the next, but we did the same thing. It turned out that the American historians had written, for the most part as an establishment—they had written out of existence the history of black people and women and Indians and Chinese people in their country. What

could be more apparent than the creativity of that? (Tom Leclair and McCaffery 270).

Doctorow is sure that the histories written by the historians had been coloured by political considerations; they had been manufactured to promote a desired view of the past. The most significant part of his argument is that he finds not much to choose between American historians who work in a free, democratic state and the historians of the erstwhile Soviet Russia, which was notoriously repressive in character.

Gore Vidal, another American novelist who has represented history extensively in his novels, states that he did it to emphasize the significance of past for understanding his present. Like the eighteenth century historians of Britain, he also wanted it to be readable: "I think recreating the past illuminates the present. We're a strange society in that we have no sense of the past. That's why I wrote my American trilogy...partly. I wanted to tell myself the story of the country because I found history as boring in school as every body else did, and it wasn't" (Stanton and Vidal 252).

Both these statements, and one could go on adding to them, make it clear that the present-day engagement of the novelist with history is different in character from what it was in earlier centuries.[11] This, however, is not meant to suggest that there is only one way in which the novelist uses history now, nor is it meant to imply that the different uses of history have necessarily led to widely-different results. The novelists' involvement with history in the nineteenth century was no less substantial than the engagement of the novelists of the present, but it has to be accepted that their cultural implications are not of the same order. This is both because and in spite of the fact that the novelist in both cases was reacting to a particular historiographical moment. If Scott and Thackeray drew the attention of the historians to some neglected areas of social and political life and helped them to evolve a pleasing method of representing the past, the modern novelists, at least some of them, virtually threaten the historians to expand their areas of historical investigation and compel their attention to developments in other fields of knowledge to improve upon their concepts and modes of presentation. Thus the main difference between the two lies in the manner in which they interact with historians and the passion with which they put forth their views.

Another difference is that in the eighteenth and nineteenth centuries, the historians showed their keenness to learn from the novelists; they did not have to be persuaded. These days, it is not historians as much as the philosophers of history who have shown keenness and openness to interact with new developments in the fields of language and literary theory. Both Hayden White and Dominick LaCapra exemplify this in ample measure, for

> they question the boundaries that separate history from literature and philosophy, to challenge what they see as the dominant trends in historiography, and to focus on the decisive role of language in our descriptions or conceptions of historical reality. Both believe that greater attention to literary critical perspectives can make historians more innovative and more aware of their assumptions and repressions (Kramer 100).

I have already stated how White uncovers the buried, hidden underlying devices and implicit assumptions in the historical works of the nineteenth century, but he consistently upholds the realizable unity of the past and the apparent order of the historical narratives that describe it. LaCapra moves beyond this position; he questions the very idea of the possibility of this unity and its representation through narratives.

LaCapra states that it is difficult to conceive of past as unity or order. Every attempt at recreating it is only an interpretation, in which the "voice" of the historian is in dialogue with the past, but "it must be actively recognized that the past has its own 'voices' that must be respected, especially when they resist or qualify the interpretations we would like to place on them" (1983, 64). Therefore, even when the historian is in conversation with the past, his involvement is much larger than merely representing it through a unified voice of an ordering device. The truth is that "the historian is in argument and even polemic—both with others and within the self—over approaches to understanding that are bound up with institutional and political issues" (LaCapra 1985, 36). If in the hands of White historiography points to the metahistorical, in the hands of LaCapra it also becomes dialogical.

The expansion in the history-fiction connection from the times of Fielding to the present, including the views of White and LaCapra, admits of a considerable change and flexibility in the conception and scope of historical representation, which brings it in line with the dominant thinking on postmodernist representation. I have already quoted the views of Doctorow and Vidal, who speak for the right of the novelist to present his version of history through fiction. Since this process takes on the shape of a self-conscious endeavour, in which attention is drawn to the manner in which the fictional mode is bent to achieve this purpose, fiction takes on the character of metafiction. Because this self-consciousness takes on the extra dimension of the novelist's visualization of himself as a historian who dilates on what history is and how it should be written, such fiction is labelled historiographic metafiction or metafictional historiography (See Hutcheon 1987, 285-305 and 1988, 105-23). Since the impulse behind writing such fiction by the novelists comes from their disagreement with the methodologies of the historians or because of their politically-motivated reconstructions, they are also revisionary in intent (see Hutcheon 1989). This is slightly different from the revisionary impulse of the historians themselves, which I have already referred to. The point that needs to be emphasized here is that though novelists write their versions to counter the overweening political slant of the professional historians, their work in turn embodies politics of a different kind: they ask for space in the domain of the historical discourse for alternate modes of representation. This makes it clear that the novelists are not necessarily better than the historians; they could be as guilty of excesses as the others.

To put the postmodernist position vis-a-vis the novelist's intervention in a nutshell. It accepts and endorses the historiographic position which posits that there can be no objective and "disinterested recordings of the past." It is especially interested in making the readers perceive how much of artifice goes in the making of narratives which present this past. Postmodernist metafiction may, therefore, include versions of the past with historical specifics, and rendered through narrative procedures which may be different from the ones used by professional historians.[12] It may also include novels which have no apparent connection with history, because they do not deal with historical specifics; they may be narratives which deal with how history is written. They are like allegorical representations of the role and function of a historian and the way he writes history. Linda Hutcheon has given examples of two such metafictions: *Waterland* and *I the Supreme.*[13] Postmodernist fictions of this kind also question and problematize the tendency of historians to present totalized views of the past, irrespective of the motivations behind it. These are contested in such fictions through "plural, interrupted, unrepressed histories" (Hutcheon 1989, 65). This particular feature also brings within its fold one of the significant ideas of Foucault who states that the historian's task of eliminating discontinuities for creating a coherent view of the past is not a mere disinterested obligation; on the contrary, it is his means of controlling the past, of gaining power over it (12; Poster 70-94).

Postmodernist metafictional historiography, therefore, is reflective of all the significant trends that stress the fluid relationship between fiction and history. By distrusting continuities and recognizing heterogeneous discourses, it also accepts that historical meaning is "unstable, contextual, relational and provisional" (Hutcheon 1989, 67). In such a framework, novels may become either alternative representations of the past, or representations of repressed voices in history, or vehicles for suggesting the provisional nature of the whole enterprise of these representations. The novels may attempt them in any combinational forms; the more multiple their aims, the more complex and problematic they may turn out to be. The interesting thing about these experimentations is that even historians have shown interest in them, to evolve new techniques for writing their accounts (See Burke 126-29).

The scenario may appear depressing to people who think that history is valuable because it provides knowledge which is firm, fixed, and stable. The upholders of postmodernism do not think so. Hutcheon, for example, sounds hopeful when she states that rather than seeing the scenario in which "fiction exploits and simultaneously calls into question notions of closure, totalization, and universality that are part of those challenged grand narratives," as being decadent or a cause for despair, "it might be possible to postulate a less negative interpretation that would allow for at least the potential for radical critical possibilities" (Hutcheon 1989, 70).

Section II

The Indian Paradigm

In the beginning of this chapter I stated that though India is an older civilization than the West, which developed several indigenous forms of art, literature, theories of aesthetics, and various complex and highly-refined philosophical systems, it missed out on developing a well-formulated Indian theory and practice of history. Because of this the possibility of an evolving debate on the relation between history and art-forms could not materialize. In a recently-published book, however, Pratima Asthana, somewhat surprisingly, claims that there is a distinct and identifiable Indian view of history:

> This view is so distinct and its voice so clear that one can hear it forever sounding across the centuries making clear the law of right and wrong. Opinions alter, manners change, dynasties come and go, creeds rise and fall, but the basic message is written on the tablets of eternity, making it evident that history is the development and revelation of providence, even though we may read it through our prejudices (iii-iv).

The passage hardly specifies what the view is; it only states that the view goes far back into time, has roots in religion, and is providential in essence. The greatest difficulty with Asthana's formulation is its vagueness, and its remoteness from the thinking and practice of modern-day historians. The last sentence of the passage makes a mystifying reference to prejudicial reading, which suggests that perhaps the view which she fails to articulate in its fullness is either not wholly true or acceptable.

Totally oblivious of these patent shortcomings of her formulation, Asthana, somewhat cavalierly, works out the implications that it has for the actual writing of history by the historians:

> The Indian view of history insists that while an historian ought to be exact, sincere, and impartial, free from passion, and unbiased by interest, fear, resentment or affection, and faithful to the truth, which is the mother of history, the preserver of great actions, the enemy of oblivion, the witness of the past, and the director of the future, the impartiality of the historian is not that

> of the mirror which merely reflects but of the judge who sees, listens and decides (iv).

This view of Asthana too poses several difficulties. First, it is so generalized in its character that it could be the view of history of any person or any country. Second, it is eclectic in its spirit and lacks specificity of ideational and cultural content. Third, Asthana does not trace any of the numerous qualifications prescribed for historians to any specific Indian source. And finally, she does not discuss or elaborate it in the rest of her book. Its chapter-arrangement, on the contrary, negates the possibility of a specific Indian view of history. For, in her very next chapter, Asthana discusses the lack of a sense of history among the ancient Indians. Then, taking a cue from the statement that ideas are the "ultimate givers of history," she refers to "Indian ideas on history and the nature of the historical" (18), in which she includes the ideas of history among the ancient Indians, the Jains, the Buddhists, and the Muslims. This is followed by her characterization of the view of history in modern India, in which she identifies three prominent strains: the spiritual view of history, the one-man schools of Nehru and Pannikar, and the view of R K Mookerji, who sees the unity of India in its geography and culture.

Asthana's discussion of these various views negates the spirit of the formulation with which she started as well as the possibility of a unified, generally-accepted Indian view of history. The truth is that no such view existed in the past, nor does it exist now. What we actually have are a number of views, which were formulated from time to time. Sometimes they supplanted each other and sometimes they coexisted over long stretches of time, because of historical exigencies. This is different from what generally happened in the West, where changes in the content and writing of history took place from time to time largely because of advances in philosophical thinking and the modes of representing reality, as for example, through novels. But in India, changes in the conception of and thinking on history were the result of the rise of new cultural forms, which remained in ascendance at different times in its history. Almost all of them were rooted in religion. However, things changed with the coming of the British. They stimulated a new awareness among people about the country's past and promoted new methods of writing history. As a consequence of this, we find that at present several views inform historical writings, which have now assumed the shape of competing historiographies, not as much for representing a specifically Indian view, though some do make such claims, as for being superior to the others. I shall sketch these views briefly, not because I am interested in them *per se,* but because these have implications for understanding the Indian novelist's interest in and use of history. It, however, needs to be stressed here that compared with what happened in the West the novelist's use of history in India has acquired an extra dimension and complexity, because of the simultaneous presence of these competing historiographies.

In his book on Indian historiography, A K Warder writes rather lamentably that "Indian historiography seems never to have been presented in any comprehensive overview before. In fact, it is even widely supposed not to exist" (1972, viii). In an earlier essay on the subject, he even stated that knowledge regarding this has been vitiated by received opinion (1961, 44-45). However, like Majumdar, he does accept that the single most important thing concerning historiography was the "encroachment of *kavya* (literary writing) on the field of *itihasa* (historical writing), the substitution of aesthetic truth for historical truth in presenting history." Although attempts have been made to rectify it by tracing "the continuity of Brahmanical historiographical traditions from the Vedic literature down to the medieval writers (Warder 1972, ix), it nevertheless remains true that the encroachment of *kavya* on *itihasa* persisted for centuries, and led to the growth and popularisation of *itihasa-purana.* Some scholars believe that these puranas were like total histories; they not only dealt with human events, but also made room for natural and cosmic happenings. It has also been suggested that in course of time they acquired the status of authoritative texts in Sanskrit, which were meant to help people regulate their everyday lives; they promoted purposive, goal-oriented knowledge for building one's character. Because of this, they became part of *Purusartha Vidyas* (Deshpande 137-66).

The original puranas were texts which contained the narratives and genealogies of ancient kings collected from various old sources and arranged and connected in a chronological sequence. It is quite understandable that they could not have been like modern-day histories. But the interesting thing about them was that these records were combined with mythology and folklore, which made them into intermixtures of fact and fiction. According to U N Ghoshal, these accounts implicitly accepted the "operation of supernatural forces in human affairs," and were marked by their "slight attention to topography and their almost complete neglect of chronology" (27). The impact of the *kavya* was so strong on them that quite often "historical events were treated merely as backgrounds for display of poetical skill, rhetorical display, or ethical maxims, and as a means of religious propaganda. Sometimes the ideal of history as an accurate delineation of past events was sacrificed in making it a source of entertainment" (170).[14] For this reason, N Subramanian compares the writers of these histories with historical novelists; they allowed "fiction to dominate facts" for literary reasons. They not only wanted to make their accounts credible and convincing, but also fit for providing delight and entertainment (332). Thus we see that even though attempts were made by ancient Indians to produce some kind of a record of events and people, it was not history as we know it now. I have already stated that gods and goddesses mixed with human beings in early historical accounts of the West too, but soon after the Renaissance the divine beings disappeared from them and human beings and their activities took their place. But in India, there was hardly any change in this for several centuries. The only exception to this trend is *Rajatarangini,* which was written by Kalhana in the twelfth century.[15] The surprising thing about it is that it did not leave any trace behind it. It needs to be mentioned here that the people who wrote and figured in these accounts were known later as Hindus. Therefore, the practice of recording things in this manner is called the Hindu view of history.[16]

Scholars have given various explanations for the lack of a properly-developed historical practice among the ancient Hindus. Most of these get connected with the philosophical foundations of the Hindu view of life. Distinguishing the Hindu view of history from the providential view of history of the Christians, the idealistic view based on reason, and the linear view of the naturalistic/humanistic kind, one commentator states that the Hindu view is cyclical, because it is rooted in the Hindu theory of Yugas, and related to the conception of Maya and the law of Karma.[17] Subramanian provides a compact statement on the distinguishing features of this thinking, by stating that Hindus:

> had a concept of time—measured in terms of Yugas, and in terms of eternity—in which the short spans of time millennia and centuries in an ordered fashion with reference to human events of no cosmic significance are naturally rejected as useless. They had a law of karma, which has, by definition, an all pervading influence on man's duties and responsibilities.... Then the concept of Maya, made famous by Sankara, held that empirical experience is unreal. Beyond the Maya is the real truth which is eternal and divine (346).

The long-stretching Yugas and Kalpas engulf the chronological time in which we actually exist. If we understand the universe from "the point of view of the Absolute," then history, as we understand it now, does not even exist (Adiswarananda 37).

If we accept the philosophical basis of the Hindu view of history, then we have to consider an important related question. Can we say that the ancient Hindus, because of their preoccupation with matters spiritual, did not possess historical sense, as we understand it now? Or is it that in spite of their world-view, they did have historical sense, but did not work hard enough to devise appropriate means for recording their activities? This is important because in the historiographical war that is going on at present these issues have been raised again and again. Several historians and commentators have it against the Hindu view of history that it does not distinguish between history and myth, because of which it legitimises a view of the past by invoking tradition and disregarding evidence. They also argue that the Hindu view is similar to the view which informs *Ramayana* and *Mahabharata,* in which fact and fiction are indistinguishable.

Several Indian and non-Indian scholars have suggested that this view is exaggerated. It is more reasonable to believe that the Hindus did not lack historical sense,[18] they just did not work hard enough to write accounts which could meet the requirements of the nineteenth-century Western conception of history. Keith, for example, states that "In view of the antiquity and the developed character of Indian civilization it would indeed be ridiculous to expect to find India destitute of historical sense, but what is really essential is the fact that, despite the abundance of its literature, history is so miserably represented..." (144). Putting it a little more explicitly, Aurobindo states that history has not been recorded in the country in the European fashion, but this does not necessarily imply that Hindus lacked a sense of history:

> ...very curiously, very fancifully, this defect has been set down to an ascetic want of interest in life; it is supposed that India was so much absorbed in the eternal that she deliberately despised and neglected time, so profoundly concentrated on the pursuit of ascetic brooding and quietistic peace that she looked down on and took no interest in the memory of action. That is another myth (190).

Aurobindo accepts that the Hindus neglected the task of recording things in precise terms, but cautions that "there is no reason why we should go out of way in this one case to attribute it to a deliberate motive or to any lack of interest in life." Several other explanations suggest that there was a deliberate design behind not recording history in the European sense; these are mostly related to various conjunctions of social and economic forces.[19] I will not go into details concerning these different positions; nor will I examine their rightness or wrongness. I only want to state that in the complex evolution of the society and culture of our country, the Hindu phase was the most ancient and lasted several centuries, without any interference from other religions and cultures. Since a large part of it was not recorded in what Aurobindo call the European sense, its later reconstructions, on the basis of evidence from various archival and literary sources, which were largely stimulated by the British historians, also stimulated investigations into the Hindu thinking on history. This eventually became one of the contesting historiographic traditions in the country.

The Jain and Buddhist views on history are closely related to the Hindu view, but I will not discuss them in detail, because they have not been influential, and do not figure in the contest I have referred to. The major view after the Hindu view is the Muslim view, because the Muslims, unlike several other conquerors, stayed on to make the country their home. When they came to India, they brought with them their well-developed historiographic tradition. This was rooted in Islamic historiography, which began from the times of the Prophet, but expanded considerably in space and time during the medieval times (See Humphreys 1991). When the

Muslims gained power in India, their chroniclers wrote historical accounts, mainly because the faith required it.[20] These were mostly about the king, his court, and their activities, and consisted mainly of what is now called political and military history. About pre-Mughal historians of India, Hardy writes that in their choice of the deeds of people and their general outlook, they were governed by religious considerations. This is reflected in the writings of Barani, Afifi, Sirhindi, Amir Khusrau, and Isami. Their histories are largely confined to the Muslims; they have been written with a religious purpose and in a predominantly Muslim phraseology. Their primary purpose, though with varying intensities, lay in serving "the cause of true religion, namely Islam. Therein lies one of the principal motives for Muslim historical writing" (Hardy 113-15). However, the situation changed with the coming of the Mughals. Historiography was rid of its heavy religious trappings and embraced new areas of social and economic experience (Nizami 154 and 225). Abul Fazal's accounts, for example, contain information which extended beyond camp and court. These included details about Hindus, especially about their religion, philosophy, and language. The result, as Mohibbul Hassan points out, was that it gradually opened up a new "rational and secular approach to history" (xiii; Mukhia 86).

The Muslim domination of the country was followed by the British. They initiated the beginnings of a systematic writing of history, through the Royal Asiatic Society of Bengal. Making use of archaeological findings and other extant literary sources, the British attempted recreations of India's past. Since they were colonial masters, these writings could not be totally unbiased. But interestingly, the true nature and real import of these histories was understood by us long after they had been written. Thus the real problematics of history in India started from the time of the British, because several accounts produced then were written from the specific object of justifying British rule in India. The writers of such histories came to be known as imperial historians.[21]

Along with the British, several historians from among the Indians developed other kinds of historiographies during the pre-independence times; they continued to flourish vigorously even after the country became free. This has led to the production of accounts of India's past from various angles. Bipan Chandra and his associates have identified several "historiographic perspectives ranging from the hard-core imperialist to the Marxist" (16-22; see also Kumar 1989, 63-69), which inform the recreations of the freedom struggle in India. These include the liberal version of the imperialist school, which denies the "existence of colonialism as an economic, political, social and cultural structure in India," and assumes that before 1947 India was not a nation, but an amalgam of several identities, largely associated with different structures based on religion, caste, class, and that there was nothing like a nationalist movement. In their view, nationalism was actually "an instrument used by the elite groups to mobilize the masses and to satisfy their own interests." This perspective is contested by the advocates of nationalist historiography, of historians like A C Majumdar and Surendranath Banerjea, B R Nanda and Amlesh Tripathi. They believe that the nationalist movement was "the result of the spread and realization of the idea or spirit of nationalism or liberty." Another school of the subaltern is dismissive of all approaches, because it considers them unrealistic and based on what they contemptuously call "elite historiography." The subalterns hold that "the Indian people were never united in a common anti-imperialist struggle, that there was no such identity as the Indian national movement. Instead they assert that there were two distinct movements or streams, the real anti-imperialist stream of the subalterns and the bogus national movement of the elite." Besides these, the other historiographic approaches include the early Marxist versions of Palme Dutt and Desai, and its later elaborations by D D Kosambi and others.

It is beyond the scope of this study to attempt a critique of these positions; I do not even want to suggest that these are the only positions, but only to emphasize that right from the times of the British, who stimulated historical consciousness in the country, history-writing became problematic. On account of this, recreations of the country's past, especially of the colonial past, and the role of different classes and communities in their fight against the British have been a source of considerable disagreement. Commenting on the present-day historiographic scene, another historian has divided the entire community of historians in the country into groups. One includes the "Imperialists, the Marxists along with the sub-class of pseudo-secularists, and finally the Muslim communalists"; their "widely different strands" get combined in their denigration of "Indian tradition"; the other group includes "the nationalists and the Hindu communalists" who "romanticise Indian tradition." The third set includes those historians who try to rise above the vitiating atmosphere and struggle to strike a new path "to write objective history with a cruel awareness of the inevitable subjective element in it" (Devahuti 1979, x).

These different groupings of historians are meant to illustrate that the process of history-writing has attained a greater degree of complexity in India than it did in the West. In a subsequent volume of essays edited by Devahuti, we get to know that the whole enterprise of historical recreations in the country has been riddled with several kinds of biases (1980, xxvii-xxviii). This difficult and complicated situation touched its lowest point when the historians of the country openly clashed with each other in 1991. The main groups in the clash were identified as Marxist and communalist historians; both charged each other with paying undue attention to certain specific periods of India's past, to legitimise their own views and positions, and paying little attention to the damage they were causing to the body-politic. Hardly a few days before this, the minister of Human Resource Development in the government complicated the situation by announcing in the Parliament that a committee had been formed to initiate a project on writing a post-1947 history of the country. It consisted of several distinguished academics, who aroused considerable controversy in the press because of their pronounced leftist leanings. Although the minister assured the members of the house that the committee would be a "completely autonomous body" akin to the "royal commission set up in Britain" (*The Indian Express*, December 25, 1991), several members expressed their apprehensions about the domineering role of the government in shaping public opinion and thinking to suit its own interests. The chairman of the committee, S Gopal, also came out in its defence by stating that it was "not a stooge organisation of the government," because he had been assured that it would have an autonomous status; he also said that it would include representatives from other educational organizations, such as the UGC, ICSSR, and the NCERT, and would not be answerable to any particular party, but to the Parliament. Some members of the committee expressed surprise over their inclusion, came out strongly against the idea, and dissociated themselves from it. They said that they were opposed to all kinds of state-sponsored history, no matter how meaningful and well-intentioned it might be.

Even before the members of the committee could write for and against it, several historians and public figures defended the position of the government in the national press. Rafiq Zakaria, for example, defended the minister's proposal on the ground that he was "trying to see that the secular character of the nation, as bequeathed to us by Gandhi, Nehru and Azad, is not destroyed" (*The Indian Express*, December 19, 1991). He admitted that it was a perfectly legitimate exercise: "Facts have many facets and historical figures are complex. Everything depends on how one looks at them" (*Ibid*).

Implicit in the formulations of Zakaria is the truth that facts can be interpreted in different ways to create a picture of the past according to one's motives and predilections. Since he wishes to promote the view that India had always been secular, he urges the historians to write histories which will meet this requirement: "Hence the past, with all its complexities, needs to be presented in a manner that will not divide our people but, on the contrary, unite them. There is enough material to highlight this" (*Ibid*). In other words, Zakaria admits that histories can be written according to a willed pattern; they can also be made to promote philosophies and ideologies which suit us. This has the further implication that histories can legitimise actions and policies of leaders and governments they represent. History is thus made into a strident resource of power. Further, it is also suggested that history is valuable not in itself, but for the views of the past it helps to present and promote.

There are two interesting, but disturbing, facets to Zakaria's defence. One, that there can be only one view of history which can be good for the nation, though the tenor of his formulation about the writing of history provides for the possibility of other views. He would like history to acquire a uniform voice, even if it meant suppressing or even destroying its complexity, its contradictions. Second, he also assumes that the state-sponsored writing of history would be used only as a resource for promoting social amity and lessening of social and ethnic strife. The truth, however, is that even after doctoring history, it may not be possible to harness the kinds of benefits that Zakaria expects from it; it may fail to promote peace and amity between social groups and communities. Apprehensions about this have been expressed by the historians themselves. Dharma Kumar, who dissociated herself from the committee, draws attention to its two major defects. First, that Indian history would be used as a political resource and not necessarily for promoting social amity: "Politicians whip up public passions by dwelling on past injustices, real or imaginary.... Now that 'historical injustice' establishes a claim to state benefits, the demand for the manufacture of usable history is increasing" (*The Indian Express*, December 28, 1991). The second defect is the illusive thinking on the part of the historians that they could counter politics involved in history-writing through government agencies: "the thought that the 'objective and impartial history' of modern India can be determined by a few academics and ultimately by MPs is frightening, besides being comic" (*Ibid*). Elaborating on this, Ramachandra Guha states that intellectuals in this country have let themselves be coopted by any political party; "they go to considerable, and often absurd, lengths to justify its policies and programmes, and are not above working in an official capacity themselves" (*Ibid*). Neeladari Bhattacharya understands the objective behind the venture, but, unlike Zakaria, does not endorse the official view: "I have no doubt that the struggle against communal visions of history is crucial at this moment in time. But the secular vision is also a democratic one. If we are silent on the way the government has acted, we weaken the very basis of those autonomous structures on which a democratic tradition can be built" (*Ibid*). Accusations of use, misuse and abuse of history by the government have increased considerably during the past several years. If the central government has been held guilty of using history for stabilising its power-base, the dismissed BJP governments of Uttar Pradesh and Madhya Pradesh were charged with rewriting, during their rule, history books for schoolgoing children with an overwhelming Hindu bias in them.

This brief sketch of the history-writing scenario in the country is meant to highlight the fact that there have been large-scale disagreements among the historians over the purpose of history and its methods of writing. This has produced divergent versions of India's past, which the historians themselves admit have been riddled with biases and prejudices.[22] In these circumstances, it is neither possible nor desirable to suggest that the novelist's interest in past—both remote and immediate—can be studied and evaluated on the basis of what he puts into his novels from what has been written about it by the historians. For what is already known through recreations is conflicting and confusing. That is why I suggest that instead of attempting comparisons between what the novel incorporates from the past and what has been recorded in historical accounts, which has been the general practice among the critics so far, it would be better and more fruitful to see in what manner and for what purpose the novelist invokes the past in his works. Does he, for example, evince any consciousness of the competing historiographies in his novels? If yes, how does it affect his own perception of what it was like in the past? Do all these considerations affect his novelistic form and style? I have already mentioned that in the West, several novelists professedly used the resources of fiction to offer alternative renderings of the past, and even problematized the very processes of historical reconstruction to provide space for marginalized groups, communities, and other underprivileged sections of the society, which the professional historians had neglected. It would be interesting to see if this kind of awareness and thinking informs the Indian English novel. We have been told by the historians themselves that existing histories have ignored large areas of social and cultural experience. But the novel, because of its traditional connection with society and its history, could incorporate a good deal of this history as well. This would be the additional gain of studying the novelist's intervention into the domain of history.

That the use of history by creative writers is valuable enough to merit serious attention is admitted by the historians of our country. In one of their annual gatherings, they devoted a special session called "History in Modern Literature" to study the "historical ideas and concepts...in literature of modern Indian languages, from the 18th century to the 20th" (Sen v). Both historians and literary critics made detailed presentations on the whole range of regional Indian literatures. In his preface to the volume in which these essays were collected, S P Sen made a mixed comment on the novelist's use of history. He conceded that the use of history by creative writers was of far greater significance than the pure history of the historians in shaping the historical outlook of a people; but he also pointed out that this use was dangerous, because writers often

> distort history according to their own prejudices or inject a heavy dose of imagination in their historical tales. This again gives rise to wrong impressions and creates misunderstandings prejudicial to social harmony. Again such literatteurs are often parochial or chauvinistic and tend to disrupt the social framework by their misinterpretations of historical facts, events and personages (v).

Sen correctly emphasizes the importance of literature in shaping the historical consciousness of a people, but his appeal to the historians regarding a careful use of literature which uses history raises several controversial issues. Implicit in Sen's cautionary advice to the historians is a sharp distinction between historians and creative writers; the former are assumed to be honest and reliable, while the latter are held guilty of distorting history, because they inject doses of imagination in them. This may or may not be true, but it raises the crucial question of the role of imagination in historical recreations. I have already shown that current thinking on this does not endorse any position in which the role of imagination is ruled out in history-writing. Further, Sen also holds the writers guilty of misrepresentation of events and personages, but does not specify what this actually implies. His remarks also make no room for different interpretations of events and people.

Sen's objections against the writers arise from his assumption that historians alone are capable of proper and valid interpretations of events and people. As against this, writers generally cause misunderstandings, which can be prejudicial to social harmony. Given the fact that historians themselves would not accept this position, one can only infer that Sen's objections are unfair and his fears unfounded. The belief that historians are honest and trustworthy because they are wedded to truth, which is the result of their wholesale adherence to facts, is also untenable. Throughout this chapter, I have pointed out that historians themselves admit that they may not be truthful and reliable. Besides, we no longer believe that we can have only one, absolute truthful picture of the past. If we accept that writers can distort history, it could be equally true of historians; they, in fact, can do so with a greater degree of sophistication and harm. Nevertheless, I do not want to suggest, as some creative writers openly do in the West, that writers are and can be better than historians because they are more sincere, honest, truthful in their intentions, and do not succumb to the pressures of ideology, and thus reverse the formulations of Sen. Nor do I want to imply, though that is also a stance very current in the West, that historians write only interested and not interesting history, which may not always lead to public good. But I do want to emphasize that our interest in and reading of the work of creative writers, particularly the ones who deal with history, should not be prejudiced by wrong assumptions about the role and craft of historians. In the context of the current views about the nature of historical discourse, Sen's remarks sound almost naive.

In spite of all the negative things that Sen has said about the novelists' use of history, he accepts that during the colonial era they used history in the novels as a weapon "to voice their nationalist aspirations" (vii). Writing with a far greater critical sympathy than his remarks would suggest, he states that if some novelists chose to include certain kinds of people and happenings in their writings, it was not because of communal considerations, a belief which is being increasingly questioned, but because they found them to be the best available embodiments of valour, patriotism, and sacrifice: they "served only as proxies of their modern counterparts all over India struggling to get rid of the British yoke" (vii).

Perhaps as a continuation of the old tradition in which *kavya* and *itihasa* had merged into each other, almost all the literatures in major Indian languages of the country had a long-standing practice of using history as a source for creating literary works. This is quite evident from the Mangal kavyas and Aitihasik gathas in Bengali, Buranjis and Rajavamsavalis in Assamese and the Bakharas and Powdas in Marathi. Under the impact of the British rule and the new modes of mixing history and fiction in England, there was a steady increase in the conscious use of history by writers in the nineteenth and twentieth centuries. This is largely reflected in dramas and novels, in which past history was used, apart from many other things, as a resource for promoting national consciousness among people.

It needs to be mentioned here that the rise of prose narratives in regional literatures, which subsequently led to the growth of the novel, was the outcome of a conjunction of several factors. The influence of the British was of primal importance, for the first attempts at writing novels were imitations of the British novels, even of the second-rate ones. Through imitation the writers became aware of the use and usefulness of realism as a literary strategy. These first attempts were primarily for the purpose of promoting social reform, but soon they moved into the realm of adventure of the heroic kind, which further led to the use of "fantasy and intimations of history" (Mukherjee 38). In several novels, the novelists brought in characters from actual history and made them interact with invented characters. This also coincided with the interest of the novelists in their past which was occasioned by a cultural crisis, which Indians had to face in the middle of the nineteenth century. Since the British had shown interest in India's past and had started writing about it, the novelists, along with social reformers, intellectuals, and literatteurs, also became interested in it. The growth of English education further stimulated in the public an awareness of history, which, in contrast to its mythic trappings, was understood in a new perspective—as the movement of events and happenings in time. Finally, it all got linked with the rise of nationalism. Thus the overall cultural mood was such that the writers found it both interesting and necessary to incorporate their country's past, recent as well as remote, in their writings; the readers, too, having developed interest in history, were willing to read about it. Thus fiction based on history "with varying degrees of historical accuracy, was a necessary part of the new situation" (Mukherjee 40). Another consideration, not linked directly with the kind of social and political situation which warranted the writer's interest in history, prompted the growth of such novels. Many novelists found the present dull, boring, and colourless, even uninspiring; this led them to find materials for writing novels in the past. Later, this situation almost reversed: the developments in the present interested them directly in writing novels in which they tried to connect the present with their past.

The most remarkable thing in the early phase of the development of the novel in India was that the novelist's concern with the past permeated all the literatures of India. One could find it in Govardhanram Madhavram Tripathi in Gujarati, Bankim Chandra in Bengali, Dbadanathakalita in Assamese, N H Kulkarnee and Hari Narayan Apte in Marathi. About Tripathi's *Saraswati*

Chandra, V K Chavda writes that apart from being a novel and a work on statecraft and philosophy, it is also an "essay on the present political conditions of British India and of the native states, a picture of the relations of the latter with the former" (Sen 134). Kalyan Kumar Dasgupta states that "patriotism, largely generated by history" was "the prime moving spirit" in major Bengali writings. Bankim's involvement with history was praised by the historians themselves: "His mastery of details and his eminent success in portraying the personality of an age elicited the praise of no less a historian than Jadunath Sarkar" (Sen 32). Gopal Chandra Misra finds a "note of robust national consciousness and social awareness" (Sen 66) in a large number of Oriya novels.

The most interesting, significant, and also controversial aspect of the novelists' work during this time was their selective use of history, for arousing the national spirit, in which they privileged some communities over the others. For example, most of them glorified the Marathas, the Rajputs, and the Sikhs. Since the principle of selection itself is now being viewed as a political act, this particular tendency had its effect on the course of events in India, both before and after its independence. When Bankim, for example, wrote about the glorious deeds of the local communities against the Muslim oppressors who had come from the outside, it may have been a strategy for expressing resentment against the contemporary British through a tactical disguise, but it earned for him the blame that he was anti-Muslim. Some historians go to the extent of saying that the rising tide of Hindutva in present-day India can be traced to these tendencies; that the nationalist spirit and hence the very shape of the nation-to-be was conceived largely in terms of a Hindu identity. Some, however, look at these practices more sympathetically, by judging them in terms of their intended effect. Analyzing this aspect of Bankim's novelistic practice, Meenakshi Mukherjee writes that Bankim's attacks on the Muslims in his recreations of the past were not because of their religion, but because they were foreigners, which aligned them with the British: "When Bankim talked of the present he could see the Hindu and the Muslim both as part of the exploited masses. But in the context of the past his image of the Muslim changed into the alien oppressor and his position automatically shifted."[23]

In the early Hindi novels of Devakinandan Khatri, Kishorilal Goswami and Gangaprasad Gupta, fact and fiction are blended in varied proportions. But in virtually all of them, in contrast to the Hindus, the Muslims are shown in a poorer light. Interestingly, in the Urdu novels of Abdul Halim Sharar, the novelist goes into the distant past of Europe and Spain to show the superiority of the Islamic civilization over the Christian.

Along with the growth of novels in different languages of the country, novels came to be written in English, too. Most of the early ones showed considerable interest in the use of history. Bankim, in fact, wrote his first novel in English. Romesh Chander Dutt translated his *Slave Girl of Agra* from Bengali into English. Its assessment by critics suggests that though it provides some details about the social life of sixteenth and seventeenth century Mughal India, its primary focus is on the love story of Sirish and Hemalatha. Historical details have been invoked only for the purpose of providing the right kind of setting for enhancing the charm of the story (Ramamurti 233). Jogender Singh's novel *Nur Jehan* is also about the Mughal past. There are varied views about its success as a novel which evokes a past era, but none of them clarifies the purpose for which history has been invoked by the novelist.[24]

The impulse for invoking the historical past for the purpose of arousing national consciousness came to the Indian English novel a little later than in the novels in other languages; for the major tendency in the first phase of its development was to produce historical romances, in which history was used primarily as a backdrop for tales of love. But the growing tide of resistance among the people against the British helped it to come into its own. In responding to the needs of the present, the novelists tried to make sense of what had happened in the past. Some went into the remote past, for awakening national consciousness among people. For example, A S P Ayyar wrote *Baladitya* in 1930 and *Three Men of Destiny* in 1939. Unlike the novelists who wrote in languages other than English, he did not use episodes from the history of Rajputs, Sikhs and Marathas to revive memories of India's glorious past, but went further back into time, when India faced its first conqueror in the Greeks. In his introduction to *Baladitya,* Ayyar clarified that he wrote it for awakening the forgotten memory of the people about their heroes. In his introduction to the second novel, he stated that

> nothing is more appropriate in the present glorious renaissance period of India, when Eastern and Western ideas are stirring people into various kinds of political, artistic and religious expression peculiarly their own, than depicting the story of the time when India first came into violent contact with the greatest and the most civilized nation in Europe then—the Greeks (Jayaraju 88).

In the wake of the nationalist struggle, the Indian English novelists got more and more involved in the momentous events of their immediate past, though, for understanding it, they occasionally went into the country's farthest past as well. This increased the range of their interest in history. In the available corpus of criticism on this novel, there is no comprehensive study on how these novelists made use of history in their novels. Several authors who figure in this study, such as Anand and Sahgal, have not been considered fit subjects for this kind of investigation. It is because, for understanding the novelist's use of history, the critics have been guided by their perception of the concept of the historical novel, which, as I have tried to demonstrate, is a limiting and unreliable category. The assumption behind the present study is that the novelist's use of history can embrace various layers of signification, which deserve to be studied because of their manifold implications. The Indian English novelists have consistently shown their interest in and awareness of history, and have used it differently in their novels. Some have evinced interest in the exciting experiments that have been made in the West in the interface between history and fiction. The present study examines the various ways in which history has been used by the novelists for different purposes.

Notes

1 This conspectus is just an outline and not a critique of the various positions that have emerged from time to time. These different and differing positions are only meant to show the shifts that have taken place in the novelist's engagement with history.

2 All the views referred to in this paragraph are in the nature of a general statement on the Hindu view of history. Its implications are elaborated in the second part of this chapter.

3 Barnes confirms this when he writes that Gibbon "had a lofty idea of the historian as the architect of a great literary and scholarly enterprise, and only supreme contempt for the mere copyist or research clerk, who has become the historian *par excellence* in our day" (159).

4 For some interesting details on the connection between history and fiction in nineteenth century Britain, see Ralph J Crane (2).

5 For a lucid elucidation of these points, see Avrom Fleishman (37-101). For Scott's varied use of history in his novels, see Harry E Shaw (51-150).

6 Quoted in Fleishman (158). For an interesting piece on how the veracious imagination has turned into a voracious imagination, see Cushing Strout (428-43).

7 For details on the interesting connection between Thackeray and Macaulay, see Christina Crosby (44-68).

8 Quoted in Fleishman (113). For elaborations on this, see Jane Millgate (119-21).

9 Discussions on the subject of history as narrative have featured in books and essays, especially in *History and Theory*. See, in particular, Maurice Mandelbaum (413-19) and "Mandelbaum on Historical Narrative: A Discussion (275-94). Polemics related to this is covered in Hayden White, "The Question of Narrative in Contemporary Historical Theory (1-33). See also his *The Content of Form: Narrative Discourse and Historical Representation*.

10 For the adverse effect of the rise of nationalism on history-writing, see Barnes (236).

11 In a conversation with Gunter Grass, Salman Rushdie observes that writers these days have a kind of historical project: "...the purpose of the fiction was in a way paradoxical, that the fiction is telling the truth at a time at which the people who claimed to be telling the truth are making things up. So in a way you have politicians or the media or whoever, the people who form opinion, in fact making the fictions. And it becomes the duty of the writer of fiction to start telling the truth. This is a kind of paradox which perhaps is true of many countries now." See Bill Bourne (54).

12 Historians too recognize that postmodernist historiography is aesthetic and accept that different interpretations of reality arise from different styles of presentation. Because of this, "representations of reality have

been taken over by the aesthetic nature of historiography." See F R Ankersmit (144).

13 (1989, 64). About the protagonist of the first novel, Tom Crick, Hutcheon writes that he is "in some ways an allegorical presentation of the postmodernist historian who might well have read, not just Collingwood, with his view of historian as storyteller and detective, but also Hayden White, Dominick LaCapra, Raymond Williams, Michel Foucault, and Jean Francois Lyotard" (56).

14 R C Majumdar (1967, 24). It is interesting to note that Nehru calls this kind of history "imagined history," and argues that "this imagined history, mixture of fact and fiction, or sometimes only fiction, becomes symbolically true and tells us of the minds and hearts and the purposes of the people of that particular epoch. It is true also in the sense that it becomes the basis for thought and action, for future history. The whole conception of history in ancient India was influenced by the speculative and ethical trends of philosophy and religion" (77).

15 R C Majumdar (1970, 5). D D Kosambi disputes Majumdar's praise for the work of Kalhana; he thinks that the historian "lapses into legend, myth, or pure romance." See his "A Marxist's Interpretation of Indian History," in Murty (37-40).

16 It is being increasingly believed that the Hindu view of history informed "the historical imagining in the nineteenth century of 'India' as a nation." See Partha Chatterjee (112). He shows how Mrityunjay Vidyalankar's history of India *Rajabala* (1808) was a "mixture of myth, history, and the contemporary" (117).

17 This is based on the long expository essay of Adiswarananda (21-58). See also, Buddha Prakash, "The Hindu Philosophy of History," in Murty (27-30).

18 Majumdar endorses this view. He uses Kalhana's example to prove that there was "no inherent defect in their mental outlook or intellectual development which rendered them incapable of producing good historical literature" (1967, 24).

19 Kalidas Bhattacharya writes that Hindus "had a clear concept of history...and also a sense of history. The absence of *historical literature* can, however, be easily explained. It is because the Indians were very much aware that the study of history as the correct record of events often revives socio-political hatred among the different groups of people in a society who after a long and bitter struggle with one another had after all got reconciled and learnt to live in amity. Social peace cum stability was to the traditional Indians, as to us even to this date, something which they were not prepared to sacrifice for anything

else" (89). Kosambi explains it to their habit of not keeping documents and records for long periods of time.

20 The strong connection between Muslim historiography and religion has been pointed out by Barnes: "The main incentives to Muslim historical writing in the first centuries after Mohammed lay in the desire to hand down the authoritative traditions of Islam...to celebrate the Muslim conquests and to laud the Muslim conquerors.... Muslim historical writing was primarily religious and political history" (94).

21 In an essay "Rewriting Indian History" (1963), D P Singhal writes elaborately on the nature of British writings on India which suffered from "prejudices based sometimes on personal bias but often on group consciousness." He also argues that the British historians presented a distorted picture of the country not only by suppressing certain facts, but also by contrasting the best aspects of the British culture and contribution with the worst features of the society. That is why he calls the imperial historiography partisan historiography (232 and 249). According to Ravinder Kumar "British historical scholarship when it applied itself to India created a literature which reflected, in equal proportions, the apologetics of imperialism and the glorification of colonial social engineering in our society" (1983, 88).

22 The complicated nature of India's past has been accurately stated by Hiren Mukerjee: "India bears the load of a complicated past, of which the depths, the contradictions and the countless thorns that prick at both ends require a monumental effort if they are to be understood" (74).

23 Mukherjee (54). M K Haldar also defends Bankim. He states that he was not a Muslim baiter, and though he "identified his nationalism with Hindu *Dharma,* his interpretation of it was different." "To Bankim Bengal is a land of Hindus and Muslims" (112 and 180-88).

24 Bhupal Singh writes that "*Nur Jehan* is a failure. Sardar Jogender Singh has little historical imagination" (307). Contesting this view, Ramamurti writes that "it has many merits and excellences which have been missed by critics" (252).

Chapter III

Making History with Anand

As one of its pioneers, Mulk Raj Anand put the Indian English novel on a solid footing and gave it a purposeful direction. He has been writing for over five decades and has produced impressive variety of fictional and non-fictional writings: over a dozen influential novels and several volumes of short stories; works on art and art criticism; and numerous essays and books on Indian history, culture and civilization. Anand has also been a responsive public figure, who has taken active part in social and cultural movements, at official and non-official levels, and has held several distinguished offices inside and outside the country.

It could be said without any risk of controversy that Anand's most durable work was produced by him before India became free in 1947 in the form of a series of socially-meaningful novels: *Untouchable*, *Coolie*, *Two Leaves and a Bud*, *The Village*, *Across the Black Waters*, *The Sword and the Sickle*, and *The Big Heart*. They are seriously concerned with the history and politics of pre-independence India. These were followed by the publication of *Apology for Heroism*, which provides a comprehensive description of Anand's literary creed: his views on the nature and function of literature and the role of a writer in society.[1] Besides, it also provides an influential statement on the responsibility of a writer in the context of the specific historical situation into which Anand was born. However, theoretical formulations on his novelistic practice and the concerns which he thought vital for a writer are exemplified in the novels he had already published. He wrote three more novels between 1953 and 1964—*Gauri*,[2] *Private Life of an Indian Prince*, and *The Road*. These too are permeated with vigorous social and political engagement which characterized his pre-1947 fiction.

Apart from novels, works of short fiction, and non-fictional writings, Anand's major work after 1947 consists of a set of sequentially-arranged novels, which form part of his long autobiographical work *The Seven Ages of Man*. Through a very thin disguise, they document in a vivid and dramatic manner his growth as man and writer. The series is not complete yet; only four of the proposed seven novels have appeared so far, but he has sketched the rest of them.[3] The four already published— *Seven Summers* (1951), *Morning Face* (1968), *Confessions of a Lover* (1976), and *The Bubble* (1991)—cover his life from childhood to the time when he chose to return to India from England and be a writer. Looking at the entire corpus of Anand's work from the beginning to the present, the current phase of his autobiographical novels could be seen as one in which he returns to his experiences of childhood and early life. Because of this, it would be fruitful to read Anand's work from his current phase to the early one: from the autobiographical works to the *Apology*, which he rightly calls the autobiography of his ideas, and then to the novels which appeared before 1947. This will provide a clear perspective on the kind of consciousness that Anand embodies as a writer, and help in explaining and illustrating his complex and multi-faceted engagement with history and the issues that have dominated his fiction.

Anand's interest in history is intimately connected with his larger involvement with the social and political issues of his day, which led him to inquire into the country's past, and to interpret it for himself, an exercise which had been undertaken virtually by all the thinking minds of his times: politicians, social reformers, and intellectuals of different pursuasions.[4] He examined the current social and political scene, and tried to understand it by relating it to India's past at several levels; starting with what he could know from within the range of his living experience, he delved into its distant and remote past. Since what he learnt went into the making of his fiction, it could be said that in Anand we have one of the best examples of a writer who is both a historical witness to the times in which India was passing through a momentous phase of her history as well as an interpreter of India's past. Through this exercise, Anand also succeeded in achieving several other things, which distinguish his work from his immediate contemporaries, such as R K Narayan and Raja Rao. By seizing on significant social, political, and cultural details related to the history of India as the material of his fiction, he transformed the novel into a powerful medium of consciousness-raising among his people.[5] This gave it a revolutionary character. The choice of these details also helped Anand to remove the residual traces of romance from the existing narrative forms and lay the foundation of a vigorous, critical realism, which gave the Indian English novel a new purposeful shape and form. This eventually stabilized it as a dominant mode of fiction-writing in the country, and continues to be one of its strains even now. It is also significant that Anand's concern with social and cultural experience led him to treat in fiction even such experiences which had not yet entered the domain of fiction and history both. For history-writing during those days lacked the comprehensiveness that we associate with it at present. His novels, therefore, also provide a rich store of novelized historiography.

Anand's autobiographical novels owe their origin to a long confessional he wrote at a feverish pace for his Irish friend Irene (1967, 28-29). They provide details about his childhood and growing up and document his involvement in several actual significant social and political happenings. The result is that a sensitive awareness of the turmoil of the times in which he grew permeates through them. He subjected to constant scrutiny what he saw and heard around him: in his family, school, and the society at large; for he did not like to accept things on the basis of hearsay or on the authority of others. He chose to judge and evaluate things on his own: at first, somewhat intuitively, but later with the help of insights provided by his scrutiny of the country's past. This is where his involvement with history acquires a significant dimension. Comprehensive formulations on what he thought of India's social and cultural past figure in the *Apology* and later in his work on Indian civilization, but this understanding informs the novels he wrote before 1947.

Anand's inquisitiveness led him to question his parents too often and invariably to their annoyance. He was struck by a divide in their thinking. His mother had a strong faith in her gods, but it was inextricably mixed up with her love for rituals and acceptance of superstitions. His father had given up the traditional affiliation of his community with the Agha Khan and had turned into a reformist Arya Samaji, but had no firm faith in the new movement, mainly because the British considered the Samajis revolutionaries and a threat to their existence in the country. Anand's neighbours encouraged him to get to know about the winds of change that were blowing across the country; they tried to make him understand and believe in the concept of non-violence. He was encouraged to read *Hind Swaraj*, for knowing Gandhi's views on the nature of the British presence in India and the ills of Indian society. He felt drawn towards the nationalists, who were organizing people to fight the British and the exploitative system they had instituted in the country. He also felt the glow of freedom, but, possibly because of his youthful zest, his early expression of it was more poetic and less substantial (*Morning Face*, 441); later, he related it to concrete and material particularity.

Like traditional Indian mothers, Anand's mother narrated to him stories of the gods and goddesses, legendary heroes, and about actual historical happenings. When she told him how the people who had been massacred in Jallianwallah Bagh in Amritsar by the British would rise in the form of ghosts, his fiery imagination could see them rising (*Morning Face*, 446).[8] He constantly felt provoked to fight the British, but was not sure of the right method: whether to fight for swaraj with the help of force or with the Gandhian method of non-violence? Nevertheless, he was excited by the political protest marches against them; at one time, he participated in a procession taken out in support of Lala Lajpat Rai. For this, he was turned out of his school, but his father's influence with the British helped him to continue there. As a college student at Lahore, he was arrested for his alleged involvement with bomb-making, but was released through the efforts of the poet Iqbal. To get away from the constricting atmosphere of his home and the repressive society which he found extremely disagreeable, he chose to go to England. There he subjected himself to self-scrutiny and realized that freedom, not just from British domination, but freedom as an informing principle of human existence, should be the most cherished goal of all human beings. Societies should be so organized that this becomes a reality. When he looked at his country from this perspective, he found its present oppressive and its past "ossified"; this led him to take vital decisions about his own future. Disregarding the wishes of his father, he decided not to seek a career in the British government, but to be a "poet of tomorrow, seeing everything *de novo*" (*The Bubble*, 9). After resolving to devote himself to his new task, he chose to return to India to become a writer. His main objective was to make his countrymen conscious of their present condition, so that they could seek ways and means for fighting it.

I shall discuss three significant aspects of Anand's life till he returned to India from England, which have a bearing on his involvement with history. First, his serious thinking on issues which were a source of conflict between his parents: the role of religion in human affairs and their attitude towards the British. I have already said that Anand's mother believed in religion, but failed to distinguish between the essence of religion and its ritualistic institutionalization. She had so much faith in the miraculous efficiency of religion for promoting human good that on several occasions she sought to cure Anand of his illnesses through the efforts of priests, even of other faiths. The reformist leanings of his father could not withstand his excessive anxiety about political expediency. This had also a bearing on the other issue of contention between him and his wife: their attitude towards the presence of the British in India. Since he was in their employ, he was deferential towards them; he made everything in his life, including his faith, subservient to the needs of his career. Contrary to this, Anand's mother, though she was illiterate and had unshaken faith in the justice and mercy of her gods, was rabidly anti-British. She often told Anand that the British were unjust: "…it is a bitch, this Sarkar….It shouldn't do so much zoolum on people!" (*Seven Summers*, 130-31). Because she was aware of the timidity of her husband, she urged Anand to model himself on his maternal grandfather and not on his father: "Be a man like my father, the Sikh Surma, who never accepted defeat even though he lost his land!" (*Seven Summers*, 131). Anand's attitude towards religion and its role in India's past and present was shaped largely by the discord he experienced in his home.

Second, Anand's attitude towards the British, which is complex. During his early impressionable years, the British fascinated him. It was not merely because of their relatively uninhibited life-style, but also because he associated them with material products, which made life comfortable and enjoyable. In fact, the effect of their material prosperity on him was so strong that he equated their home Vilayat with a dream-world of new and colourful products:

> These wonderful products of western civilisation illuminated the course of my imaginings so intensely that I built up a vivid dream-world Vilayat.... The fervour of these early desires sank into the labyrinths of my mind, soaked me in the colours of this fantasy and filled me so that though it became a less superficial and more conscious inclination afterwards, my first goings into dreams...(*Seven Summers*, 99).

During his college days in Lahore, the poet Iqbal drew his attention to another aspect of the West: its belief in progress through human agency, which sharpened his rebellion against his gods and their deputies on earth, the brahmins and mullahs. The poet encouraged him to imbibe the new attitude the West symbolized for him: "We must change our outlook...we must take fresh inspiration from the West. We may differ from them. But they have shown that the world is made by man. Not by God. Man makes himself" (*Confessions of a Lover*, 158). This new perception about the liberating influence of the British was combined with another facet of their stay in India, which was exploitative in the main. Anand understood it partly through his own experience and partly through Gandhi. These two aspects about the British—their exploitation of the Indian people and their liberalising influence on his attitude and thinking—constitute an important part of his mental make-up, which shaped his understanding of India's past and contributed to his thinking on the reconstruction of Indian society.

Third, Anand's attitude towards the lower rungs of Indian society. His autobiographical novels and the volume of autobiography he wrote about his childhood days provide vivid details about Anand's sympathetic attitude towards the lowly and the humble. In violation of the express commands of his parents, he associated with them because he loved them and felt happy in their company. Bakha, the protagonist of *Untouchable*, is modelled on his actual childhood companion. The most significant thing about his attitude towards them is that he invests them with qualities and virtues which his countrymen at that time would have thought simply unimaginable:

> How much kinder and more prodigal in their generosity were these humble, poor sepoys, workmen and untouchables than my own parents, who regarded themselves as their superiors and always forbade me to touch anything belonging to them!...I learnt a great deal of what I know from these people, the gift for making things, of telling a tale as well as making tea, and all my manhood was built up on the experiences of these...moments spent in truancy (*Seven Summers*, 150).

The purpose of isolating these three strands in the formative years of Anand is to emphasize that these influenced his choice of inquiry for examining the past of his country and shaping his views on the society and culture of his day. *Apology*, which is a fairly comprehensive chart of his intellectual development, provides details about both, but the seeds of his ideas were already there when he started writing; these inform his pre- and post-independence fiction. Since he had been taught as a student that Indian history and tradition were inferior to the Western ones, he resolved to examine critically the tradition into which he had been born and to understand its history. He needed this also for locating himself in the very process of history.

Apart from his dissatisfaction with the institution of religion, which had fostered unhealthy practices, and which he got to know through first-hand experience, by visiting temples, mosques, gurudwaras, and churches, Anand found himself extremely uncomfortable with the Hindu religion into which he was born. Its most distressing aspect for him was the view of man and history implicit in it. In the face of Vedantic Absolutism, the universe shrank into the "tiniest speck in the aeons of the historical process in which all things were tending towards the Divine" (1986, 69). The eternal cycle of birth and rebirth, which was the only available way for getting absorbed into the divine, reduced human beings into ciphers. Anand called such a tradition a "negative tradition," because it diminished a human being into "a frantically agitated, impetuous, fictional being" and "dwarfed [him] into insignificance" (1986, 70). Anand had a similar complaint against Christianity, because it wrapped human beings in an eternal cloak of sin: "...the whole presumption about man being born in sin, which lay at the root of Christian ethic, seemed obnoxious" (1986, 75). Though Christianity had ceased to have a cramping effect on people in the West, Anand found that the people of his country continued to suffer because of their religious beliefs.

Anand understood that the repulsive aspects of the society of his day had their roots in the past, but he did not condemn the heritage of his country outright; nor did he accept the values of the West indiscriminately. In this he can be placed squarely with the critical modernists or syncretists, with people like Ram Mohun Roy, K C Sen, G K Gokhale, though he differed from them in many ways. Considering the nature of the colonial situation in the country, the manner in which the British had gained control over the people, and also the degradation in the very fabric of Indian society, Anand could not align himself with the traditionalists, who were for the wholesale acceptance of the country's old past. In fact, he rejected the view that its past had been consistently glorious and without a blemish and that the British occupation of the country was no more than a temporary irregularity. Nor could he totally be with the modernists, who believed that there was nothing worth keeping from the past, because it was deformed and disfigured and totally irrelevant to the needs of the present. Instead, he pleaded for a serious, critical reexamination of the past for its balanced and realsitic appraisal. He wrote about it with unequivocal clarity:

> We in India had done a great deal of thinking about qualitative aspects of the universe. The great religious and cultural tradition of India was of immense consequence to us; and we were concerned to rescue it from debasement in the currency of ordinary practice and to take from this heritage of ours what was useful to us to-day. But we were not willing to let our preoccupation with the values of our past prevent us from achieving new ones (1986, 89-90).

He also stated clearly the reasons for doing this: "...to lift ourselves from the degrading, sub-human levels at which our masters preferred to leave us, to a human awareness, to the mastery and control of ourselves as well as of the natural forces which surrounded us, to a new synthesis of values" (1986, 90).

Being acutely aware of his location in time, in which the British had become a part of India's past, and had already shaped the thinking and attitudes of its people, Anand does not merely delve into the ancient past of the country, but in its British past as well. That is why he states: "So I struggled to weigh up the double burden on my shoulders, the Alps of the European tradition and the Himalayas of my Indian past, all my senses aching to realize the significance of the history of my country, all my heart and brain devoted to the search of those causes which had led to its present degeneracy; and ...to prepare for the future" (1986, 104).

Anand's main purpose in going into the past of his country was to find out why things had come to a sorry pass; he wanted to know what could be retrieved and retained from it for shaping a new future. His approach was pragmatic and dictated by the needs of the times; it had also a specific purpose, which determined the scope of his inquiry. He found that for reshaping the future of the country, he needed to contend with the colonial situation and the mess in its social structure. He understood the presence of the British in India largely in terms of the Marxian framework. Their exploitation of India had started off with the efforts of their merchants; they had converted the country into a dumping ground for their products, destroying in the process whatever capabilities it had for sustaining industry of any kind and scale. All this had worked for them because of the absence of an organized middle class. I do not go into the details of his analysis, because my main interest is in the conclusions he reached. Having found that the colonial structure was totally exploitative, Anand thought it necessary to explore why the Indian people had accepted the British for so long without much resistance. In effect, he was looking for a more plausible explanation for the growth and expansion of the British control in India; the Marxian explanation did not seem to reach the essential core of the problem. For this, he chose to reach the wellsprings of their thought-patterns, to probe the very roots of their actions and the way they related themselves to the world around them. He found that the main cause of their present condition was the acceptance of the divine intervention in human affairs; they had believed that God was always present in history and human actions were subservient to His will. In other words, they had believed in the divine interpretation of history, in which events and happenings were governed by forces beyond the control of humans. That is why he wrote in *Apology*: "We put too much emphasis on the unknown fate and prostrated ourselves towards the deity, under the guidance of our priestly mentors.... We became bound in the cycles of *Karma*" (11)[6]. It needs to be mentioned here that Anand's enquiry is largely directed from the viewpoint of a Hindu, but the conclusions he arrived at had relevance for all communities. Colonialism for a vast majority of Indians was divinely ordained. The British understood this and exploited it fully to strengthen their position.

Anand also found that this attitude to history, in which the sources of change lay outside the domain of human will, had a bearing on the second part of his inquiry, which was to find out why the deformed social structure with its dehumanizing practices had flourished for long, especially among the Hindus. He found that people had accepted gross inequalities in social structure because a selected few had exploited people's belief in the force of faith to their advantage: "...One had grown up in a muddled society, where the realities of life lay buried beneath the thick crust of mendacity and superstition, of dogma and unreasoned belief, where knowledge had been sedulously built up only in the interests of the few, where the whole tendency to light was unconsciously choked up amid the perversions of faith, in order to avert a change of the current social order" (1986, 112).

After understanding the reasons of India's political and social degradation by analyzing its past, Anand realized that any change in the present in a desired direction could be possible only through an effective intervention into the very tide of history. For this he envisaged a massive transformational programme: "Nothing less was involved than a reorientation of one's outlook on history as well as a complete transformation of present-day society from the new point of view" (1986, 11).

Anand's ideas on historical change, which embraced social, religious and political reality are subsumed under his programme of humanism, in which he offers an alternative view of history, which is man-directed. Being different from the divine, deterministic view, which had resulted in the ossification of the country's social and political structure, it had several new features, which are woven into the very fabric of the fiction of his first phase. In his full-length study of Indian civilization, Anand documented its growth, the changes that had taken place in it, the influences it had absrobed from non-native sources, and the kinds of humanisms it had thrown up from time to time, as sources of hopeful change. But he carefully distinguished his humanism from that of others, including the ones recommended by his contemporaries, especially because he thought them inadequate and wrongly-conceived. For example, he distinguished his version from the ones of Gandhi and Tagore, because it rested neither on divine sanction nor on any intimations of the mystical. Instead, he based it on a judicious combination of reason and imagination and in human capacity to seek beauty and perfection:

> ...the humanism I put forward is against all organised faiths, though I feel that, by relegating religion to private conscience, the tasks of social reconstruction are more easily possible. Freedom of conscience is, however, itself a touch-stone of humanism. Only, it is gradually more amenable to the sanctions of enlightened emotion, reason, science and imagination, and goes to make that something unconquerable in the spirit of man, which is proof against perversions, untruth, social injustice and oppression (1963, 156).

Anand believes that creative writers are uniquely gifted to take active and effective part in cultural reorientations by changing people's attitude towards history. They can "relate the inner and outer forms of human experience" and integrate "thought and reality more constantly in their work than any other person." The writer, in fine, is eminently suited to be the "conscience of the race, the guide, the mentor" (1986, 146-47).

One of the twelve premises of Anand's humanistic philosophy is its opposition to "all theories of fatalistic acceptance of God, predestination and determinism." He believes that human beings possess genuine freedom of creative choice and action, and "every man is master of his own destiny" (1963, 159). That is why he emphasises that change can and should be directed by human beings and not dictated by divine forces. All that it requires is that people should build faith in institutional structures which can direct the processes of history in a desired direction. In this, Anand is like Gramsci, though the latter wrote about it in a different context:

> History is a continuous process of development and hence is essentially unpredictable. But this does not mean that...history ...is the domain of arbitrariness and irresponsible caprice. History is at once freedom and necessity. The institutions in whose development and activity history is embodied emerged and con-

tinue to exist because they have a task and a mission to accomplish (75).

As an extremely responsive and responsible individual, Anand began his writing career fully conscious of the role of a writer with a strong sense of engagement, which encompasses his engagement with history. It would not be an exaggeration to state that this is the *raison de etre* of his novel-writing. He bent the existing form of the novel to make it into a vehicle for intervening into the very processes of history. I have already shown how the novel in the West changed from time to time, both in its form and content, because the novelists made adjustments in their modes of writing to respond to the historiographical moment of their time. Anand too made changes in the art of fiction-writing in India to make the novel responsive to his new vision of history. This not only involved making changes in fictional strategies and the choice of experiences for inclusion in his fictional universe, but also formulating a new theory of the novel, which is revolutionary in character. The very conception of Anand's novel as also his novelistic practice is directly related to his engagement with India's past and present.

Anand considered novel-writing a suitable mode for working out and transmitting his understanding of his present in terms of the country's past. This had a direct bearing on the distinct shape and character of his fiction. It led him to think on the role of a writer in the context of his historical situation and issues related to social and cultural transformation. When he began writing, he posed a question to himself: "Was I to be a pure artist or would I have to play some part in the political life of the day" (1986, 79)? Rejecting the notions of Proustian aestheticism and the growing isolationism of the Western writer which had been the result of the ascendance of the ahistorical character of literary works, he chose to write in the new mode of "poetic realism" with a clear conception of the "exact function of the artist in contemporary society" (1986, 127). Clarifying the distinctive features of the new mode, he stated that the novel was neither to be a "reportage about social conditions" nor "the phantasmagoria of one's psychological states, particularly the subconscious, dream, or clinical experience," nor a means for providing escape for the readers. Along with defining the character of his novel, he also enunciated the function of a writer and the areas of experience he needed to treat in his fiction for effecting social and cultural transformations.

In this context, it is relevant to examine how Anand changed the existing form of the novel into a new medium. While analyzing the style of narration common in earlier works and the one proposed by him, he made a distinction between the recital and novel, which he related to the old and new attitudes to history. To quote him: "In the old recital or narrative there were generally three elements: the bard or strory-teller, the characters and the audience. The recitalist interrupted the story to give discourses on the philosophy of life, preached sermons, or drew out the moral lessons for the audience or 'dear reader'" (1970, 116). Anand admits that Bankim and Tagore made several changes in this schema, and infused new life into the old recital, for making it relevant to the actual needs of the people of the times. He praises Tagore for introducing new elements like the "culture of our primitive, closely-knit communities," into literature, because of which "alone a renaissance can be built up" (1946, 17). Tagore also succeeded in incarnating "some of the chief types of the emerging middle and lower middle sections of Bengal in his writing and [in] reintegrat[ing] the arts of poetry, drama, story, and particularly the novel, in our country" (1946, 20-21). In spite of these advances, which made literature in general and the novel in particular realistic enough to cope with the needs of the times, for which Anand gave him due credit, traces of the old form persisted in his writings, which militated against the new aspiration of the novel. That is why he writes that Tagore is "mainly a romancer who is extending the old myth and legend of India, and the recital element survives in his work almost as in the lay of the ancient bard, minstrel or troubador" (1946, 32). When his heroes look for new ways of life by embracing new values, Tagore surely breaks new ground in the conception of the novel, but traces of the past baggage, such as "mementos, charms, and tokens etc," (1946, 35) persist in his writings.

Anand moved ahead of Bankim and Tagore, and gave the novel a new, healthy shape.[7] The most important step in this direction was his insistence that writers needed to reorient their perspective, so that they could see the human condition in historical time and not in a kind of timelessness, as they had done in the past: "... the most important shift in the mental make up of this intelligentsia was to accept historical time in the European sense as against the timeless world of the Indian inheritance" (1977, 15). Thus the narrative changed from the recital into the novel. This led to changes in the conception of the character as well:

> My characters were not meant to be revised versions of old mythical symbols of the epics. I think that human beings change, in a changing universe, even if ever so little....My characters are conceived as human beings of a different historical age which is not the changeless samsara of tradition. They struggle in this life, on earth, in the here and now, even as their struggles end in failures (1983, 9-10).

In his choice of a new kind of narrative and a new approach to character, Anand formulated the blueprint of a vigorous, critical realism, which was his healthy response to the dictates of historical imperatives. He utilized the new medium for understanding India's past in relation to its present and for sharing it with his readers for raising their consciousness. This makes Anand a culture-figure in the Gramscian sense: an intellectual who works assiduously for shaping the currents of history. Gramsci writes that culture is not to be equated with mere acquisition of knowledge, in which case it would be a kind of "weak and colourless intellectualism." Far from it, it is "organization, discipline of one's inner life, a coming to terms with one's personality; it is the attainment of a higher awareness, with the aid of which one succeeds in understanding one's own historical value, one's own function in life, one's own rights and obligations" (11).

Another feature which flows directly from Anand's renovation of the genre, to make it relevant to the requirements of history, is that he brought within the folds of literature "whole new peoples who have seldom entered the realms of literature in India" (1986, 119). Gramsci calls them *emarginati*, the ones who live outside the margins of respectable society. In according them a place in his fictional universe, where they are treated with sympathy and respect, Anand did several things simultaneously. He brought within the folds of literature the experiences of people who had been marginalized for centuries. Since they had also remained outside the domain of history proper, he also alerted the historians of their existence. Anand also made people aware that historical change is the result of the will of all classes in a society and not merely of the select, privileged few. Since social change in India had moved unevenly for various ideological reasons, he also made the people aware of the coercion inherent in the old mode of thinking on history, which he vigorously contested in his fiction. All these considerations made the novel into a new medium, and gave it a revolutionary character. It discloses the "way to a new life," and the novelist stands as "an inspiring force behind all those men and women who face the task of reconstructing the future society out of the shambles of a near prehistoric present" (1986, 134). The novelist assesses the past, provides guidelines for a new future, and thus, in a true sense, becomes the maker of history. He not only provides a sense of direction, but also builds a new sense of confidence among people in a process which for centuries they had thought was beyond human control.

On the basis of Anand's autobiographical novels and his non-fictional writings, I have tried to demonstrate that Anand's theory of the novel is embedded in his strong awareness of Indian history and people. What follows now is a discussion and an illustration of the salient features of this awareness in his novels: to show how they are permeated with his sensitive understanding of India's past and present and build into them a strong element of historical specifics and a critique of various positions that people adopted to grapple with the problems of their day. For a coherent focus, I shall isolate three particular strands from his fictional universe, which have a bearing on the issues I have already referred to: 1) Anand's understanding of India's colonial past; 2) the view of history implicit in this understanding; 3) the significant aspects of his focus on the lower and exploited sections of society and their implications for social history. I shall also discuss the dialectics of historical change in his novels and his response to the ideas and thinking of Gandhi.

Almost all the novels of Anand are located in historical time: the pre-independecne ones, mostly between the 1920s and the 1940s, when India was under the British rule, what Anand's characters call the Angrezi sarkar; the later ones go into the 1960s. The locale is not meant merely to provide the environment in which his characters come to life; it impinges on their lives. Anand deftly connects the individual past of his characters with their cultural and historical past. That is how Englishmen enter their consciousness; they recognize their presence, which transforms them in many subtle ways. Through the exploration of their lives, the direct comments of the narrator, a specifically-drawn character meant to represent his views, and finally, the truth of his presentation, in which realism also becomes a mode of critique, Anand incorporates into his fiction his understanding of the colonial situation in India and its implications for the society in general. His overall view of colonialism is a negative one. He brings out the exploitative character of the British presence in India and dramatizes the demoralizing effect it had on the psyche of the Indians. Probing a little deeper, he also unravels the causes which made the Indians accept the overlordship of the British for too long a time. Anand thus goes beyond the surface, material explanantion of colonialism, which we normally find in history books.[8] He emphasizes this because it is seminal to his understanding of the historical consciousness of the Indians. Anand's inbuilt plea in his novels is that this understanding is essential for effecting changes in the thinking and attitude of people.

In Anand's first two novels, *Untouchable* and *Coolie*, the British are very much in the background. In the first one, there is only one major Britisher, a padri, who tries vainly to soothe Bakha's hurt feelings, by inviting him into the merciful fold of Christianity. Anand describes the efforts of the padri with amused contempt, especially because Bakha is baffled by Yessuh Masih and the padri's insistence that he confess his sins. Similarly, in *Coolie*, the nightmares of Munoo dominate the narrative, but Englishmen do surface occasionally to confirm that they are in charge of the country. In fact, in W P England (Cowasjee 1977, 68), whose very name suggests that he is a type, Anand draws the portarit of a typical colonial officer. Suppressing his honest instincts, he assumes a pose of superiority, by keeping Indians at a distance. He deliberately avoids being familiar with them, so that he can live up to the prestige of his position: "... his compatriots at the Club had always exhorted him to show himself off as the son of King George himself if need be" (*Coolie*, 53). Anand establishes that such behaviour of the Englishmen prompted many Indians to seek their company, and led to the growth of a class who would not hesitate to fawn and cringe before them, because their sole obsession was to please the British in any way they could. Because of this, even

England found them "embarrasingly obsequious." The sole ambition of Baboo Nathu Ram is to make him accept his invitation to tea at his home. Even a man of Todar Mal's eminence and affluence pines for the "vision of himself driving through the bazaars of his native city next to an Englishman" (103).

Coolie also provides a brief glimpse of the corrupt and unscrupulous Britishers who exploit the poor textile workers in their factories in Bombay. This is elaborated into a veritable picture of the colonial set up in *Two Leaves and a Bud.* This short novel is located in a tea plantation, where the planters enhance their profits by cashing on the misery of poor Indian coolies. As a microcosmic picture of the colonial situation, the novel dramatizes two basic features of the British presence in India: their dissemination of the theory of racial superiority for legitimizing their rule and the immoral and exploitative nature of their policies and practices. Both are thoroughly exposed by Anand. Croft-Cooke and his assistant Reggie combine in themselves the theory and practice of colonialism. Croft justifies the British presence in India by stating that "Indians could not rule themselves" because they were "shocking barbarians in point of intellect and civilization, while the coolies were sub-human creatures, contemptible and bare" (31). As a more strident and active agent of the establishment, Reggie considers his relationship with the coolies that of master and servant, because of his firm belief in the theory of racial superiority. De la Havre, through whom Anand deflates the views of the colonials by building a contrast to their thinking, fails to convince them about the wrongness of their assertions. But he helps us see that their superiority was only a pose, which they cultivated for justifying their stay in India: "The prestige of the Englishman in India could only be kept up by associating strength and wisdom and justice with the English as a superior race" (157). Havre uncovers the "layer upon layer of the superciliousness, the complacency and the assurance of the spirit that built the Empire"(49). These traits are represented in their fulness and foulness by Reggie. Havre also exposes the falsehood and ruthlessness with which they perpetuated themselves in power; they let "lies pass for truth"; made "deceit a virtue"; and exalted "the worst to the best" (65).

Anand attacks both the theory and practice of the Raj through Havre, who draws attention of the officers to their trickery and deceitful ways, their "open loot and bribery and corruption." He questions the assumptions behind their thinking and practices and organizes the coolies against them. When he does not get adequate response to his appeals, he undertakes a detailed study for finding out the reasons which had contributed to the success of the Company in India. In his Journal, Havre records that "The black coolies clear the forests, plant the fields, toil and garner the harvest, while all the money-grubbing, slave-driving, soulless managers and directors draw their salaries and dividends and build up monopolies" (123). That they could do so for a long time leads him to study the Indian character. He comes up with several interesting observations, the most important being about the disheartening passivity of the average Indian. Anand complements the findings of Havre about the British by providing a graphic picture of their exploitation of the coolies, and their biased judicial system which exonerates a cruel and lecherous Englishman, even though he had committed a murder.

Havre's understanding of the Indian character is Anand's understanding too: that Indians accept things in hopeless silence. The planters were shrewd enough to understand this and also the reasons behind it. That is why they followed the policy of the administrators to keep themselves in the saddle: "...the white race could only rule them by putting the fear of God into them and by dealing with them severely when they played any monkey tricks, and with generosity when they behaved" (269-70). But Havre considered Indians human beings and "believed that they had a right not only to rule themselves, but to rule themselves justly..." (30).

In the first two novels of Lalu trilogy, the British are in the background. In *The Village*, the main focus is on the exploitation of the villagers by landlords, moneylenders and lawyers. The British invite censure because this exploitation takes place under their administration. In *Across the Black Waters*, the sarkar emerges as an evil force through the perceptions of Lalu, who constantly compares the British with the French and finds them wanting. His exposure to European ways of living and thinking also changes his perception of the Britishers, which is used to great advantage in the next novel, *The Sword and the Sickle*.

After being a prisoner of war in Germany, where he got an opportunity to meet several members of the revolutionary group which worked for the independence of the country, Lalu returns to an India which is seething with discontent against the British. His perception of these changes is enlarged upon by Anand in *The Sword and the Sickle*. Immediately after his arrival, his friends and acquaintances provide him information about developments in the country. He learns of the brutal tragedy in Jallianwallah Bagh, and the iniquity of the British administrative and judicial machinery, which included their opportunistic Indian agents. He gets a taste of the ungrateful and tyrannical sarkar when, instead of being rewarded for his bravery in Europe, he is demobilized, which gives him a big jolt. He gets involved with the peasant movement, which had been launched in various parts of the country to protest against the exploitative system instituted by the British through Indian landlords. Through earthy similes and metaphors, the peasants express the impoverishment of their country by the British. Hindustan is visualized by Harnam Singh as "a lean bullock that has been reduced to the bone by the Angrezi lion" (64).

The value of the novel also lies in its comprehensive dramatization of the popular discontent that the British government bred in the country and the various alternative strategies that it promoted in the shape of varying political movements. That is why the novel is full of confrontational politics, in which actual people like Gandhi and Nehru are brought within the corpus of its action. Apart from this, the novel is also dominated by debates and discussions in which the relationship between the British and Indians is discussed from different angles, which throw up different solutions to meet the need of the times. It is the only novel of Anand which documents the political creeds which flourished in the 1920s and 30s, representing the various contesting views on nationalism as well. These are animated in the concrete historical setting of peasant movements and kisan sabhas. All the debates and discussions are presented through Lalu, who is at the centre of the novel's overall design. The mode of presentation is in the spirit of a critique of the various positions, so that the reader is able to judge for himself their relative strengths and weaknesses.

Comrade Sarshar is a firebrand communist who thinks that a full-scale revolution is the only way in which the country can be liberated. He accuses the Count of taking his political programme non-seriously. The Count is a professed communist and a thorough activist, but possibly because of his birth and upbringing, there are vestiges of feudal culture in his personality and style. He uses the Marxian jargon, especially in his denunciation of the policies and programmes of the Congress party, but is ambivalent towards the use of violence for bringing about a revolution. This partially explains why several of his programmes against the landlords end in dismal bunglings. However, his denunciation of the British and their agents comes through effectively. The theoretician Verma only talks and formulates proposals and plans of action, but is incapable of doing anything. That is why he invites the Count's reprimand: "If you remain too addicted to theory, action is poisoned at the source" (54). The Congressites are represented by Tiwari, who preaches non-violence for achieving social and political goals, but he is laughed at by all others. Gandhi too comes in for severe criticism for reasons to which I shall return a little later. The achievement of the novel lies in working out fine discriminations between alternatives that have been effectively concretized. I do not think that it upholds any specific ideology, particularly the Marxian one, as some critics tend to suggest. It is true that Lalu talks too often about revolution and Roos, participates in organized campaigns against the landlords and the British administration, but it does not necessarily imply that he favours any ideological position. He shows his preference for radicalism of any kind, mainly because his primary motive is to come to grips with himself, to rid himself and his companions of the shackles of fate-oriented thinking. Revolution and Roos provide him handy symbols for a fresh orientation. We have only to examine carefully his comments to know the real impulse behind his actions and thinking. When he tells Maya that his dream is to see his country transformed into Roos, his conception of Roos is very different from what it was for the upholders of communist ideology. For him, it symbolizes a place "where there are no divisions of religion or property among people, where women, who were sold to the highest bidder, have become free to choose their own lives" (103). The emphasis here is to draw inspiration from the emancipatory energy of communism, because the essence of Lalu's thinking is to urge people to make their own lives. This is further confirmed by the manner in which Lalu understands revolution: "This strange job of helping to bring about Revolution, to gather the peasants in a union, so that they could defend themselves against the assaults of their enemies, the officials and the landlords, fairly well defined his own yearnings whatever the word 'Revolution' might mean to others" (102).

That this is the real position of Anand is clarified further in *The Big Heart*, in which Ananta, another sympathetically-drawn character, also talks about revolution. The central thrust of the novel is to deal as much with political change as with the problem of social change, which involves the larger question of striking a balance between tradition and modernity. The relation between the two was at the heart of the intellectual debate during the pre-independence times. As a leader of the community of thathiars, Ananta has to take a stand on the use of machinery. This implicitly gets involved with politics, and the novel suggests various ways in which this could be tackled. There are elaborate debates between workers and proponents of different views: the Gandhians, the Communists, the Arya Samajis, and extremist anarchists. All the views are presented in their roundness, with their positive and negative aspects. Although Ananta is for the machine to stay, he does not uphold any of these rigidly-defined positions. In fact, the novel is a dramatization of his conflict which arises from these conflicting positions; he does not want to own any one of them in totality. In a moment of lucidity, he comes out with a significant statement: "If our hearts are sound and we are pledged to make a 'Revolution,' there is no question about being tainted by the Roosis, the Chinis or ferungis" (153). This clearly suggests the essence of Anand's position; we do not need to import programmes of change from the outside. Implicitly, and what is confirmed by the drift of the action of the novel, it also suggests the primacy of dialogue and discussion over hasty and impulisve action. I think that instead of pushing through a definite ideology, the Marxian or any other, the novel encourages people to recognize and examine different alternatives, and then possibly make an appropriate choice for effecting changes in the existing social, economic, and political order.

The pre-independence novels of Anand thus incorporate his understanding of the colonial situation, his exposure of its baneful aspects, the political and social ferment that it produced among the people, and his estimate of the various political formations that it engendered. But consistently, his emphasis was more to critique them than to endorse any position. This holds true even when he was somewhat sympathetic towards the leftists.

From among his post-independence novels, there is one novel which illustrates Anand's interest in political history. It is about an Indian prince, and has an interesting title: *Private Life of an Indian Prince* (Cowasjee 1977, 140). It suggests that the primary focus of the novel is on the private life of Maharaja Ashok Kumar, also called Vicky, the prince of Sham Pur. But the word prince in the title also draws attention to a historical phenomenon, which was unique to our country. The princes, whose number exceeded five hundred in pre-independence times, formed an important part of the Indian polity and played no mean role during the colonial period. Since almost all of them were like feudal lords, who held their subjects under a tight leash, and lived a life of adventure, romance, and of excessive indulgence, they became a subject of great interest to the British. They studied them also because they wanted to utilize them for consolidating their power in the country. Because of the extraordinary tenor of their lives, the princes were also projected into a stereotype: as glamorous, autocratic, highly romantic, callous intriguers.

The main thrust of Anand's novel is to break this stereotyped image of a prince by writing a realisitic account, in which Vicky has been portrayed as a human being, in a concretely-realized setting, and as part of a political structure of India in transition. Vicky, of course, has his share of mortal weaknesses; he has several Ranis, because his mother wanted to ensure that he is married into the right kind of families for producing a proper heir to the throne. He is also in love with a nymphomaniac, Ganga Dasi, who delights in keeping him in thrall. Since she is ambitious and wants a secure future for herself and her child from him, she seizes on all possible opportunities to advance her cause, which leads to several embarrassing moments for him. Her wayward and unpredictable nature involves her with several men; Vicky interperets her actions as betrayals, which have a shattering effect on him. The novel dramatizes very sympathetically his steady disintegration, which culminates in his madness. Psychological studies of this kind were normally against Anand's grain and contrary to his professed views on the novel, but the present one, written under conditions of personal strain, succeeds in destroying the stereotype of a typical prince by deromanticizing and deglamorizing him.

As a period-piece, *The Private Life of an Indian Prince* is authentic. The large frame within which the actions of Vicky and the political climate of the times have been realized is a composite one, based on the lives and situations of several known princes; one could easily trace individual scenes and happenings to the ones that really happened to this or that prince. The problems posed to Vicky by the freedom of India are also the ones which were faced by several princes. The kind of political stand that Vicky takes, which is to work out an arrangement which could free him from the control of the newly-constituted Indian union, is also based on actual happenings. The Maharaja of Jammu and Kashmir, for example, dragged his feet for several months over the question of accession, before he was compelled by circumstances to join the Indian union. All these are historical details of great interest. Even the role of Sardar Patel in using his extraordinary skills for making the princes join the union has been brought within the action of the novel, though there is no single, specific instance which is invoked to portray the relationship between him and Vicky. When the prince is summoned to Delhi to sign the instrument of accession, he is made to go through a humbling experience, because the Sardar does not see him at his will; he has to wait for his call. The meeting is finally held at five in the morning. The unusualness of the hour and the brutal pointedness of Sardar's candour are also based on actuality. But this is not probably what Anand is keen on emphasizing. That is why the narrator, whom Anand considers a character in his own right, though he represents his views on many things, tells us about the Sardar: "It is possible that I fancied all this about the Sardar, that I was making up the kind of pattern about him which I knew would fit his legend. But any such meeting with an historical personage becomes personal-impersonal and somewhat symbolic, like a landscape into which one can read any meaning one likes" (243). The comment clarifies that in drawing his picture of the Sardar in the novel, Anand was governed by what he had learnt about him and his actions, though, as I have already tried to suggest, much of it is grounded in actuality. Anand's purpose, however, was to use the Sardar to cut Vicky to his size.

Apart from providing an authentic account about the place and position of princes in the Indian polity and the problems they posed for the Indian union, the value of the novel lies in subjecting the institution of royalty to a critical scrutiny and to show how the princes figured in Anand's scheme of social and cultural reorientation of the country. These are made availalble mostly through exchanges between Vicky and Dr Kumar and the latter's comments and reflections.

Dr Kumar constantly subjects the institution of the Maharaja to a rigorous appraisal, by examining closely the role of Vicky as the head of a state. He finds in him an absurd mixture of old and new things, a result of his anchorage in the tradition of his forefathers and his exposure to new Western ways. These account for contradictions in his personality, which have serious implications for his people. Kumar constantly talks to him about the new vision of a healthy synthesis between the Indian and the European, which is the mainstay of Anand's thinking on the cultural reorientation of the country:

> I do not think things strange because I am a silly modernist, for whom everything European is good and everything in our own heritage bad, but because I have begun to see that the confusion arising from the clash of all the centuries with our own, in India, is bound to become worse unless we seek a synthesis of Europe and India, unless we evolve a new sense of values to live by and generally know the direction in which we are going (69).

But Vicky does not have sense enough to see things from this perspective, nor does he perceive contradictions in his thinking and behaviour. He professes love for his people, but is autocratic in his ways. He is utterly oblivious to the goings-on in his state and allows misuse of power by several of his state functionaries. The novel figures scenes of popular discontent, in which people voice their protest against the Maharaja because they are poor and subjected to forced labour and other kinds of exploitation. Instead of devoting attention to these urgent problems, the Maharaja spends his energies on cultivating the Americans, for retaining his independent status. Above all, the Maharaja is also the victim of his frustrating love affair with Ganga Dasi, which leaves him no time for anything else. Although Anand is sympathetic towards him because of his suffering, he has no respect for him for his lack of will and imagination to move ahead with changing times. That is why the final word of judgment against him is delivered by Kumar, when he explains to him the concept of the world in a "state o' chassis," after the Irish writer O'Casey. He makes him see that the institution he represents is out of tune with the times: "You are unable to give up your past and to accept the broadening of life, which is releasing the oppressed. And there are quite a few others like you. And their stubborn self-will makes them abnormal in our age. And hence the distraught atmosphere of our time" (247).

Thus we see that though the novel is mainly a psychological study of a love-stricken prince, so that we sympathise with his condition, it also locates the institution of royalty in the historical time of India's transition into a free country. In the context of his views about cultural change, he condemns it, because it is retrogressive and unhealthy.

I have already stated that the main thrust of Anand's concern with the colonial situation in India is to probe the reasons which helped the British to take root. This leads him to uncover the attitude of the people to history: the passing events, their movement and their control. His novels confirm that people put up with all forms of oppression, both at the hands of the British and their own fellow beings, with "resigned indifference." Take the case of Gangu in *Two Leaves and a Bud*. When his visions of liberation are snuffed out by the brute British force, he understands his situation only in divine terms, as the working of "an inevitable, inexorable fate, imposed by the Omnipotent, Omniscient Providence, of whom Siva and Vishnu and Krishna were the supreme incarnations" (261). In a tone of passive resignation, he tells his companions: "...brothers, there is nothing to be done except to make up our minds to settle down here and smoke the hookah, and mention the name of Ram" (213). Anand suggests that in the popular imagination, the British were the kinsmen of God, and therefore to be obeyed. Lalu thinks of George Panjim as the incarnation of God. The soldiers who fight for the Britishers in France "obey the orders of the Sarkar and of God who made us servants of the Sarkar for our past deeds. " They think that they are "without a will of their own," and therefore act like "soulless automatons."[9]

In *The Sword and the Sickle*, Lalu's perception of the sarkar is presented through a powerful image, in which it is invested with divine force, which inspires awe:

> ...one could merely stand aside for a moment and contemplate its potencies, stand aghast and gaze, wide-eyed, at its invisible, insidious presence, gaze at it as one gazes at a god, merely to see its magnificent, all-embracing, omnipresent, omniscient being in action and to seek to understand its inscrutable, inexorable presence, to realize the reality behind its various manifestations (188).

The most striking thing about this image is that Lalu associates all the divine attributes with it: it is all-powerful, omniscient, and inscrutable. It compels obedience in the same manner in which people generally pay obeisance to gods. Anand is suggesting unequivocally that the Indians have accepted the British as divine beings. As such, they were part of the inexorable wheel of time, outside their control.

Having established that the British and the gods cohabit in the psyche of the majority of the Indians, Anand develops the action of his novels towards stressing the need for a fundamental change in their attitude. This he accomplishes successfully by making his protagonists come to terms with themselves, and thereby providing for the recognition and gradual acceptance of an alternative mode of understanding the processes of history. Let us look at the Lalu trilogy. In the first two novels, Lalu totally submits to his fate. So much so, that when he returns from France to India, he looks back on his life up to that point as a movement within the inexorable wheel of time, the pitiless fate, which had consumed several of his companions. But he also experiences the first stirrings of that spirit with which one could shake off this burden and break the chains of that fate which prevents people from shaping their own lives. In the thick of the turmoil in which he is caught in India after his return from France, he resolves that he would "look for it, he would track it down, the oppressor that drowned the agonies of the people—he would know it and seek to master it" (66). This contrasts with the view of his uncle, who sticks on to his earlier thinking of the "pessimistic faith in renewal, in the going back to God, who seemed to the devout the beginning as well as the ultimate end of the journey" (67).

Throughout the novel, Anand elaborates these contrasting views in such a manner that they develop into two conflicting positions, signifying two constrasting attitudes towards man's onward march in time. The dialectics which Lalu has to resolve is whether he should believe in the divine interpretation of history or the one directed by man. Through his struggle and the understanding he finally arrives at, Anand endorses the latter:

> The Sahibs were no gods, as he himself had seen at close quarters in Europe. The days were gone when he would be cowed by the red-faced monkeys or by rich Indians, like Harbans Singh and other greasy sycophants. Why, the Hindustanis were a separate nation like the Germans and the Francisis and the Angrezi people!...They had the right to be a separate nation and, what was more, they had the right to their own land! (82-83).

When Lalu learns to disentangle the presence of the British in India from the belief that they were gods, he develops confidence to think of ways and means to combat them. This helps him gain self-confidence. In fact, Lalu realizes that the major reason of his failure for long had been his lack of faith in himself. He consistently feels that he needed "confidence in his own capacity to control his destiny and to help others to do the same" (144). An interesting point on this is Anand's belief that this attitude can be promoted through radical thinking, which includes Marxian thinking. This, in fact, provides the basis for a comparison between the Congress and Communist ideology in the novel. When Tiwari, for example, taunts the Count by telling him that Communism cannot flourish in India because it is anti-God, the Count tells him that they are anti-God because they recognize history as a man-directed force: "...they merely explain how and why religion came to be....They deny God, because they understand history. They don't need the drug of religion, because they can discover the capacity to live intensely in the new world which they wish to create. .." (163-64). The spirit behind this viewpoint is, once again, to emphasize that human beings should build in them the confidence to shape a new world by moulding the processes of history. Since the colonial bondage was the most pressing challenge before people, their first priority was to fight it, in whatever way they could.

A more concentrated treatment of these two constrasting notions of history, is at the centre of *The Big Heart*. It takes off from a crisis in the community of thathiars: whether or not to accept the use of machines in their trade. Ananta the protagonist of the novel is for their use, because he thinks that they have become a part of history. But he tells his fellow artisans that they have to work unitedly to prevent the owners of machines from exploiting them. Ananta understands the constraints of objective reality, because of which the machines had come to stay, but maintains that even then one could control and direct change. In contrast to this is the view of Viroo, who says: "I got my trust in my kismet and my God," and of Ralia, who extends its scope to the whole range of human activities: from playing cards to fighting his masters. Ananta thinks differently about gods and fate: "God won't help us because, as far as I have known Him, he has always preserved a discreet silence in the affairs of men. And Fate, like money, seems to be bitch goddess, favouring the few who can invest capital and then call in its aid" (197). He does not merely dismiss God's role in human affairs, but also suggests that the idea of the role of fate in our lives has been exploited by vested interests to gain access to wealth and power. Even the Britishers had used the idea of providence to legitimise their rule over India. Anand's sympathies are with Ananta, when he says: "It is a good thing that we are not like wax in the hands of Destiny... we can now make a choice in this world of evil and destruction, if we have heads and hearts" (198-99).

Anand's debate on the right kind of attitude towards history is connected with the larger question of the place of modernity and tradition, which has been an important issue in the social and cultural history of India. This is where Anand comes into frontal clash with Gandhi's views on history and cultural change. Anand's steady emphasis on man's capacity to bend his present and future to give a self-directed motion to events is largely the result of exposure to the West. He believes that the influence of the West alone can build in people their eroded self-confidence, which had been destroyed by their excessive reliance on their faith in the role of gods in history. This had been instilled in them through habit and force of authority. Anand believes that religion, as it had been understood and accepted by people, was responsible for diminishing people's faith in themselves. This could be fought by accepting the confident postures of the Western civilization. Gandhi took an entirely different view in the matter. He blamed all the ills of our country to the baneful effect of this civilization. The sickness and palor of our country came from there: "Those alone who have been affected by Western civilization have become enslaved" (Gandhi 93). If Anand considered religion as an obstructive force, Gandhi considered it emancipatory energy. Contrary to the views of Anand, in Gandhi's transformative programme, "Religious, that is ethical, education will occupy the first place" (145). A further extension of this was Gandhi's attitude to the use of Western modes of production. He, for example, held that "It is machinery that has impoverished India" and "represents a great sin" (148-49), but we have already seen that Ananta is not against the machine. In fact, Anand brings in the Gandhian viewpoint in the novel only to be contested by Ananta. In a big debate, Ananta passionately pleads that the machine is not an evil in itself; it needed to be controlled by people who were sincere, honest, and compassionate. Although Anand admired Gandhi for his intense humanism, he did not accept his view on the machine. It is significant that the anti-machine people in *The Big Heart,* who constantly invoke the name of Gandhi to fight Ananta, have no other affinity with Gandhi as people or programmers.

The tension in Anand's attitude towards Gandhi is connected with Gandhi's complicated views on history, to which a reference is made, though not very directly, in Lalu's meeting with him in *The Sword and the Sickle*. When Lalu goes to invite him to join the crusade against the British and the landlords they supported and protected, he finds Gandhi dictating his views about the value of cattle to one of his assistants. Lalu is baffled by his extraordianry love for the cow and his calling himself a "Sanatani Hindu," a sect which he thought "was notorious for its conservative fanaticism." Lalu is also struck by the incongruity of his interests, which he thinks ranged from the "sublime to the ridiculous, and from the puerile to the profound" (199). But what troubles him most is Gandhi's insistence on suffering as the most important agent of change: "No country has ever risen without being purified through the fire of suffering.... It is impossible to do away with the law of suffering which is the one indispensable condition of our being. Progress is to be measured by the amount of suffering undergone, the purer the suffering, the greater is the progress..." (199-200).

Lalu's discomfiture arises from the fact that this part of Gandhi's teaching closely resembled the view of his uncle, a view he had already left behind him because it was rooted in religion and favoured self-torture: "[his] teaching was no different from the teaching of all his father's saints, who enjoined people to purify themselves through asceticism. All these priests, yogis, sadhus and beggars who tortured themselves! What was the difference between them and this enlightened man" (200)? A little later, when Lalu gets a chance to speak to him about his mission, Gandhi tells him that the essence of his creed was non-violence, which he defined thus:

> 'Non-violence does not mean submission to the will of the evildoer, but of pitting one's whole soul against the will of the tyrant. Working under the law of our being, it is possible for a single individual to defy the whole might of an unjust Empire and lay the foundation for that Empire's downfall or its regeneration' (201).

Gandhi also tells Lalu that he did not believe in the efficacy of mere mechanical action to yield results and that non-violence was another name for God.

Lalu's rejection of God-oriented view of history collides with Gandhi's belief in the supremacy of spirit for attaining human goals. This is because, through Lalu, Anand endorses a view of history which rejects religion. But religion is central to Gandhi's project. His understanding of history is rooted in his philosophy, which could not fit into Anand's thinking. According to Gokhale, the "seminal ideas in Gandhi's philosophy...were a sense of guilt or sin [the result of the acquisitive spirit of human beings], the need to return to God, the pre-eminence of non-violence as an instrument of human progress, and the value of bread-labor as the basis of peace in society" (Gokhale 216; see also Raghavan Iyer 319-20). It is quite understandable that seen from this philosophical perspective, Gandhi's views on history were extremely unconventional, more so in the 1920s and 30s when most of the Indians had accepted Western modes of history and historiography. Contrary to these ideas, Gandhi regarded all histories of this kind non-histories; for him they were just a record of wars and as such "a record of an interruption of the course of nature. Soul-force, being natural, is not noted in history" (Gandhi 120). Since the struggle of man's progress towards his spiritual growth, which involved mastering his hold over the practice of truth and non-violence was not recorded in such histories, he dismissed them as being useless. For him myths and legends of the great religions and the life stories of great spirits were better samples of history (Gokhale 217). Gandhi's views, thus, come very close to the traditional Hindu view of history, in which history was less of a fact-oriented account, and more of a *vidya*, which helped human beings to learn to live life in an ideal manner. Gandhi, in fact, paid a special compliment to his Hindu ancestors for giving him this particular insight: "'It is my pet theory that our Hindu ancestors solved the question for us by ignoring history as it is understood today and by building on slight events their philosophical structure. Such is the *Mahabharata*....That which is permanent eludes the historian of events. Truth transcends history'" (Gokhale 217).

Thus we see that Gandhi finds no use for history, because the real truth about man is available in allegories and parables, and "myths and legends whose chronology is stated not in terms of centuries, decades, years, and dates but in periods and cycles of ages which are parts of cosmic processes" (Gokhale 219). We have already seen that Anand is opposed to this view of history, because he had accepted the Western naturalistic kind, which grew out of the recognition that we should understand the movement of events in a comprehensible time-frame. It is because of this that Anand's Lalu finds Gandhi unacceptable. In fact, he finds Gandhi's emphasis on spirituality and his constant reference to God mystifying. Anand's Ananta believes that anything which is outside a comprehensible time-frame and invokes the spirit and God creates scope for exploitation of illiterate masses. This partly explains why Gandhi does not find much of a place in Anand's views on history and economic programme, both of which are crucial in his plan of historical reorientation of Indian society and its people.[12]

Though Anand does not share Gandhi's views on history, he fully endorsed his condemnation of untouchability as a symptom of the degenerate Hindu society. His interest in untouchables was a part of his larger concern with the exploited sections of our society, whose speedy improvement figured prominently in his plan for its healthy reorientation. It is therefore significant that he made first use of his literary skills to write a novel about untouchables. In this he sought and received help and guidance from Gandhi.[13] The novel, which he appropriately called *Untouchable*, is the account of a day in the life of Bakha, based on an untouchable boy he had known in his childhood. But the title suggests that it is much more than the story of a single individual. Anand's choice of details about Bakha's experiences makes it clear that though they are specific to him, they are true of other untouchables too. As such, his story resonates the story of a class, who have suffered at the hands of their compatriots for generations on end. Through a personalized and dramatized narrative, the novel thus incorporates into it significant aspects of the cultural history of our country. Anand's main purpose in this was to make the readers understand the societal forces that make an untouchable and to draw their attention to the tragedy and waste the plight of such people embodies.

Untouchable is designed as a double-layered history. As an account of a day in the life of Bakha, the narrative unfolds his personal history through his exposure to a series of situations and his memory and dreams. But these details have the imprint of a particular class. Even the details about his past are actually a part of his collective past, a past he shares with other untouchables. Anand thus does not focus on an individual consciousness, but a kind of figural consciousness, which tries to link and interpret the narrative present and the figural past. The situations in Bakha's present take on the aura of reenactments of situations which have recurred for countless generations. We share Bakha's pain and anguish because he is a part of our own time; but because he also represents archetypally the painful existence of his forebears, we also see the deformities of the institutional framework within which he comes to life.

Anand prepares the reader for this double response from the very beginning of the novel. He makes Bakha into a "child of modern India" (13), who likes to imitate the ways of the British, because they are different from the people he has to deal with everyday. His parents, especially his mother, are "Indian to the core and sometimes uncomfortably so" (16). When Bakha is treated kindly by Charat Singh, his patronising grin, the narrator tells us, "symbolised two thousand years of racial and caste superiority" (19). With a single sentence, Anand alerts the reader that he is not merely reading the story of Bakha, who has been individualized to the highest possible extent, but of all those untouchables who have lived and suffered like him for over two thousand years. In the course of his journey, Bakha also goes through a moment of recognition, in which he becomes aware of his condition. This awareness, it is significant to note, is about his social condition in the main, because he recognizes his position only in relation to the people of the superior caste, with whom he has to live in a state of perpetual bondage. His awareness has been dramatized effectively and is epiphanic in its import. Like "a ray of light shooting through the darkness," it flashes upon his mind, and he cries: "For them I am a sweeper, sweeper—untouchable! Untouchable! Untouchable! That's the word! Untouchable! I am an Untouchable" (59). This is a searing illumination and reverberates with resonances, which sharpen our awareness of the shady and cruel past in which this class came into existence. For the readers, it provides a moment of re-cognition, which is like the re-cognition the audiences experienced in a Greek play, when the already-known stories were experienced by them through their re-enactment. Anand's accent is on revivifying a part of the institutional past of the country through intense dramatization, so that it makes an impact on people in the present.

For the purpose of arousing the consciousness of the readers towards the plight of Bakha and stimulating them to action for ameliorating the lot of the people he represents, Anand ensures that details pertaining to his life also function as details of the social history of untouchables. Bakha's relationship with superior caste people is one of master and slave; but his servility is not rooted in his present, he has "inherited [it] from his forefathers" (20). Because of this we see him as part of a hierarchical, stratified, tyrannical structure, in which his place is pre-determined. Even his reactions and reflexes are conditioned by it. When he hears a kind word or gets a sympathetic look from his superiors, he is elated; like a slave, he feels "overjoyed at the condescension of his master" (20). Although he is a sensitive and healthy being, and has even an air of nobility about him, because of which he could be a match to anybody from the upper-caste people, he knows that he has to live with his social disabilities, because they are the disabilities of the group into which he has been born. He has learnt about these things right from his childhood, and the narrative provides a sensitive dramatization of these by relating them to his raw experience, so that we experience the anguish these things cause to untouchables. Judging from the manner in which Bakha's father responds to these situations, we have to assume that in course of time, Bakha would also learn to let these things sink into him, making them a part of his second nature. Already he has learnt that he has no freedom of action and certain places are out of bounds for him. He has also learnt to regulate his behaviour according to a set pattern, to ensure that he does not touch people and invite their displeasure and wrath. He knows that if he drew water from a well, "the Hindus of the three upper castes would consider the water polluted" (26). He also knows that he has no access to education. Worse still, for the superior castes, he is a mere object—an object of derision. They let off their steam on him, by showering their choicest imprecations on him: "cock-eyed son of a bow-legged scorpion," and a "dirty dog! Son of a bitch! offspring of a pig" (53)!

Whenever Bakha mistakenly transgresses the limits of his freedom, he has to seek forgiveness for his actions. Even after that, the superior castes do not feel pity for him; nor do they feel remorse for their cruel actions. Anand suggests that the social structure in which Bakha has been reduced to the position of an abject slave is one in which relationships between people are governed by power. The hurling of abuses and the physical beating of Bakha are symbolic acts, through which the superior castes exercise their power over the weaker sections of society. At one point in the novel, we see that even "those who were silent seemed to sense in the indignation of the more vociferous members of the crowd an expression of their own awakening lust for power" (55).

The most significant aspect of the novel is that Anand locates it in the time when lot of effort was being made by several leading men and women to work for the betterment of the untoucables. The best strategy for doing this was to retrieve their history so that people could be made aware of the heinous effect that the institution had on the society in general and on the untouchables in particular. Anand's novel performs this function quite successfully. As an account of a day in the life of Bakha, it succeeds effectively in making the point that his day is like any other day of his life, and that his routine is the routine of any other untouchable. That is why there is nothing extraordinary or unusual about his happenings. In order to emphasize that the oppressive system is well-entrenched, Anand also shows that Bakha's anger against it proves futile. His rebellious outbursts are no more than expressions of his impotent rage.

Anand also suggests that the evil of untouchability has its roots in religion. Bakha's father tells him that people are generally kind to them; if they are not, it is because of their religion: "We must realise that it is religion which prevents them from touching us" (93). In this Anand is dramatizing one of the influential positions on the problem taken by Gandhi, who understood untouchability within the framework of Hinduism. It is both interesting and significant that he lets Gandhi appear at the end of the novel to address a big congregation of people, in which he condemns untouchability. The words spoken by him are a mixture of several speeches which Gandhi had delivered before the Suppressed Classes Conference, and were later printed in *Young India*.[14] Since Gandhi approaches and understands the problem from within the Hindu fold, he speaks against any kind of official interference in it. In his speech he specifically mentions how he opposed the British Government policy of alienating them from "Hinduism by giving them a separate legal and political status" (167).

The thrust of Gandhi's address is to present the problems of untouchables in the form of a human story, so that it produces a desired response in people. He relates to his audience, which includes Bakha, the story of Uka, an untouchable he had known as a small boy. He tries to make the people understand that the practice of not touching these people had no religious sanction and was, therefore, satanic. To make them discard the practice, he uses the strategy of reinterpreting religion from a new perspective. At the end, however, he reinforces his plea by making an appeal to their conscience:"...If I have to be reborn, I should wish to be reborn as an untouchable, so that I may share their sorrows, sufferings and the affronts levelled at them, in order that I may endeavour to free myself and them from their miserable condition" (164). In this appeal Gandhi's reformist programme is constricted to the arousal of conscience in the tormentors of untouchables. This may be morally correct, but not necessarily efficacious. That is why in his critical analysis of Gandhi's discourse on untouchability, Bikhu Parekh remarks that while "it had the great advantage of focussing attention on the centuries of Hindu oppression, it also had the demerit of treating the harijans as passive objects helplessly waiting for their masters to get off their backs" (242).

It is significant how Anand makes Bakha respond to Gandhi's words. Although he feels happy about what he hears, he is mystified by his heavy reliance on soul-force. He is also troubled by the fact that Gandhi wants him to keep on cleaning latrines. Anand also stresses that for the people listening to him, Gandhi is much more than a mere reformer: he is a mystic, an avatar, and a voice—all rolled into one. This makes the Gandhi episode one of the most complex parts of the novel, because of which it is not possible to suggest a straightforward interpretation in which one could say that Anand supports Gandhi's understanding of the problem and his solution for the removalof untouchability. Bakha's response is ambivalent, and should discourage us from such a facile inference. By ending the episode with a dialogue in which the Gandhian position is discussed from two contrary angles, and also considering that Bakha shows more interest in the suggestion of the "clever poet" who talked of a machine to remove dung without touching it, it seems that Anand is not taking a final position on Gandhi's programme. Perhaps that is not the intention of the novel. Anand's main purpose, as I have tried to suggest, is to dramatize the condition of the untouchables in history and to bring out forcefully the inhumanity at the root of the institution of untouchability. He brings Gandhi within the fictional space of the narrative to emphasize his role in the reformist programme, as a part of the ongoing national effort in this direction. It is both an acknowledgement of Gandhi's contribution towards the removal of untouchability as well as an implicit critique of the manner in which he wanted to deal with it. It is significant that even in the 1960s the persistence of the menace of untouchability moved Anand to write another novel *The Road*, but it lacks the passionate involvement and urgency of the first one.

The attempt at negotiating the difficult terrain between modernity and tradition is also at the centre of Anand's concern with women, whose social standing he summed up in a single phrase—"the eternally wronged women"—which he used in his postscript to a later edition of *Apology* (198). Considering that the social history of women in the country remained a neglected field till the 1970s (Basu 181-82), it is significant that Anand was alive to their pathetic plight and clubbed them with untouchables and other downtrodden sections of our society. In his pre-1947 novels, women figure consistently as victim-figures of male power and lust (Berry 56-57). In his heroine-centred novel, *Gauri*, Anand sums up the history of women in India as victims of patriarchy. Suggestive references to this effect can be found in a novel like *The Big Heart*, in which Maya tells Ananta that in India women had been denied the freedom due to a human being, because they lived in a male-dominated society. When she chooses to live with him, in violation of all the restrictive social norms, even the most ardent votaries of freedom despise her; some even call her a prostitute.

In *Gauri*, a novel cast in a village, where nearly eighty per cent of our womenfolk live, the protagonist, also called Gauri, is married to Panchi through an arrangement in which she has no choice. From that point onwards, the drift of the narrative is to dramatize her suffering as a woman who has to live within the constricting bounds of the patriarchical system, whose perverse aspects have been thoroughly exposed by Anand. He makes it clear that Gauri has to live according to the norms of this system, because women have been taught by their parents and the society at large to respect them. Even the stories of gods and goddesses, puranic kathas, and the lives of the saints, which are the only other means of education they have access to, are heavily tilted towards patriarchy. That is why, Gauri, like Savitri "believed in the worship of her lord and master, and wanted to conquer him [her husband] with her devotion"(100). Visualizing herself in the mould of Mira Bai, she works hard to win the heart of her lord.

Panchi is least appreciative of Gauri's persistent efforts to please him, because his upbringing too has been according to the norms of patriarchy. He considers his wife an object of pleasure as well as a fit thing on whom he can let out his steam. At one point, when Gauri shows her anger, Panchi silences her by invoking the aid of *Dharam*, which enjoins upon the husband to "chastise the wife if she goes wrong" and also gives him the power to decide about it (51). However, Anand does not confine Gauri's problems to the ones created by her husband; he extends the scope of the novel to make her contend with other manifestations of male power. Her uncle Amru represents the demon-like "malignant power of...man's physical authority." He terrorizes Gauri and her mother; considering her a mere commodity, he packs Gauri off to Jai Ram Das's house, where the seth tries to rape her, "sanctifying [it]...with holy verses."

Unlike what he does in *Untouchable*, in *Gauri*, Anand aims at suggesting a way out which could give a new direction to the painful history of women, but in this he fails to move out completely from the constraints of tradition. When Gauri leaves her husband for the first time, because he poses a veritable threat to the child growing within her, she does not give him up. In fact, she tells her mother in no uncertain terms that Panchi continues to be her husband. Besides, Anand makes Gauri fight male tyranny by invoking the resources of the tradition into which she has been born. She fights the Seth by seeking the help of Parvati; she fights the overtures of Batra by seeking the aid of Kali. Anand also sees to it that she does not suffer sexual exploitation, so that she could go back to Panchi with a position of strength. In fact, when Panchi doubts her purity, she invokes the image of Sita. It is only when he threatens to throw her out, like the mythical Sita, that she takes the extreme step of leaving him, and gets transfigured from a gentle cow into a woman with a will of her own. But the very fact that Gauri takes this step after she fails to convince Panchi shows that Anand is not ready for a radical orientation in man-woman relationship. He would have been happy with adjustments—that woman has to have dignity and respect within the existing structure.

Notes

1 Several critics have attempted explications of Anand's literary creed. Margaret Berry thinks that Anand's art "undergoes shifts of emphasis, passing through three stages, not mutually exclusive: a brief, relatively unimportant idealism, followed by revolutionary Socialism, thence broadening into what the author calls 'comprehensive historical humanism'" (27). Saros Cowasjee does not agree with this: "I personally see no significant changes in Anand's theory or attitude to the

novel from the time he first began to write fiction." (1973a, 66). Cowasjee comments on Anand's social impulse, emphasizes his sense of compassion, but does not pay adequate attention to history as part of Anand's engagement. He has however an essay in which he writes how Anand fuses fiction and history (1989, 17-26).

2 Published originally as *The Old Woman and the Cow* in 1960.

3 For information on the ones which are to follow, see Marlene Fisher (149-51).

4 This exercise was stimulated by what Nirad Chaudhuri calls "the two great external facts of their existence: alien rule and the impact of Western ideas and culture" (15). For details on the various ways in which this inquiry was conducted, see Bikhu Parekh (35-70).

5 In one of his letters to Cowasjee, Anand rejected the various labels and categories which have been used to describe his novels; he also states that his aim is not "merely to shock, but to stimulate consciousness at all levels" (1973b, 116). See also Anand (1965, 53).

6 Anand captures the essence of the traditional thinking of Indians on time and history: "Time is the cause of all, it is time that creates and destroys, that binds men by its links and causes the joys and sufferings of men, regardless of their actions. According to this conception man is purely and simply delivered up to fate, and his actions and efforts are powerless to alter his lot" (Pannikar, 67).

7 Jack Lindsay has pointed out how Anand moves beyond Bankim and "brings together Tagore and Prem Chand, and proceeds to evolve something new, his own work" (14).

8 Ravinder Kumar has an interesting observation on a creative writer's ability to see more than what a professional historian can: "The creative writer...seeks to grasp reality through cognitive processes different from those of the social scientist or historian. His perception does not depend upon an initial process of disaggregation, for purposes of ready analysis, and the subsequent aggregation of fragmentary insights into a mechanical whole. Instead, the imaginative writer seeks to explore reality as a totality. He, therefore, reveals a sensitivity to problems of consciousness and identity which is seldom equalled by the more formal disciplines of social sciences" (1989, 75-76).

9 *Across the Black Waters* (133 and 136). Quoting Francis Hutchins and Lewis D Wurgaft, Ashish Nandy writes that "colonialism encouraged the colonizers to impute to themselves magical feelings of omnipotence and permanence" (35).

10 D Riemenschneider considers this drive in Anand's protagonists to be at the core of his fiction, and an evolutionary principle in his novels. See his *An Ideal of Man in Anand's Novels.*

11 (Gokhale 217). Ashish Nandy writes that Gandhi's rejection of history and affirmation of the primacy of myths over historical chronicles is his indirect reply "to the colonial homology between childhood and political subjugation" (55).

12 My main argument is that it is not correct to say that Anand accepts Gandhi uncritically. Through his characters, he subjects his ideas and philosophy to scrutiny. It is because there is a high degree of complexity in Gandhi. In this I differ from a critic like Rama Jha, who concentrates mostly on working out parallels between Gandhi's ideas and their use by Anand in his novels. In the same manner, it would not be right to say that Anand is an unqualified champion of Marxian ideology, a view projected by Suresht Ranjan Bald in *Novelists and Political Consciousness.*

13 This is one of the commonplaces in Anand criticism, which has been widely documented in Cowasjee, Fisher, Rama Jha, and several others.

14 These are collected in M K Gandhi, *The Removal of Untouchability* (3-9).

Chapter IV

Disguising/Interrogating History with Sahgal

Like the novels of Anand whose shape is determined largely by their involvement with the history and politics of pre-independence India, Sahgal's novels weave aspects of India's social, political, and cultural history into their narrative framework and subject them to a close critical examination. The period covered is roughly between the 1930s, when there was a mass awakening in the country to fight the British, and the time of emergency in 1975, when its democratic character was rudely shaken—the period that Rushdie covers in a single novel *Midnight's Children*. Sahgal is different from him and the other novelists discussed in this study in two significant ways. First, she writes about the past without invoking it directly, that is, avoiding, as far as possible, direct reference to actual events, happenings and people, but in a manner that they become recognizable. Secondly, instead of dealing with long stretches of time, she concentrates on short periods or specific tendencies or issues of crucial import, which have their basis in actuality. She analyzes them in depth, so that the period, the tendency, or the issue is dealt with in its comprehensiveness.

Since Sahgal uses conventional, realistic narratives, which teem with well-developed men and women characters to realize her ends, critical response to her work, with the exception of her last two novels, *Plans for Departure* and *Mistaken Identity*, has focussed on analyses of themes and her fictional technique.[1] Because her novels make covert and some rare overt references to significant political happenings, especially the novels she wrote during 1970s and 1980s, critics have also considered her a political novelist or a novelist with political consciousness. Her two early and major critics consider her a novelist who holds together private and public concerns in her fiction. Krishna Rao writes that besides dealing with individual lives, her novels "dramatize the contemporary *zeitgeist* and the traditional *elan vital* of India" (Rao 1976, 7).

Jasbir Jain states that her work "reflects not only her personal values but also the changing values of a country exposed for the first time to both freedom and power" (9). Sahgal's active involvement with the civil liberties movement in India and her public opposition to Mrs Gandhi's emergency consolidated her reputation as a political novelist. She figures prominently in a study of political consciousness in Indian English novel by M K Bhatnagar, though she gets less space than Bhattacharya and Malgonkar.

Interestingly, dissenting voices about her abilities as a novelist have also been heard. In his essay on politics in the English novel of India, Makarand Paranjape writes that as a political novelist, Sahgal is "without special insight or profundity," because her novels "do not offer a convincingly valuable reading of current political affairs." He even suggests that her novels "may be considered boring and uninspiring" which have been written according to a "dishonest formula" (221-22).

Rao and Jain partially accommodate Sahgal's interest in history, but do not pay special attention to it. Since Paranjape's assertions are not supported by adequate discussion, which makes them more like opinions than properly-argued viewpoints, they are sweeping and generalized, which also makes them unfair. The purpose of this chapter is to demonstrate that in spite of their limited range, Sahgal's novels explore seriously and in a substantial measure several significant aspects of the social, political, and cultural history of pre- and post-independence India and also incorporate her understanding and assessment of its complicated past. Right from her childhood, she was a witness to momentous changes in India's history and had the rare opportunity of watching first hand and interacting with major national figures of the times. This stimulated her to study and form her own understanding of the several layers of India's past. Since she constantly connects the immediate past of the country with its older past in her novels, they assume the nature of historical constructions. However, she does not write about the past like a traditional historian, who constructs his account from actual happenings and people. She uses invented characters to weave a narrative, which recreates a disguised picture of the past she chooses to write about, in which significant aspects of both the immediate and older past of the country get illuminated. What makes her writing interesting and important is not merely the insight she provides into the times she writes about, but also the manner in which she subjects issues and concerns related to them to constant questioning. That is why I state that she disguises and interrogates the past. The disguise in fact is a strategy for interrogating it.

Sahgal's novelistic world is dominated by the selected upper crust of our society, which includes bureaucrats, politicians, businessmen, big officials, and women, mostly from higher classes. This distinguishes her from a novelist like Anand, whose novels deal mainly with the lower strata of our society. Since her novels also investigate the cultural consequences of the Indo-British connection, English people also figure in them. Like several other novelists, who wrote before and after her, she mixes private and public histories in her work in a pleasing form. Just because she makes use of psychological realism in her presentation of characters and avoids the kind of sweep that one associates with novelists like Rushdie and Tharoor should not make us overlook her claim as a novelist who makes conscious use of history. Her novels may have a facile exterior, but they are not superficial. If we pay adequate attention to the subtle disguise she resorts to, we can see that her surfaces hide serious explorations into public history. She shows a sensitive response to the social, political, and cultural currents of her immediate past, which she examines and analyzes within the framework of a larger historical past of the country. Even when she deals with the immediate social and political history of the country, her very mode of making sense of it, by seeing it in the context of an older past, gives it the orientation of a historical inquiry.

The major feature and strength of Sahgal's fiction is that she relates the different levels of the country's past through the credible mechanism of a web of human relationships built around avid, thinking, and responsible characters. Drawn as part of a specific time-space continuum, the characters are moulded by events and happenings around them and show a strong awareness of their situation in all its varied dimensions. They constantly interrogate events, happenings, and problems, which are rooted in the actual; they hint at possibilities which could have matured, but did not. Often they even suggest the possible turn of events.[2] Because of this steady and constant interaction between the past and the present in her novels, they come very close to the conception of a novel in which the two are in a constant dialogue.

A synoptic overview of Sahgal's work will reveal that right from the time she wrote her first volume of autobiography to the time of the publication of her latest novel, she has shown consistent interest in the history and culture of her country. The two autobiographical works, *Prison and Chocolate Cake* and *From Fear Set Free*, paint vividly the changing social and political climate of the times in which she grew up. They also provide clues about the essential core of her thinking which informs her understanding of India's past, which she constantly invokes in her later novels, to make sense of the post-independence times. In her first two novels, *A Time to be Happy* and *This Time of the Morning*, the complexities of the Indo-British encounter are analyzed with discrimination. She dramatizes its effect on the institutional framework of the country, which in her view is of key importance for understanding the turn of events in post-independence times, because it passed on, virtually without any significant change, from the colonial set-up into the administrative machinery of free India. The novels also bring out the contrast between the pre- and post-independence India in terms of the tension between Gandhian and non-Gandhian ideologies of political practice. The next four novels—*Storm in Chandigarh, The Day in Shadow, A Situation in New Delhi*, and *Rich Like Us*—have at their centre several interesting aspects of the history of post-independence India, with special focus on the problems of political governance. In all of them, the narrator or the protagonist, who functions as a central consciousness, is connected with a significant moment or situation, which is rooted in the actual. By connecting his life with the lives of other characters, this particular moment or situation—whether it is the division of Punjab and the problem of political reorganization of the country, the instability caused by the death of a Prime Minister of a long standing, or the declaration of the state of emergency by Mrs Gandhi—is subjected to a thorough scrutiny through their actions, attitudes, and thinking. The mechanism is usually the same: the characters are sufficiently individualized, but linked closely with the socio-political scene. They are affected by it; in some cases, even changed and moulded by it. This framework has its limitations. It may not provide the kind of freedom which grotesque characters provide Rushdie in his novels. But it has its own compensating advantages. Sahgal's work acquires a greater degree of credibility and plausibility. Her last two novels are more self-conscious attempts at dealing with the problematic nature of historical reconstructions.

Before dealing with her novels, I make a brief reference to Sahgal's autobiographical work to demonstrate that the practice of mixing private and public history in her novels virtually flows from these writings and also to construct the normative core of her beliefs and values which she invokes to evaluate happenings and trends in the immediate and remore past of India. In both *Prison and Chocolate Cake* and *From Fear Set Free*, Sahgal uses her memory to recreate significant moments of her life and weaves them into a narrative. In the process, a large part of the history of the country also gets mixed with it. In *Prison*, she describes the process of recreation of the past as "putting together the pieces of a jig-saw puzzle" (vii). It suggests that it involved arranging experiences in a manner that they could acquire a desired shape and make intelligible whatever she thought was important in her and India's past. The possibility of the country's past becoming a part of her own past arose from the particular situation into which she had been born. Members of her family from her father's and mother's side were actively involved in the struggle for the freedom of the country. Its ups and downs impinged heavily on their lives and through them, on her own life too: "Our growing up was India's growing up into political maturity.... We learned to take pride in our parent's contribution to the struggle and to feel that it was our own" (15). When Sahgal writes elaborately about traditional Indian living styles, her participation in Hindu and Muslim festivals, and special occasions like weddings, and their carefully and sensitively-drawn comparisons with marriages in the West, she documents significant aspects of social and cultural history too. Sahgal also writes elaborately on the distinguishing features of the man-woman relationship within Indian (Hindu) culture, and provides interesting and informative details on the folk music and dance forms of the country.

The volume also provides evidence of Sahgal's involvement with and her impression of the two most important leaders of modern India, Gandhi and Nehru. Though she was struck first by the ugliness of Gandhi, she soon discovered his magnetism and his compassion and love for people of all classes and communities. She also found that though he was a devout Hindu and used Hindu symbols to mobilise people into a strong force to fight the British, "there was no trace of bigotry in the Mahatma" (17). In this, she differs from several present-day historians and novelists, such as Tharoor, who think that his methods spread disaffection among the non-Hindu population of the country. Sahgal points out that in the early phase of his career, some people made fun of him and his ways; even then one could not ignore him, "just as one cannot ignore a sudden shower during a dry season or the early and unexpected appearance of buds on a tree" (139). In a very short time, Gandhi became a strong force and an unavoidable presence. She sums up his major achievement by stating that "millions of people would have been ordinary folk, living their humdrum lives unperturbed but for him. He had come to disturb them profoundly, to jolt them out of indifference, to awaken them to each other's suffering, and in so doing to make them reach for the stars" (190). Sahgal thinks that the faith he awakened in people to better their lot is his precious legacy of hope for the people of India.

Like *Prison*, *From Fear Set Free* is an account of events and happenings in Sahgal's personal life. It also incorporates, in a more analytical manner, events from India's social and political history, because of which we get to know more details about her views on several issues, which form the central core of her later fiction. The title sums up the burden of her narrative, which is to demonstrate how the most vital concern of her growing up was to learn to free herself from fear, which had also become the aspiration of the vast majority of people in the country. The main impetus for her was her intimate association with Nehru, her mother's brother, who inspired by his personal example. This was strengthened by exposure to the teachings of Gandhi, whose main aim was to make people learn to live fearlessly: "The development of that inward freedom is the kernel for which economic advance can only form the shell. The survival of India's people can matter only as long as her spirit survives —the spirit of Gandhi, and older than this, the fathomless spiritual reservoir from which he drew his faith and inspiration" (6).

Sahgal's admiration for Gandhi is reflected in her focus on his well-known achievements: his work for the uplift of villages and their inhabitants, for drawing attention to the urgent need for taking care of the underprivileged and the untouchables, and for strengthening the spirit of all Indians. The most distinguished aspect of his work, in her view, was his purely native mode of response to the needs of his times. Unlike her Nanuji (Moti Lal Nehru), he succeeded in realizing his objectives because he thought himself one with the multitudes of India, "rooted in the same soil, nourished on the same simple diet, reared in the same beliefs and virtuous by the same standards. He did not impose alien standards on India" (102). This not only increased his popularity and appeal, but also provided the basis for a debate on the relevance of his ideas and ideals in post-independence times. It constitutes an important part of the intellectual history of the country, which her novels incorporate in a substantial measure.

Sahgal's treatment of India's social and cultural past in her novels is shaped by her understanding of two important issues, to which she draws attention in this volume. The first is her conception of India as a single, unified nation, which provides for the coexistence of pluralities. She is very firm on this and writes about its desirability in very positive terms:

> The human being could best express himself in his own medium and no language, however well taught, however important or influential, could take its place in reflecting the many-faceted culture of a people. Nor could one language, one culture or one religion ever be the formula for India, unless a great deal of value was leavened and lost in the process and the very foundation of India destroyed (203).

Sahgal is realistic enough to visualize the possibilities of conflict between people of different groups, faiths and beliefs, but derides solutions based on emotional considerations. I specify these details, because they provide the normative basis of her interrogation of events in India's history after 1947.

Another issue concerns the place of women in the Indian social system, into which Sahgal had been born and brought up. She comments elaborately on the views she inherited from her parents. She felt that her mother's ideas on marriage were old-fashioned, for she thought it absolutely essential that women should marry and that only arranged marriages were safe and durable: "They just go smoothly along. Excitements like poisonings and thrashings are for love matches" (50). Manu was invoked to tell her that a single woman had no life of her own; she "belonged first under her father's protection, then under her husband's, and if fate condemned her to widowhood, she must lean on her son" (51). Sahgal is more sympathetic to her father's view, because he upheld the Vedic ideal of woman as the equal of man. This detail is important because Sahgal consistently dramatizes the predicaments of her female characters within the cultural practices of our society. She analyses and critiques their coercive assumptions, and even suggests ways and means of fighting them.

Sahgal's first novel, *A Time to be Happy*, is located in the time immediately following the freedom of the country, but its narrative space is dominated by pre-independence times. The protagonist recalls his past life, especially the changes in his thinking and actions brought about by Gandhi's call to the people of India, and combines it with the story of the children of one of his close friends, concentrating in the main on the youngest son Sanad, who finds himself a total misfit in independent India. The narrative has the character of a historical construction, because the narrator shows awareness of the manner in which he writes his account. He recreates past events partly from his memory and partly on the basis of details provided by Sanad.

The novel takes off from a crisis in Sanad's life, when he seriously contemplates giving up his job with a reputed foreign company. He finds that the "veneer and gloss" of Englishness which he had acquired during the British rule looked totally unnatural and artificial in independent India. Though it is Sanad's personal problem, Sahgal treats it as the problem of a large section of people in the country, and a cultural issue of far-reaching significance. For understanding it in its wholeness, she locates it in the concrete historical context of pre-independence times, in the 1930s, though, as I have already pointed out, she does not invoke actual names or incidents, and concentrates on the significant changes that the British rule brought about in the cultural climate of the country.

The opening chapter of the novel clarifies that because of vast differences in the levels of living and thinking of its people, there was a simultaneous coexistence of several layers of pastness in the country, which made people respond differently to the British. They either chose to remain unmoved and fixed, like Sanad's father, who, in spite of the social and political ferment around him, opted for a "leisurely neutral life," or evolved new ways for combating their influence by invoking a part of their native tradition, which also created possibilities for reforming their society. Some, like the protagonist, gave up their rich and prosperous life for joining Gandhi's social and political programme. Others, like Sanad, chose to follow the British blindly, because they considered it both enlightening and rewarding—a civilized mode of living and an effective road to success. The changes stimulated by the response of the Indians to the British presence in the country left their mark on the post-independence times as well. The narrator clarifies that these changes were not confined to big cities, where the British presence was quite strong; their impact was visible even in small places like Saharanpur, where Sanad took his first job. The novel elaborates these strands as products of history, because of which its action constantly moves between the present and the past. This method of understanding the present and the immediate past by relating it to an older past, but without using any recognizable actual events and happenings, is the method of disguise that Sahgal consistently uses in her novels.

The British presence in the novel is exemplified in Tom Grange. His first encounter with India confuses and puzzles him, but soon he succeeds in becoming a stolid functionary of the empire, by casting himself into the mould of a colonial Britisher, in which "the traditional pattern of behaviour in India had been handed on from one generation of Englishmen to the next, and each newcomer had carried it forward" (11). He learns that in India he was more than an individual being; he was part of a large set up, in which "his very presence was accomplishing a mission" (11). Cyril Weatherby, another colonial administrator, followed the same elaborate pattern of behavioural codes, which saved him from making many adjustments, so often needed in a foreign country. Even on an unusual day, such as August 9, 1942, when people were protesting against the British, he looked normal. As part of his ordained role, he knew that "In India there were no new situations. Generations of Englishmen before him had smoothed the path for him, building up a code of manners and morals to deal with any situation that might conceivably arise" (115).

The narrator's father represents the growing class of Indians whose admiration for the British was total. This includes Sanad's brother and their uncle Harish, who accept the British ways in an unabashedly uncritical spirit, which the novelist disapproves. Harish's mother provides the right clue for understanding this tendency, when she expresses her fear of the cultural consequences of the Raj. As the replica of a bara sahib, Harish is a total stranger to her; she is puzzled by the fact that the likes of him had taken to British ways without any struggle or experiencing any conflict between their native and adopted ways. She also fears the true import of this transformation, because she knew that her son's "traditions were as remote from Britain's as any could be, whose intrinsic temperament and attitudes bore not the slightest resemblance to those of the British, yet whose entire outlook and manner had been so moulded as to leave not the suspicion of an Indian about him" (19-20). She partially understands it in terms of the educational system specially introduced by the British to keep the Indians ignorant of their country and its tradition. That is why she says in anger: "'Do they live in England that they know nothing of what goes on in their own country? Do they know what crops grow on their father's land, or even what this land was before the foreigner came to it? What kind of learning do they acquire in school?'" (21) This education is meant to help them become loyal servants of the government, who follow a routine of business and pleasure, the "glittering cocktail-party-gymkhana-club-Government-House Circuit" (27). Such people are not merely out of tune with the happenings in the country, they also fail to adjust with people who do not accept their ways. Harish, for example, fails to make it up with his wife Maya. The narrator laments ruefully that the two "who should have been ideally suited were, in fact, as remote from each other as strangers" (43). What is being emphasized time and again is that their incompatibility does not arise as much from their temperaments, as from their cultural differences. Harish is Westernized, sophisticated, flamboyant, and given over to British ways of living; Maya is subdued, cool, a little remote, who loves her pujas and festivals. Harish has no liking and use for her ways. Sanad's problem is that, like his brother, he modelled himself on his uncle.

Sahgal uncovers the politics behind this polarity. For perpetuating themselves in power, the British wanted to create a class of people from amongst Indians who would be like them and yet not be them. But they motivated the Indians to follow their ways by inventing a rational argument. McIvor uses it, when he tells Sanad that such people could provide "the link between India and the rest of the world," because "the world is in need of a universal culture, a universal language, if not in literal terms, at least in terms of thought and values" (151-52). Sanad's brother too speaks for homogenized universalism as the need of the hour, and expresses his disapproval of the appalling variety that the country already had, with people in dhotis, pyjama-kurtas, loincloth, and suit and tie.

The burden of Sahgal's novel is to examine this view in its wholeness. Through Sanad's constant interrogation, she draws attention to its serious implications. In spite of the arguments of the British and Indians for the validity of such a stance, he considers it a masquerade, which prevented Indians from seeing the piles of corpses outside their pleasure haunts in Calcutta. Their aping of the British resulted in "mimic uniformity." Taking things from their culture "lock, stock, and barrel" was just "pathetic" (96). It made them cast their life in a rhythm set by the British, to conform to their modes of thinking and go against their "own roots." This created a class of Indians who neither belonged with the English nor with their fellow beings, especially the ones who belonged to the lower rungs of society. They did not know even the language of their own people. Sanad thinks that they symbolized cultural confusion of the worst kind, because they had mistaken modernity for Westernization.

Sahgal clarifies her position through Sanad, who is drawn as a complex character. Though he follows the ways of his brother and uncle, he is alive to the problematic nature of his actions; that is why he questions them at every step and makes efforts to combat their evil influence. Even though he conforms to the accepted behaviour-pattern of this class, he asserts his individuality. Disregarding the advice of his father, he confronts his British employer as a free being and not as an enthusiastic convert. His awareness of his situation, however, takes on the proportions of a crisis when he meets Kusum, who belongs to a family firmly rooted in the culture of the country.

Kusum's father, Madan Sahay, is a teacher of history. As a sympathetically-drawn character, he represents the views of the novelist about the true character of India's past. Sahay imagines it as a dynamic force, which could be felt only when one endeavoured to "pierce the dry barrier of facts." Sahgal too believes that the best way to approach the past is to see "behind the facts and dates," so that it is possible to "imagine the state of mind that inspired the impassioned edicts engraved on rocks and pillars all over the country…" (184). Sahay also voices the assimilationist view of the composite culture of India, in which his Vedic ancestors and their temples coexist with Muslim sultans and emperors: "Some magic assimilative quality…made sons of them all, the native-born and the stranger. Even those who came here as conquerors, flashing swords and spilling blood, remained to become Indians and to contribute their genius to this country. What is India but the combined product of them all" (191)?[3]

Sanad's continued association with Kusum intensifies his alienation. He struggles to fight the oppressive nature of the Englishness which has burned into him: "…we're branded with it. My body is in India, but my brain doesn't belong here. I might as well be an Englishman except for the colour of my skin" (234). Sanad is willing to take hard decisions to fit himself into the new free India. Sahgal suggests that many unreformed Sanads continue to operate in post-independence India. As an influential part of the society, they also exercise control over the lives of people and much of the mess in the country is of their making.

Through the career of its protagonist, the novel also exemplifies the power the Gandhian ideology had on a large number of people in pre-independence times. Gandhi helped him see the true face of India, "the village India, her desperate plight, her crushing burdens of debt" (9). He also testifies how Gandhi "made symbols of the lowliest commodities, salt and cloth, both vital necessities of life, and both heavily taxed." For a more effective dramatization of the influence of Gandhi on individual lives, the novelist creates the character of Sohan Bhai. For him Gandhi was just not a politician; he was a healer who cleansed people's minds. He converted the

Congress from a political party into a "channel of service." Through his efforts, Sohan Bhai learnt to overcome his personal sorrow and make common cause with people who had nothing, exemplifying the Gandhian credo that pain can be sublimated through service. Even *charkha* becomes a "medicine both for the body and for the mind. It keeps idle hands busy and calms the mind" (89).

Thus we see that Sahgal provides a multi-layered social and political history in the novel. It documents the diversity in people's response to the changes that took place in the country around the time the British rule was about to end. It also demonstrates how the British shaped a class of people, totally out of tune with the needs of the country, who created new islands of power and values in Indian society. These, Sahgal labours to point out, continue to flourish even in free India.

In *A Time to be Happy*, Mark McIvor tells Sanad that at the time of its independence, India would inherit two institutions, "a trained army and a trained Civil Service. These are the elements that will run the new regime" (150). Located in the years immediately after India's independence, *This Time of Morning* deals elaborately with the various facets of the role of the civil service in the country, which impinges heavily on the country's choice of a suitable political and administrative structure for its new needs. For examining different facets of the Gandhian mode of governance as one of the options, a good part of the pre-independence past of the country is brought into the narrative. The novel also records the growth of resistance to the idealistic moorings of this option by political adventurists, whose role in the polity has become quite visible, in spite of the strong presence of an idealistic Prime Minister.

The most significant feature of the novel is that it drew attention to the pivotal role of civil servants in the Indian state at a time when they did not figure in the writings of the historians. This is where Sahgal scores over tradition-bound historiography. Although a part of the larger package that the British left behind, of the "Army, the parliamentary system and the English language" (7), the civil service had an influential bearing on the existing and future political structure of the country. The novelist records that

> The old Civil Service jealously guarded its rights and privileges against the encroaching new services, both foreign and internal, and the polite tension between the old and the new affected this and every other Ministry as India struggled to squeeze a revolution into the bureaucratic mould and adapt dramatic plans and programmes to everyday consumption (129).

Arjun Mitra represents the graces as well as the absurdities of the service. The most absurd aspect of their functioning was that the civil servants had to work with the very same people they had put in prison during the colonial times. Secondly, even under the new dispensation, they continued to hold on to their pre-colonial life-style and the belief that modernity "went hand in hand with Westernization." Because of their power and prestige, they exerted a baneful influence on the administrative structure of free India, by tempting the new recruits to emulate them and to consider themselves part of a "goosey goosey gander generation." Apart from the rich slice they took from the national cake, they clung to old ways and hardly ever thought of reorienting themselves to the changed times. That is why a new recruit Rakesh says: "How full of inconsistencies we are and surely the biggest one is trying to administer an independent country through the framework of a colonial system" (129).

It is through this firmly-entrenched, though tangled, bureaucracy that Sahgal builds into the novel the conflict between Gandhian and non-Gandhian modes of political governance of the country. Though symbolized in the person of politicians like Kailash and Kalyan, who are finely drawn individuals with strong convictions, the behind-the-scenes work is done by the civil servants, who support them for the furtherance of their ends. By focussing on the leaders and their thinking, the novel captures a slice of the cultural history of post-independence times, when reexamination and reassesment of the relevance of Gandhism was attempted with a greater degree of rigour and realism. Although in the action of the novel it triumphs, the novelist makes it clear that its influence is on the decline. This is because many political leaders are openly critical of it and are aided and abetted by the old bureaucrats.

Sahgal's admiration for Gandhi and his relevance to Indian conditions is dramatized through Kailash, who re-lives Gandhi's life and its charisma through a long memory recall, from the days of his stay in South Africa to his role in India, where he brought about a revolutionary change in the values of people and gave a new character to the struggle for independence, by making it into a "quest for truth." He thinks that Gandhi played a crucial role in rescuing Indian people from "the spirit's stagnation, from the crippling malady of resignation, because non-co-operation was a courageous and determined resistance to evil" (48). Kailash is conscious of some of the outmoded aspects of Gandhian thought, but thinks that its main plank of reaching the very last human being in society is of perennial relevance. He is pained to see that whatever resistance there was to Gandhism was not because of this, but because the people in power wanted to promote ideologies for their social and political advancement. This created politics of domination and dictatorship.

This tendency is represented in the novel by Kalyan Singh, who had no faith in Gandhi's method of fighting the British and had championed India's cause of freedom from the American soil. He felt that by emphasizing the value of suffering in his programme, Gandhi had only perpetuated a lie that religions normally do. In his view, "suffering is evil. It must not be endured or sanctified. It must be torn up by the roots, brutally if need be" (73). In post-independence India, Gandhites were no more than "old fossils," who obstructed change. He thinks that Gandhi's greatest disservice to the country was that he

> emasculated us.... If a saint is indeed what he was, then saintliness was an intolerable intrusion into everyday life. But for Gandhi there would have been a revolution like any other—if not with guns, then with sticks and stones, teeth and nails—and there would not have been these anomalies to contend with today, this oil-and-water regime that could command no singleness or unity of purpose (136).

Sahgal, however, is keen on showing that Kalyan criticized the Gandhian mode only for providing a rational excuse for his ambitious designs, in which he is supported by unscrupulous leaders like Hari Mohan and several ambitious and discredited civil servants. Sahgal sees the rise of leaders like Kalyan as part of the general degradation which had overtaken even the Congress party, forcing one of its veterans Prakash Shukla to say that politics had become a dirty game.

If the first two novels deal with the effect of the colonial encounter on the pre- and post-independence India through the institutional structures which the British had established in the country, the next four novels deal with deterioration in the political and social culture of new India, which reached its culmination in the emergency times of Mrs Gandhi. Sahgal's method, however, remains the same. Without naming actual people and events, she concretizes trends and tendencies and subjects them to a keen, thorough examination. By linking them with the older past of the country, she not only examines them in a historical-cultural perspective, but also brings out the divergence between the promise the new free India had held and the dismal rot that had actually set in it.

Storm in Chandigarh focusses on the crisis in Chandigarh, which has arisen from the division of Punjab into two states, of which it is the joint capital. The immediate cause of the crisis, however, is the belligerent posture of the chief minister of Punjab, whose actions the novelist considers reflective of a slide in the country's faith in the philosophy of non-violence. The novel, in fact, projects the view that social and political violence has become endemic; it is perceived in its fullness by the home minister of India, who is one of the few remaining Gandhians. With despair, he refers to "brutal, calculated violence," which has become "routine and expected" and given different names: "indiscipline, unrest, disorder" (8). Vishal Dubey, who has been sent by him to Chandigarh to resolve the crisis, explains the rise of violence to fall in people's level of commitment to causes and issues, which were expressed earlier in words like "dedication, sacrifice, austerity," but had lost their meaning, because they were a part of, what Sahgal consistently invokes as a dying norm, a "big vision,"—the vision of a united, integrated India. Because Indians had lost sight of it soon after attaining independence, the country had lapsed into a "welter of separate, sensitive identities" (15). Unlike several contemporary historians, Sahgal does not view this phenomenon as an expression of people's thwarted aspiration or a genuine yearning for true freedom, but as an undesirable collision between the grand vision of a single, united India and the parochial ambitions of politicians, who wanted its division into smaller units. Almost all the major characters in the novel except Gyan understand it as an assertion of power and authority of a "dictator, a regular hell-raiser," who cannot brook any control on his power. Sahgal considers the partition of the state a wrong political act. Her disapproval is reflected in her comparison of this event with the first partition of Punjab in 1947. Both were wrong, because they were the result of egotistical belligerence and represented a reprehensible tendency. If the first one marked a relapse into a "primitive century," because religion was used as a resource of power over each other's mind, the second one used language as a weapon for dividing people who had been living together for centuries. On both occasions, things had changed because of the confounding sentiments voiced by a strong person. Because of this, the crisis in Chandigarh, though considered political, had actually turned into a "clash of personalities." The issues had given way to squabbles. That is why Harpal Singh, the chief minister of Haryana, who had opposed the division, says that "there was something sinister at the root of the Partition mentality and those who upheld it. Mankind's journey was towards integration, not the breaking up of what already existed" (30).

Vishal Dubey considers the Punjab chief minister's attempt to demonstrate his strength a glaring example of fall in higher morality, the one which represents "a search for value, and an attempt to choose the better value, the real value, in any situation, and not just what's done or what is expected" (82). Going beyond its immediate cause—which is fall in the level of awareness among people—he looks for its actual cause in the older past of the country, in the changing veins of its culture. Dubey thinks that in India several cultural strains had blended without producing anything different. As a result a "monolithic slab of antiquity had survived the ages. A way of life, wrongly called a religion, lay embedded in it. Against it the intellect foundered and the emotions were reduced to insignificance" (88). Although there lay vitality underneath it, it had not been tapped. On the contrary, it had been used, and was still being used, for unhealthy purposes, which had created problems. Gyan had pleaded for the division of the state by invoking the aid of history. When he called himself a simple man fired with a purpose to call "his soil his own in the language of his forefathers," Dubey could see in it "a strange mixture of truth and imagination that had the lure of a revival" (121). Gyan conjured past glories of an old, large Punjab, a state which had existed long back in time. Dubey could also see, and this is where Sahgal proves a perspicacious diagnostician, that the simple argument could later be converted into a larger one, in which things would follow logically from one to the other: "His next official act would be to start religious instruction in the schools." And this "could be followed by asking for a separate army and a flag for the Punjab" (145 and 147). Rushdie too traced the rise of linguistic states in India to the revivalist fever among several sections of Indians, which was actually a cover for their lust for power. The novel documents several scenes of brutal and insane violence which are directly related to Gyan's attempt to hold on to power.

The novel also clarifies that fall in the standards of political morality was not confined to the states; it was in the centre too, in its political set-up and bureaucracy. The central leaders, who were supposed to make the vision of integrated India into a viable and purposeful reality, without compromising on values, failed to do so, because they were solely guided by the consideration of perpetuating themselves in power. The top bureaucratic officials too had ceased to be humane, cultivated, and broadminded; like politicians they had learnt to keep themselves in power by playing safe.

Sahgal demonstrates that violence has spread into social relationships too, especially in relations between men and women, which she has consistently explored and commented upon in several novels. The valuable thing about her treatment is that, like what she does about other aspects of India's social and political life, she traces its roots in the country's past. Dubey explains the depressed position of women in Indian (Hindu) society to the same "monolithic slab of antiquity" of Indian culture, to which he traced the divisive tendencies in its political set-up. His regret is that its richness had not been used in an "enlightening way"; it had been used only for supporting feeble issues, like the preservation of cows.

In several vital areas, where it was necessary to climb "out of stagnation onto the high road where the fresh air blows," Indians had shown utter lack of imagination in holding on to unhealthy fixities and rigidities. This is exemplified in the marriage situation of Inder and Saroj. Inder's problem with his wife arises from his view of the destiny of women which has descended down the generations, in which she has to live according to a fixed role, pre-determined for her by the male-dominated society. The result is that he is not able to reconcile himself to a woman who, before she got married to him, has had a life of her own, when she had known another man. Inder fails to see Saroj in the present, as a pleasant, trusted partner, only because he cannot get over her past, which haunts him like an unpleasant obsession. The result is that a shadow looms large in their otherwise successful relationship.

Although Inder starts spending some of his time with a married woman Mara, who treats him like a friend, he cannot bear the idea of Saroj being friends with Dubey. When she goes for long walks with him, he is incensed. This leads Dubey to analyze her situation, so that he could go to the very root of her problem. His finding could safely be described as the synoptic history of the situation of Indian women:

> ...creatures not yet emerged from the chrysalis, for whom the adventure of self-expression had not even begun. Whatever womanhood had once meant in India had been lost in the mists of antiquity. In its place there had long been a figure of humility, neck bent, eyes downcast, living flesh consigned to oblivion.... They were wives, daughters, mothers. They belonged to their men by contract or by blood. Their sphere was sexual and their job procreation. They were dependents, not individuals. When you wanted them it could apparently only be for sex. You could lust after their bodies.... The one thing you could not crave, the thing that was a crime, was that they should inhabit the world as your equals, with the splendour and variety of human choice before them.... A woman was not entitled to a past, not entitled to human hunger, human passion, or even human error. In the fires and desolations of living she ranked as not quite human (191-92).

The passage brings out tellingly the disadvantaged position of a woman in Indian society, which is linked to her tradition-bound role. At considerable risk to his person and reputation, Dubey encourages Saroj to reexamine her situation, even to leave Inder, at least for some time, so that he can see the unreason and oppression in his thinking about her. Dubey speaks for the novelist when he says that there should be openness in the relationship between men and women; for too long they had "contorted into moulds, battered into sameness." The novel thus takes off from a situation from Sahgal's near past which she analyzes in depth by linking it to the country's earlier past.

The Day in Shadow, once again, connects the issue of female domination with changes in the political scenario of the country. At the core of the novel is the fast-deteriorating relationship between Som and Simrit, who have been married for long years and have three children. As a businessman, Som's sole ambition in life is to move up fast; for this he makes and unmakes friendships and alliances with people without any compunction. At one point, Simrit is shocked to find that she has become irrelevant in his scheme of things. After moments of hesitation and with guilty feelings, she finally walks out of her home, because she finds a supportive friend in Raj. Even after leaving him, Som takes advantage of her ignorance and burdens her with tax obligations, which make her independent living very near impossible. Since Sahgal does not want that we read her story merely as the predicament of an individual being, she connects it with a specific socio-cultural location, whose origins have been subjected to a sustained interrogation.

Simrit's unhappy married life is located in the early phase of the Nehruvian era, when Gandhian principles had started losing their appeal. In the foreign and economic sphere, it is marked by the rise of the influence of the erstwhile U.S.S.R. In the action of the novel, we find that Gandhi is still being invoked by some politicians, but only to catch public attention. As a "cynical bunch of manipulators," they are incapable of providing any meaningful direction to the country. This situation and the plight of Simrit are explained in terms of India's cultural past, which has been dominated by the Hindu mode of thinking.

As a character through whom Sahgal projects her viewpoint, Raj believes that nations need constantly to be vitalised. Gandhi did this at the most crucial time in India's history and succeeded in awakening people to fight the British. The need for such a periodic vitalisation was greater in the case of India, because of its predominantly Hindu character. As people, the main preoccupation of Hindus had been to survive the onslaughts of time, by developing "an endless spongelike capacity to absorb" (13). Nothing had struck them as being dangerous or challenging. Because of this, Hindus had also developed the unhealthy trait of passivity, which made them put up with several kinds of shocking things. That is why India's past had become riddled with unhealthy practices and thinking. I have already pointed out how Anand links the deformities in the Indian social and political system with the deeply-entrenched passivity of its people. Raj considers it the root of all the ills of the country—the mess in its politics and the relations between men and women: "The Hindu race!—mute, acquiescent, letting things happen to it, from a country to the mind and body of a woman" (37).

Raj encourages Simrit to make sense of her condition by connecting it with the cultural malaise of the civilisational past of her country. When she looks back into her past life with her husband from this new awareness, she realizes that most of the time she had been like an "animal, only a nice, obedient, domestic one, sitting on a cushion, doing as she was told" (57). Som had not considered her worthy of being told about his business; her "usefulness to him had never extended to the areas of her mind." He considered woman as a "moron," "an object of pity and tenderness." Simrit has to go through suffering and anguish before she can see the lie in the fact of her life with Som. And in her situation, Raj "sees the mirror of the whole culture, people—especially women—forever taking things lying down" (140). Since Simrit had all along followed the beaten track, she hesitates to act, even after realizing how futile her life with her husband had been. Raj has to work hard to bring about an attitudinal change in her, to help her overcome hesitations and guilty thoughts. When the successful moment comes, she chooses to be "separate, excluded, rebellious."

Sahgal suggests that unless change of this kind comes on a mass scale, there is no hope for the country. In a fast-changing world, we need to be "free-willed and creative, not the playthings of chance. We've got to take matters into our own hands" (43). The newly-acquired freedom has no meaning if people continue to have unquestioned faith in their inheritance as they had in the past. There was also the danger that "If the inert mass of them did not wake up to the fact that they were their masters, the brutal and single-minded among them would" (43).

Som is a frightful example of such brutality. He has rightly realized that he has to lift himself from his origins, but because his effort is no more than an example of "isolated forcefulness, isolated currents of energy undirected by vision or compassion" (44), it turns out to be an act of aggression on his environment, which includes both men and women. Part of this can be seen in his attempt to rub out his past, which he carries to the dangerous extreme of destroying his memories. He follows the pursuit of money with rigour and single-minded devotion, only to create a new resource of power and authority. In this plan, he is guided by no ethical or moral considerations; he sacrifices friends, even his wife, without any qualms of conscience. The cult of aggressive individualism that it promotes is defined in his advice to his son: "...Prove yourself. Be tough. Be a winner. Be a man. The kind of man who batters his way through opposition—and arrives" (59). Raj considers people like Som dangerous, because their desire to lift themselves from their past passivity is not "tempered by humanity"; it has no worthwhile social dimension and therefore no healthy impact on society. In fact, it only replaces old tyrannies by new ones, in which the weak are trampled upon, the way Simrit was.

In the political field, a similar situation is typified by Sumer Singh. Sahgal adds an extra dimension to it by positing a difference between two kinds of politicians. The first category is of the older ones, who had learnt from Gandhi the proper modalities of change, to plant new dreams in a manner that they became part of the evolving movement of India's fulfilment. They are symbolized in the person of the Prime Minister, who resembles Nehru. The second is of the new brand of opportunists, represented by Sumer Singh. Like Som, he takes a dismissive attitude towards the past, because he equates it with old people, the "fringes of society" who needed to be "carted along like unprofitable baggage" (129). In his reductionist view, the past becomes a burden of authority, dominated by the old; he wants it to be "dismembered and ground to fine dust." Sumer realizes that one way of getting over it is to take a leap like Som into a totally new terrain. He does this by shifting to a new style of economic and political culture, which is symbolized by his signing of a new deal with Russia. He is abrasively confident of the success of this new direction and suggests that people should throw "away sentiment, the weak, worn-out liberalism of the past, time to bury Gandhi and write a new page of Indian history" (186). That is why he says that the country needs a "clean-up, a break away, an end to the Gandhi syndrome, that supposedly long, shining chain of service, begun by the Mahatma that he himself had spun out ad nauseam in speeches" (192). Since Sahgal is opposed to this tendency, Sumer Singh, like Som, is drawn by her like a caricature; he is mocked even by his uneducated mistress Pixie.

Sahgal's way out of this is not by recommending a total annihilation of India's cultural past, in which many tides and currents had blended with the native, but by suggesting that we try out new mixtures. Part of it stems from her anxiety that India might go the Communist way. Ram Krishan, Raj's friend, is confident that a possibility lay already there in the Hindu approach. If Gandhi succeeded in showing the way by taking just one or two ideas from it and giving them a new meaning and force, it could be done even now. "It's this that will provide the stamina, the sticking point, the boiling point we need to resist what we don't believe in, and give us the will to act" (234). Another possibility could be to sort out irreconcilables in two religions, say Hinduism and Christianity, for evolving the basis for a new meaningful action.

In *A Situation in New Delhi*, Sahgal makes a larger inquiry about post-independence India, in which she posits the idea of a clear distinction between Nehruvian and post-Nehruvian times. Instead of concentrating on a single trend or tendency, she attempts a comprehensive perspectival statement on the country as a whole. The title of the novel suggests that the situation in New Delhi epitomizes the situation of the entire country. For this, Sahgal weaves a narrative around a number of characters: Devi, the sister of the dead Prime Minister Shivraj, who is Nehru in disguise; her son Rishad, a young college-going boy, member of a Naxalite group, who dies in an explosion in a cinema hall; her friend Usman, the Vice-chancellor of Delhi University, an admirer of Shivraj's policies, who, like Devi, is disenchanted with the changed regime; and Michael Calvert, an old acquaintance of Shivraj and Devi, who returns to India from England to write his biography. During Shivraj's tenure in office, Devi was his friend and companion, who shared in his dreams and gave him constant support. As a minister in the new government, she is witness to the rapid changes that have taken place after him. This makes her eminently suitable for comparing the two periods, with regard to the quality of leadership and the policies and programmes of the government. But Sahgal supplements her view of the changed situation by the observations of Calvert. As one who had returned to India after several years, he could understand these changes with a greater degree of clarity and objectivity.

The novel attempts an estimate of the dead leader's personal qualities, his approach to nation-building, and his power to influence the lives of people. Largely on the basis of this, it builds a contrast between the times before and after Shivraj. The principal feature of the post-Shivraj India is a steady erosion of all that he had stood for: robust and healthy democratic fervour, value-oriented thinking, and a purposeful drive towards future advancement. That is why the prevalent cancerous filth: widespread corruption, political interference in areas which had better be left free, and growth of manipulated violence. This is reflected in unrest and indiscipline in the universities, senseless, conspicuous consumption of the business class, and insecurity and unease of people who have minds of their own. All this is suggested not merely by Devi's image of her times as a "world falling around her," but also by the bewilderment of Mansa Ram, who symbolizes the common man: "There were things happening around him he could no longer understand." This is not just because of decline in the quality of leadership, but also because the new group in power has muddled and confused thinking. The result is that the country is in the grip of a crisis. It cannot think of a proper mode of change for carrying it forward. The novel documents two alternative strategies to meet this situation. The one represented by Rishad recommends violence, which has its basis in actuality. The second one is of Usman, which envisages a new revolution, anchored in the retrievable elements from India's past, and having affinity with the plans and projections of Shivraj. The novelist examines the assumptions behind these alternative strategies, but makes it clear that the mode of change suggested by Usman is not acceptable to the new group because they have broken away from the policies and programmes of the dead Prime Minister. That is why the chances of the violent possibility overtaking the peaceful one were there. The burden of the novel, therefore, is to suggest that there was a marked difference in the style and functioning of the ruling party during the times of Nehru and the leaders who came after him, especially Mrs Gandhi.

The novel is quite flattering to Nehru's personality and style. Calvert thinks of him as an outstanding Asian, "a symbol of the fight against colonial rule, a hero who had resurrected a legend so much of Asia shared and given it modern meaning.... And for Indians, a man who took the people with him on uncharted journeys, on the frail, unbreakable, so very unpolitical bond of trust" (6). As a distinctively self-conscious individual, he was no camp follower, a fate which leaders of the newly-emergent countries could not easily avoid. That is why for the Westerners, he was enigmatic, especially "because he wore no disguise"; for the Communists, he was a source of unease, because they had "no use for the contemplative view or vision." His work was marked by enervating freshness, because he insisted on using his mind and not taking "chewed and half-digested bits of other people's"(7-8). Devi praises him for his success in welding together a vastly heterogeneous people into a unity, not with the help of "any hidebound principle or rule from a book" (42), but through his imagination.

Sahgal's admiration for Nehru borders on idolatry; she condones even his wrong acts. Through Devi, she admits that he made compromises, but explains that he was forced to do so either because he was too ill or because he wanted to save his party from falling apart. In her view, he was a thorough democrat, who worked consistently to let free institutions "become part of the soil, become a way of life and thinking that no future could destroy" (93). Devi stresses that the foundations of a firm democratic structure which he had laid with great care were being undone in the new times. She points out that he had succeeded in his efforts because of the support and cooperation of his associates, who were men of distinction: "Each had made some peculiarly personal contribution.... They had been representatives of the intelligentsia themselves but like Shivraj they had been identified in work and sympathy with too many kinds of classes of Indians.... There'd been no sheep and goats in Shivraj's time" (129). In contrast to him, the new leader was a non-entity, because of which he/she is not even sufficiently individualized. His/her associates are ordinary and pedestrian. They talk with pride that they are with the poor and the small, but say so in a manner "as if they had discovered social justice all by themselves"; worse still, they did not have "one good sound sensible programme to put before the country."

One could read Sahgal's elitist bias in Devi's remark, in which she looks like running down ordinary and common people in the new government, but it is not so. She has nothing against being a commoner. In fact, what she laments is that in spite of being ordinary, the new people in power did not act like humble, ordinary beings. They thought themselves part of the "new aristocracy," because they were the "new privileged around the cabinet table." Their ordinariness was reflected in their inefficiency and ineptitude. Because they lacked the ability of their predecessors, they stopped giving press conferences and took to addressing mammoth meetings at well-known places, such as India Gate and Red Fort. This led to the emergence of a new style of leadership and introduced militant populism into the political culture of the country.

This partly explains the rise of the influence of communists in the power structures of the country. Devi puts this in perspective by admitting that Shivraj too consulted the communists, but "firmly ruled them out as mature partners in the government" (16). But the new government was under their influence, because it depended upon them. The novel documents vividly the dangers this new alliance between the two posed to the country.

As a fresh convert to the new creed, Rishad expounds its basic philosophy, which is quite appealing. His argument that old modes of thinking in the country had proved inimical to change is similar to the one of Raj in the earlier novel. Rishad includes in them the belief in cosmic dispensation in which each individual has to work out his destiny. He thinks that it suited only the fat rich and not the hungry desperate, who could not "live on a diet of philosophy. They needed another easier-to-grasp prescription for change." All this fits in with Sahgal's ideas on social change. But they lead Rishad to a view of India's past, which the novelist does not accept. Draining it of all the significant changes that had taken place in the country, he understands it only in economic terms, as an uninterrupted period of grievous exploitation. India's freedom struggle, which covers a long and momentous period in the awakening of its people, does not figure in such a view of history. For Rishad, the country's freedom in 1947 is virtually "pre-history, an event whose antiquity had no relation to the present and with which he had no ties.... When he said 'India' he meant something different" (74).

On account of this one-dimensional view of India's history, Rishad thinks that the major problems of the country are hunger and inequality, which could be solved only by breaking the existing structures. His party's plan for this is to administer shock to people, spread panic, and resort to wholesale destruction of men and materials: "To build a new world the old one had to be razed to the ground. The way to do it was through the systematic creation of panic. Panic to chaos to ruin. And out of ruin open revolt and power. Only then could the new social order arise. Not utopia. Just food in the stomach and a decent wage. Utopia for the poor and the downtrodden. An Indian utopia" (58). Rishad thinks that all the existing political structures had proved ineffective in coping with the problems of the poor and the weak. In fact, by categorising them as the underprivileged and weaker sections of society, political parties had deliberately kept alive the contrast between the rich and the poor, and exploited it for making bids for power. Rishad thinks that the poor and lowly were hardly human; they had been pushed to the very edges of history. By incorporating Rishad's views in their fullness, the novel is quite sympathetic to his creed, but it does not endorse its constricted view of history; nor does it approve of its violent ways. The novel dramatizes several scenes of violence connected with the activities of Rishad's group to suggest that they are only senseless and sensational acts. Rishad's death in one such violent incident symbolizes the danger inherent in such a programme of change.

Usman's alternative strategy for social change derives from his perceptive understanding of the malaise of the new times: the rise of the power of the state. He fears that soon it would threaten and engulf private lives. Because of this, he feels that what people needed urgently was a mechanism for ensuring the devolution of power to the smallest possible unit. This he locates in the country's past: he finds that power could be filtered down to its oldest known unit—the village. That is why he advocates going to the "village past, for another form of government, one that didn't build up and up into a formidable state apparatus" (83). Usman disapproves the revolutionary fervour of the new "crop of interpreters" who dominated policy and practice and suggests that instead of faking revolutions, which did away with the entire "previous human record," it was better to develop a "native variety of communism," which would have its "roots in the village and its inspiration drawn from the Indian heritage."

Sahgal's support for the viability of such an alternative reaffirms the viewpoint she made in *The Day in Shadow*: that the Indian tradition had the potential for providing a meaningful possibility of change, which would also provide a safeguard against violent socio-political alternatives. In this respect, she links Usman's thinking with the thinking of Nehru. When the ambassador of Britain tells Calvert that recent changes in the set up of the country—such as curbs on press and platform and the imposition of censorship—were reflective of the waning of the British influence, which had been quite strong on the late Prime Minister, he disagrees with him. On the contrary, he tells him, that many things that the late Prime Minister had believed in did not come from the British, but from the tradition he had inherited. It is true that the tradition had some ugly features too, but it did provide for values like tolerance:

> That way of life and thinking still exists, and not only in the village. It's there in the factory and the bazaar. It's there if you scratch the surface of anyone who calls himself a modern Indian. It's a colossal storehouse, some of it evil and repellent, and some of it as fine as the world has produced and very relevant to modern times.... They've got five thousand years of tradition to dip into. And nowhere does it come up with intolerance (107-8).

Calvert asserts that Indian tradition has several redeeming features, which Indians could fall back upon. The measures taken by the new government were undemocratic and unhealthy; they clearly hint at the repressive measures of Mrs Gandhi. He spells their disastrous effect on the body-politic: "When this kind of thing begins to happen, interpretative writing disappears. Second-hand stuff, official handouts take its place. Scholarship becomes a farce" (108). These tendencies led ultimately to the declaration of emergency in the country, to which Sahgal devotes an entire novel.

Rich Like Us is in a way a climactic sequel to the three novels I have already discussed. It is imbued with such a strong moral passion that, for once, Sahgal throws up her cloak of disguise to make more than usual direct references to people and events, and expresses her disapproval of the emergency let loose on the country by Mrs Gandhi in unequivocal terms. But she does not give up her technique of enmeshing public and private histories. She intertwines this part of India's history with the history and fortunes of two families, whose members cannot help getting involved with the new situation. But it proves to be a time of unequal opportunity for them. To some it brings profit and gain; to others, especially the women, Rose and Sonali, it brings pain, hardship, and frustration. For Rose, it is a veritable nightmare, which finally consumes her. They try to cope with it by delving into their familial past, which gets connected with the older past of the country. They use it as a resource for countering their oppressive and tyrannical present. Through a skilful interplay between various kinds of histories, Sahgal vividly dramatizes the historical scene and comments elaborately on some of the crucial issues thrown up by the times. In the family of Rose, pressures from the outside world change the very shape and direction of the family history. It culminates in her gruesome murder, which is recorded as an accident, because her stepson, who first deprived her of money through fraud which the banking officials refused to investigate, is now a cabinet minister and, therefore, above law. The covered-up history of the family metaphorically represents the covered-up history of the nation; Sonali perceives their ominous connection: "Here in this house the revision of history had begun and there would be no end to the lies" (253).

The entire action of the novel deals with the changes the emergency brings in the social and political fabric of the country by analyzing the response it evokes among individuals, classes, and groups. For this purpose Sahgal provides for two narratives, the main narrative and the shorter narrative of Sonali. If the first documents responses to emergency from various angles, and are generally of approval, Sonali's dramatizes its reprehensible aspects. The emergency is seen by the novelist as an event which marks a clean break from the past; like the room of Dev, it bore "No echo of time past or things to come." As an active supporter of the new regime, Dev justifies it by stating that it had brought stability to the country and created healthy climate for business, trade, and industry. He even suggests that it should have been declared earlier: "...this emergency is just what we needed. The troublemakers are in jail. An opposition is something we never needed. The way the country is being run now, with one person giving the orders, and no one being allowed to make a fuss about it in the Cabinet or in Parliament, means that things can go full steam ahead without delays and weighing pros and cons for ever. Strikes are banned" (10). If Dev justifies it on economic and business considerations, politicians consider it a logical outcome of the evolving process of the political structure of the country. Some even establish its hoary links with the Vedic times. The minister who comes to inaugurate the new project of Dev makes the connection with unbelievable ease: "...the Vedas, the undimmed glory of India's heritage, the high place of selflessness and sacrifice in her tradition and the brightness of the future assured by the emergency" (49). One can perceive Sahgal's fine irony in the minister's sweeping counterfeit connection. In tune with the radical orientation that the official media gave to the emergency, the minister characterizes it as a liberating force, which was being utilised for ameliorating the condition of bonded labourers and weaker sections of the society. In fact, he visualizes it as an emancipatory wave, which was being obstructed only by vested interests: "Radical change was the order of the day and a country united under one party and one Leader would help to bring it about. He ended on the warning note that vested interests had not been entirely vanquished. Left adventurists and Right reactionaries waited to seize their next opportunity to create chaos..." (49).

The official version of the emergency, touted by politicians and businessmen, who used official patronage for carrying out secret business operations to make profit without doing anything which could be called productive, is countered mostly by Sonali. She understands its true character: that it meant the establishment of "modern authoritarianism" and the official apparatus needed for its smooth continuation: censorship, flouting of all established democratic practices and norms, and the creation of an atmosphere of hate and fear. She also visualizes its long-term effect of destroying the dream of hope and promise of people like her father, who had fought for the freedom of the country. It was a dream which she too had shared with him: the dream of Indianizing India.

As an honest, outspoken, spirited person, Sonali finds that the reasons given by the government for the imposition of emergency were not true. That is why she says: "We were all taking part in a thinly disguised masquerade, preparing the stage for a family rule. And we were involved in a conspiracy of silence.... So long as it didn't touch us, we played along, pretending the Empress's new clothes were beautiful" (29). This is a serious criticism of the civil servants, who just closed their eyes to the dangerous designs of the government for safeguarding their private interests. She is appalled by what she calls their "collective will to cowardice" and their readiness to accept the dictates of "one and a half people," that is, Mrs Gandhi and her son Sanjay.

For Sonali, it is both a humbling and a learning experience. It makes her sensitive to the use of power and authority. She begins to understand the pain and suffering in other kinds of oppression, to which she had not given much attention till then. For example, she understands the frightful experience of bride burning, the torture of people by the police, and the liquidation of small farmers by big landlords. But her major lessons are about the true character of Indian polity and its institutional structure: that it virtually supported the anti-people policies and programmes of the Prime Minister.

The novel also records how the Prime Minister got unstinted support from the civil servants, confirming Sahgal's earlier finding that they represented the thinking and mentality of the precolonial times, that ordinary people needed to be controlled and directed with a strong hand. Some officers, like Ravi, undertook to motivate people to organize small professional groups, like medieval guilds, such as the forums of lawyers, teachers, entrepreneurs to "strengthen the hands of the Prime Minister." They did not stop at that. They even invented a rationale for the action of the Prime Minister, by propagating a new philosophy of government, especially among the lower rungs of society. At one place, Ravi explains it to the taxi-drivers: "... what were the Government, the Cabinet, the Ministers, the States, the municipalities? They were there to do Her bidding. What was the country? It was She, who like the many-armed goddess would be ever victorious against those who were plotting to dethrone her" (169). This deification of the Prime Minister, in which she was equated with the country, and had therefore to be protected against all attacks on her, became the basis of the slogan that India is Indira and Indira is India. The implicit exercise here is to build the idea of a leader as a person to be looked up to.

One of the dismal features of the times, the novel stresses, was that Madam (Mrs Gandhi in the novel) succeeded in getting the support of lawyers, professors, newspaper editors, and other liberal and progressive groups for her unrestricted use of power. Sonali contemptuously calls them "opinion-makers of our society." Some professors of Delhi university, who owed unstinted loyalty to her, defended her by suggesting that she had been led to take the extreme step because of her son. To show that the son was right in this, one of the newspaper editors justifies it as the new style of functioning, "which would teach that bunch of stooges who was boss. Decision was the thing, not like grandpa with his view-sharing and soul-searching, his to-be-or-not-to-be and comrades-all in the struggle" (92). This clearly contrasts the style of Nehru with that of Mrs Gandhi and her son and a brazen endorsement of the latter. For Sonali, such statements blew up the myth which had been in circulation for long that people in the top classes were rational, intelligent, and humane, and the rest cunning and corrupt. She now finds that people of these classes found nothing objectionable in the efforts of the mother to ensure that she was succeeded by her son. In a tone of scathing sarcasm, she remarks that these people thought that the "dictatorship around us was one of nature's marvels, not man-made, not 'made' at all. It had the naturalness, the mother-and-child-ness of a crop and was cultivable…" (91).

The novel also suggests that the emergency ultimately turned into an elite game, in which, from the comforts of their drawing rooms, the wives of high-level functionaries and top businessmen organized what they called soirees for popularizing the programmes of the new government, in which planting more trees and preventing the birth of more babies were lumped together. In their enthusiasm to show proof of their achievements, in which they would try their best to outsmart each other, they perpetrated coercion of despicable proportions. To increase their family planning figures, they did not spare beggars and people who just happened to be on the roads. The worst part of their actions was that they did everything only for promoting their interests—to get monopolistic control over activities, by edging out competitors.

Sahgal's most scathing comments are on the communists—the CPI in particular—whose support of the Prime Minister was obscenely enthusiastic. Her anger against them is so strong that the novel records their past misdeeds through Sonali. She provides details about the disgraceful role the communists played in the Quit India movement in 1942. She also finds that even when they talked for the proletariat, in spirit, their ideology was overwhelmingly dictatorial. Through her, Sahgal also confirms, as she did in the earlier novel through Usman, that their philosophy and thinking ran counter to any attempt at working out a native solution to our problems: "...I couldn't understand why we had to keep cutting and pasting Western concepts together and tying ourselves to them for ever as if Europe were the centre of the universe, and the Bible and Marx were the last word on mankind" (113). In a tone which anticipates Vijayan, Sonali writes that "Establishment Communists were cheering monarchy, and [stating that] the millennium had arrived disguised as an emergency headed by a Mother Tsar whose ignorant little peasants were quite happy with mother's blessing" (95).

The burden of the novel is to suggest that this was a difficult time for people, because resistance to authority led only to suffering and torture. This she documents through several characters. Although Sonali is an IAS officer, she has to pay heavily for not joining the brigade of sycophants; she is "demoted, punished, and humiliated." Others, who did not have official positions, were jailed, tortured, brutalized and even sterilized. The travails of Kishori Lal typify this tendency of the times. Though he survives his first brush with authority, he cannot escape the growing shadows of the arbitrary use of power. When he is arrested next time, he is slapped, pushed, prodded, humiliated, and, finally, put in a lockup because he is branded an RSS man. Like several others, he is charged with being a "saboteur, part of a conspiracy to overthrow the government" (190). Kishori Lal understands his situation in terms of a historical parallel, which also serves the purpose of clarifying the attitude of the novelist; he thinks that what was being done to him was like what the Russians did to the Germans.

The officials in charge of carrying out the task of the government dug up old and tried-out methods of torture: "upside-down hangings, rods up anuses, lighted cigarettes held to tender organs" (207); they also showed keenness to make new experiments, so that they could improve upon them. Inside the jail, Kishori Lal meets a young Marxist, who conceives of a surrealistic play in which the dictator is part man and part woman, and the audience roars with laughter all the time. In fact, this is their standard response to all the pronouncements the Prime Minister makes about her programmes. Through this, Sahgal is suggesting that the tyrannical structure had assumed such bizarre proportions, that it could be represented only through the surrealistic mode. Kishori Lal also helps us perceive two features of the dismal reality of the times. The levels of degradation had touched a horrifying low, because "righteousness had decayed and rotted. And there was no sign of renewal or rescue…" (214). But to cover it up, the official media had started legitimising its actions and the turn of events, by offering their version of things. That is why he fears "that history would now be revised and rewritten. All dictatorships meddled with history" (175).

Unlike Sahgal's normal practice, the novel incorporates one scene of actual resistance to the tyrannical policies of Mrs Gandhi. This in itself indicates how passionately Sahgal was against her and the respect she had for Jayaprakash Narayan, who took the lead, in spite of his failing health, to fight the authoritarian tendencies of the body-politic, even before the actual declaration of emergency. On the dais where from he spoke were written the words of the poet Dinkar: "Vacate the throne for the people are coming." Though it was a slogan raised against the British, Sonali finds that it had become relevant once again.

The most noticeable feature of Sahgal's strategy in the novel is to establish that the emergency was not just a political event, for it did not stop at activating official agencies into perpetrating repression on innocent people. Like a virus, its baneful effect spread far and wide, and contaminated private structures and institutions as well. It disrupted value-systems, encouraged hostility between individuals, fostered unscrupulous behaviour, and turned people into selfish monsters, who did not hesitate to commit murders for petty gains. The family of Rose illustrates this in its completeness.

Right from the very beginning, she suspected that there was something fishy about the business of her stepson, because she knew that there was no business which could make people rich overnight. She rightly guessed that it was sustained by graft, which was channelised through the "conveyor belt of bureaucracy." Gradually, she also learnt that Dev was defrauding her of her money, even when her husband was still alive, though in a state of coma. Sonali tries to help her, but without any success. Dev had risen so high in the rungs of power, that he had gone beyond the reach of law. Rose learnt that even within her private home, she could not help being affected by what was happening outside. Her very existence depended upon whether she was on "the right side of power and omnipotence." She could also understand "how many little victims the snapping jaw of the emergency were claiming in the course of an ordinary working day, how many big and small tyrants one act of whimsy had created" (224).

Sahgal also tries to suggest that in situations of oppression and tyranny, history can provide a means of hope, not just for surviving, but for getting enthused to fight, for the worst of tyrants had ultimately to yield to popular will. To escape her oppressive present, Rose goes into her private past, which, once again, gets mixed with the national past. She remembers, how she came to India, got used to the new ways of her husband, and learnt to live with very many obstacles because her husband had already an Indian wife. This recall gets connected with the pre-independence past of India, which expands the historical core of the novel and at the same time provides a significant contrast to the new times of the emergency. For the older past is a part of the nationalist struggle of the people of India against the British, the rise of the influence of Gandhi and even the role of Jinnah in dividing the country into two bits. For Rose, the imaginative recreation of this past is a healing experience, because it affirms that the forces of resistance ultimately triumphed. Since Sonali does not have much of a past to go back to, she dips into the past of her father, by reading through his papers; she learns how as a young boy of nineteen, he had valiantly prevented a woman from being burnt as a sati. This provides Sonali a moment of illumination. She understands that though history has recorded examples of cruelty in the past, it also shows that they had been fought, and needed to be fought. That is where hope is, has to be.

Notes

1 For details on critical works and essays published on the novelist before 1985, see Hilda Pontes (84-94). For a compilation of more recent essays on the novelist, see R K Dhawan.

2 Sahgal's interrogation of selected aspects of India's history, which she undertakes by seeing them in a larger historical perspective, helps her to anticipate even the future course of events. At one place, she has written that "Fiction often foreshadows fact. *The Day in Shadow* had had an accompanying backdrop to Simrit's divorce settlement, the growing Soviet influence on our subcontinent and a definite Indian tilt in that direction. I finished writing the book in 1971. The Indo-Soviet Treaty, a landmark of its kind, embodying this tilt, was not signed until August that year." See her *A Voice for Freedom* (20).

3 This is similar to what Nehru writes at one place: "I was also fully aware of the diversities of Indian life, of classes, castes, religions, races, different degrees of cultural development. Yet I think that a country with a long cultural background and a common outlook on life develops a spirit that is peculiar to it and that is impressed on all its children" (39). In an interview with Rama Jha, Sahgal has admitted that "my whole idea of India, what it should stand for and how it should grow was shaped by him [Nehru] (7).

4 It is relevant to mention here that like Rushdie, Sahgal sees a downward slide in post-independence India, especially after the passing away of Nehru. Concentrating mostly on the political culture of the country, she sees a qualitative change in leadership, especially in the times of Mrs Gandhi. Because of her involvement with the social and cultural consequences of this, she wrote a book-length study entitled *Indira Gandhi's Emergence and Style* (1978). The contrast of styles, which is at the heart of the novel, is summed up in a passage in this book: "After independence the Indian scene remained unusual in Asia because of the restrained educated tone the leadership employed in seeking the cooperation of a vast, unlettered electorate for the understanding and solution of long-term problems. In search of support, Mrs

Gandhi had found the CPI, anxious for political respectability and power, eager to cooperate. The skilful use of economic conditions and the vivid vocabulary of class war as political weapons yielded rapid initial dividends. The campaign of street arousal introduced a throbbing undercurrent of exaggeration, excess and violence waiting like electricity to be switched on" (50-51). The expanded version of this book appeared as *Indira Gandhi: Her Road to Power* in 1982.

Chapter V

Problematizing/Critiquing History with Rushdie

Rushdie's rise to eminence as a fictionist of stature began with the publication of *Midnight's Children* in 1981, and was further consolidated by the appearance of *Shame* in 1983. Though a British naturalized citizen, Rushdie's links with the subcontinent are strongly in evidence in his first novel; they have a significant bearing on his understanding and assessment of the social and political situation of Pakistan in the second one. It is because of this, and not just because of his Indian birth, that critics in and outside India have considered him an Indian English novelist. In a book of critical essays on the Indian novel of the eighties, Viney Kirpal singles out *Midnight's Children* as a trail-blazer and trend-setter, which infused new life into the novel and "made a tremendous impact on a whole generation of writers both new and established."[1] This is reflected in the contents of the volume too: five essays deal exclusively with Rushdie's novels; they also figure prominently in virtually all the other essays, which deal with themes and techniques of this novel. Critical response to his work has focussed mainly on the experimental nature of his fiction and his efforts at bending the English language to the needs of the subcontinent.[2] Several critics from outside the country hold that Rushdie brought the Indian novel into the mainstream novel of the world, and in line with the aesthetic and cultural style of postmodernism.[3] While it is true that his fiction takes on some features of the contemporary Western fiction, it is equally true that he builds into it a rich mass of historical detail related to the subcontinent, which he interprets in his unique style. More importantly, *Midnight's Children*, in particular, bears a strong impress of the problematic cultural scene of India. This gives a singularly new dimension to Rushdie's attempt at problematizing history through fiction. For dealing with the varied aspects of Rushdie's involvement with history and historiography, this chapter will discuss the nature of his connection with the Indian novel, the affinities he has with postmodernist fictionists of the West, both at the level of form and content, particularly with regard to the problematizing of history, and the range and extent of the impress of the cultural scene of India on the formal and thematic aspects of his fiction. It will also attempt an assessment of his evaluation of the historical specifics he isolates for comment in his two novels. The assumption behind this is that besides problematizing the historical discourse, Rushdie also critiques the history of the two countries.

Rushdie's involvement with the subcontinent is borne out fully in *Midnight's Children* and *Shame*, which deal with its history, culture and politics with passionate concern. This makes him different from a host of other writers who have written about them as outsiders. Rushdie is more of an outsider-insider, which distinguishes him from a writer like Naipaul. In a later non-fictional work, he expresses his solidarity with the people of Nicaragua by invoking his ties and involvement with the subcontinent: "I was myself the child of a successful revolt against a great power, my consciousness the product of the triumph of the Indian revolution" (1988, 12).

In spite of this avowed connection with India and Pakistan, it is significant that Rushdie chose to set himself apart from the influential group of early Indian English novelists, who contributed to the establishment of the genre:

> Writers like Mulk Raj Anand and Narayan have many more affinities to Indian writers in the Indian languages than they do to a writer like me who just happens to be writing in English. Apart from the accident that we all use English, I don't think there's a great deal in common. *Midnight's Children* was partly conceived as an opportunity to break away from the manner in which India had been written about in English, not just by Indian writers but by Western writers as well (1982, 19).

Rushdie consciously broke away from the realistic tradition of novel-writing, which is still current and popular in the country, because he thought that his involvement with historical and cultural questions related to the country called for new experimental strategies. This makes him different from Indian and non-Indian contemporaries, and is adequately reflected in his modes of narration, use of fantasy, the novelty of his images and metaphors, and a highly suggestive use of language, which encompasses several registers of actual spoken English. It is largely because of this new orientation in *Midnight's Children* that Rushdie was hailed as an international writer, who had more in common with Marquez and Grass than with the novelists of India.

Rushdie has an interesting point on his international connection in one of his essays. He writes that as an Indian living in London (this in spite of his British citizenship), he is a part of a large group of migrant writers from all over the world, who have the unique privilege of choosing their literary parents (1992, 20-21). Numerous critics and reviewers have chosen these for him from time to time. Marquez and Grass have featured prominently in the list, though assessments of their influence on his work have differed (Merivale 12). Rushdie has not been particularly enthusiastic about being bracketed with them. His preference has been for a different set, though this too has varied. At one time, it consisted of Sterne, Dickens and Swift (Pattanayak 20); at another time, of Rabelais, Gogol, and Bocaccio (Rushdie 1982, 20); at yet another time, it was Gogol, Cervantes, Kafka, Melville and Machado de Assis (Rushdie 1991, 21). His reason for this is that "at a time when the novel has never been a more international form," writers cannot help being international. Interestingly, in this group, Rushdie includes an Indian parent in G V Desani, whom he regards highly for his innovative use of language (Cauto 63-65).

Although *Midnight's Children* looks like the baggy monster of a novel from the West, it has several characteristically Indian features, about which Rushdie has written on several occasions. He acknowledges that the shape of the narrative in the novel conforms to the shape of traditional Indian oral narratives, which are repetitive and marked by swoops, spirals, and loops. Rushdie considers this affinity of greater importance than his international literary pedigree: the novel "derives out of an Indian tradition which, to my mind, is much more important than this...list [and it] conforms to the architectural idea of a Hindu temple" (1985, 6 and 8). He also refers to the mixed and plural tradition of India, which he constantly invokes in the novel for assessing historical events and attitudes (Rushdie 1991, 16). Since the novel also incorporates a profusion of mythical incidents and illusions, several critics have considered it a totally Eastern book (Swann 352-62). The fact is that it is an interesting mix of elements from the West and East, particularly in its problematizing of history. In this, Rushdie evinces a strong awareness of the crisis of historiography in the West and the response it has evoked among the novelists there. But it has also a deep impress of the East, which goes beyond Rushdie's professed adherence to the formal features of an oral narrative, and embraces concerns which arise out of India's complicated multiculturalism.

Rushdie's involvement with the subcontinent in his novels is further confirmed by his views regarding the kind of audience he visualized for them. As an international novelist, he did not usually write for any specific audience: "I have ideas, people, events, shapes, and I write 'for' those things, and hope that the completed work will be of interest to others" (Rushdie 1991, 19). But in the case of *Midnight's Children*, he was conscious of the subcontinental readership: "I certainly felt that if its subcontinental readers had rejected the work, I should have thought it a failure, no matter what the reaction in the West" (1991, 20). Keeping in view the reception it got in our country and the critical debate it has generated, it is very much an Indian English novel. *Shame* is in many ways its complement; together they complete Rushdie's interest in the subcontinent.

Rushdie's central concern in both novels is to dramatize his encounter with history. This has several dimensions. He mixes the public history of the two countries with the private histories of individuals and families. Both novels have in them a hard core of historical specifics, which have been worked into the narrative either realistically or through the mode of fantasy, or through a promiscuous intermixture of the two. A specific standpoint informs his choice of their incidents and happenings, in which prominent personalities of the two countries also figure. Rushdie builds into the narrative an ethical framework for judging the rightness and wrongness of their actions. Mixed with all this is Rushdie's involvement with the very process of history-writing, which is closely connected with the crisis of historiography and controversies regarding the value of history. In his treatment of these concerns, Rushdie has many similarities with the novelists of Europe and America. But another aspect of this, which has not been adequately stressed, is that in *Midnight's Children*, the crisis of historiography takes on an added specifically Indian dimension, which arises from the distinctive texture of the culture of our country. I maintain that Rushdie's choice of narrative strategies, protagonists, and other devices in the two novels is largely determined by these multiple concerns.

It needs to be stated here that though *Midnight's Children* and *Shame* share common concerns, they differ in their character, scope, range, and purpose. The strategies employed in them also vary. Some of the formulations that I have made about Rushdie's subcontinental connection would apply more to the first than to the second. Both, however, are characterized by a high degree of self-consciousness; both use fantasy, though it is more concentrated in the second than in the first. The narrative in *Midnight's Children* has a leisurely pace about it, and embraces a variety of scene and incident. *Shame* is a more concentrated work, with a tighter plot and fewer incidents and characters. In the former, Saleem is at the centre of most of its action; we understand the entire novel through his perceptions. But Omar is like an outsider, and at the periphery of the happenings in *Shame*; his only claim to attention is his link with its two leading families. In *Midnight's Children*, the problematization of history through Saleem gets a fairly large space; in *Shame*, the historical specifics, which have been incorporated through an elaborately framed disguise, receive more attention than the discourse proper. Because of this concentrated thematic focus, *Shame* virtually turns into a work of satire, in which Rushdie comes heavily on the shameful aspects of the social, political, and cultural life in Pakistan. Though there is a pronounced streak of satire in *Midnight's Children*, too, it is of a different order.

As a first step towards understanding Rushdie's involvement with history and historiography and the methodological and cultural issues related to them, we need to analyze the narrative strategies and the kinds of protagonists he employs in his novels. *Midnight's Children* is a first-person narrative in which Saleem Sinai writes his private history, which is inextricably connected with the history of his country.[4] Since his birth coincided with its independence and his destiny got irrevocably handcuffed to history, the narrative and the thematic progression in the novel are characterized throughout by a continuous oscillation from his personal story to the story of his country. The opening chapters hint at the narrators he has in mind, such as Valmiki and Scheherazade, who set the pace and tone of the narrative. He also clarifies that it would be a promiscuous mixture of various kinds of stories: "an excess of intertwined lives events miracles, places, rumours, so dense a commingling of the improbable and the mundane." The result is that the novel unfolds in a series of episodes with heavy trappings of fantasy and the historical details which figure in it are seasoned with varieties of spicy stuff: anecdotes, mythological lore, and very diverting comedy.

The most important and effective part of the narrative in *Midnight's Children* is the carefully-built narrator, Saleem. Rushdie's involvement with history is realized largely through him. Saleem's personal history is quite fascinating and full of unusual and humorous incidents, though there is also an edge of pathos to it. We get plenty of details about his parents and grandparents, his birth in Bombay, his growing up, and the interesting people he comes across: uncles, aunts, classmates, social and political celebrities, and many more. Though his association with them gives him the semblance of a human being in real life, he is unlike a character in realistic fiction. Saleem's story is not exactly a human story, for Rushdie's purpose is not to explore his psyche, the way Henry James does in his novels; nor does the novel attempt an exhaustive analysis of human relationships, like it is in realistic, psychological novels. On the contrary, right from the time of his birth, the novel consistently draws our attention to the fact of Saleem being a grotesque; he adds to his deformities as he grows. "If I seem a little bizarre," Saleem tells us, "remember the wild profusion of my inheritance...perhaps, if one wishes to remain an individual in the midst of the teeming multitudes, one must make oneself grotesque" (108). The speed and scale of his enlargement is a pointer to this:

> From my very first days I embarked upon an heroic programme of self-enlargement.... By mid-September I had drained my mother's not inconsiderable breasts of milk. A wet-nurse was briefly employed but she retreated, dried-out as a desert only after a fortnight.... I moved on to the bottle and downed vast quantities

> of the compound.... I expanded almost visibly, enlarging day by day...waste matter was evacuated copiously from the appropriate orifices; from my nose flowed a shining cascade of goo. Armies of handkerchiefs, regiments of nappies found their way into the large washing-chest of my mother's bathroom... (124).

This is an excellent piece of magnification, reminiscent of Swift and Rabelais. Saleem's grotesquerie is Rushdie's ploy for gifting him with extraordinary omniscience: for making him see, know, and report more than an ordinary mortal can, a substantial part of which is national history. At one point, Saleem says that his life "has been transmuted into grotesquery by the irruption into it of history" (57). Variations on his miraculous powers, because of which he reports and comments even on those happenings which take place in his absence, recur in the course of his journey from birth onwards. His dip into his pre-natal past brings into the novel the story of his grandfather's fantastic love affair, the equally unbelievable story of his mother's first husband, and several actual historical incidents, connected with India's colonial past. As a child, he is given a mature, adult voice for reporting critically on people, situations, and events, both private and national. He has a Ganesh-like Gargantuan nose, which is capable of miraculous sensitivity, and gives him unbelievable powers of discrimination. As an extraordinary voyeur, he sees through the deceptions which Lila Sabarmati practices on her husband; on occasions, he gets transformed into an enlarged peephole, and sees more than what is on the surface. With a prophetic voice and a sensitive receiving-mechanism, he communicates with the other miraculous children of his country. His powers of telepathy turn him into a kind of container: "The inner monologues of all the so-called teeming millions of masses and classes alike, jostled for space within my head." Spying on his mother, he becomes a private eye. After his nose is drained off of its miraculous goo, it acquires new powers of knowing: he sees through the games of love and hate, sniffs truth and falsehood, smells what is in the air, and follows trails. He is, in short, a window to the world around him.

Though Saleem has the semblance of a normal human being, he does not have a life of his own. "From ayah to Widow," he tells us, "I've been the sort of person *to whom things have been done*"(232). For he is made to report and comment on people and happenings; sometimes he has to participate in events of crucial importance. Whenever the novelist wants it, he makes him perform impossible tasks. On one occasion, he is made invisible, so that he can be transported from Bangladesh to India. Like conventional victim-figures, he has also to suffer dismantling: he loses his goo, his hair, and finger. In short, though we see him walk in flesh and blood, he is no 'character' at all. He is an embodiment of history, and no more than a voice. He says about himself:

> Who what am I? My answer: I am the sum total of everything that went before me, of all I have been seen done, of everything done-to-me. I am everyone everything whose being-in-the-world affected was affected by mine. I am anything that happens after I've gone which would not have happened if I had not come...to understand me, you'll have to swallow a world (370).

Saleem is a world in himself—history encapsulated into a human frame. Every passing moment makes him full and heavy. The cracks and fissures in his body are constantly widening because of its pressure. "History pours out of my fissured body," he tells us quite often.

Saleem's connection with history is also suggested by the amalgamation of the public and the private in his person:

> How, in what terms, may the career of a single individual be said to impinge on the fate of a nation? I must answer in adverbs and hyphens: I was linked to history both literally and metaphorically, both actively and passively, in what our (admirably modern) scientists might term 'modes of connection' composed of 'dualistically-combined configurations' of the two pairs of opposed adverbs given above. This is why hyphens are necessary: actively-literally, passively-metaphorically, actively-metaphorically, and passively-literally, I was inextricably entwined with my world (232).

The different types of the active and passive connection between Saleem and history are both interesting and problematic. As an embodiment of history, Saleem is made into a receptacle of what has happened and is happening around him. This makes him into a passive being, even a kind of victim. Because he is also placed at the centre of all the happenings in the novel, he gives history shape and meaning, which makes him into an active agent.

This active part of him becomes the nucleus of the problematizing of the historical discourse.

Saleem is a part of Rushdie's larger fictional strategy, in which realism is mixed with heavy doses of fantasy. It helps him build into the narrative several myths, stories, legends, and even gossip (see Nair for Rushdie's use of anecdotal history, 57-75). We also get bizarre, dreamlike situations, which are shocking as well as surprising. The overall style corresponds to magic realism. On account of this, critics have associated Rushdie with writers like Borges, Marquez, Grass, and Angela Carter. It also brings him within the ambit of postmodernism.

Midnight's Children and *Shame* exemplify in a substantial measure the aesthetic style of postmodernism. Both are characterized by a high degree of self-consciousness, because Rushdie uses the techniques of defamiliarization and self-reflexivity. In *Midnight's Children*, the narrative is addressed to Padma who as an interlocutress also stands for a listener/reader who has old-style notions about art. In response to her constant questionings, Saleem explains and clarifies his art of writing to her, even while writing his account. Through this mechanism, Rushdie forces the reader to participate in his creative process and increases his responsibility for understanding the novel (see Wilson 23-37). He draws attention to its artifice, and destroys the illusion of the 'reality' of the novel as it is conventionally understood. By focussing on the very process in which it comes into being, the novel, in effect, becomes a work of metafiction. And because this self-consciousness is extended to the domain of history-writing, concentrating in the main on the problems involved in writing about the past, it also becomes a work of metafictional historiography or historiographic metafiction. This is the postmodernist fictional frame for the novelist's active intervention into the problematics of history. In the words of Linda Hutcheon, such fiction consists of novels which are "intensely self-reflexive," and "re-introduce historical context into metafiction and problematize the entire question of historical knowledge. Like those recent theories of both history and fiction, this kind of novel...forces us to recall that history and fiction are themselves historical terms and their definitions and interrelations are historically determined and vary with time" (Hutcheon 1987, 285-86).

Implicit in Hutcheon's characterization of historiographic metafiction is the belief that it is the result of two significant and simultaneous developments: change in the thinking of historians towards their craft, following the decline of positivistic historiography, and advances in literary and fictional theory. This new mode is the novelist's response to these developments. Stated broadly, these assume that the boundary between history and fiction is not rigid, but flexible, and accepts that there can be several valid views of the past. Underneath every view, there is a buried substratum of unstated assumptions and arguments. It also recognizes that because of this, there has been a strong and vitiating connection between history and politics. In response to these ideas, the novelists have written self-reflexive novels, in which they use the modes of parody and magic realism to contest the very idea of realism as a reliable method of representing reality. The works of historiographic metafiction thus either offer alternate recreations of the past, mostly of repressed voices or the ones marginalized in available histories, or become vehicles for suggesting the provisional nature of historical representations; in most cases, they combine the two in varying proportions. Rushdie's novels fit into the historiographic metafictional mode in several ways. In *Midnight's Children*, Rushdie views the history of India from a specific standpoint, because of which he gives a singularly new interpretation of India's past. The novel also problematizes the nature of historical discourse and pays attention to the problems which are unique to historical reconstructions in India.

In *Midnight's Children*, Rushdie deals with a chosen period in India's past; the main impulse behind this choice is clarified by him in one of his statements: "...it seemed to me that the period between '47 and '77—the period from Independence to the Emergency—had a kind of shape to it; it represented a sort of closed period in the history of the country. That shape becomes part of the architecture of the book" (Pattanayak 21). The shape that Rushdie perceives in the thirty-year period of India's past is the outcome of a distinctively specific point of view that informs his understanding and, therefore, his reconstruction of it. The very choice of the period is significant; the historical space it covers is enclosed by two momentous events. The first one marked the end of a long period of colonial rule and the beginning of free India; the second put an end to the short but controversial period of Mrs Gandhi's emergency rule, during which the hard-won freedom was severely threatened. It is Rushdie's understanding of the import of these two events and the connection he perceives between them which determines the shape of this period for him. I emphasise this, because it leads him to an interpretation of India's pre-1947 past, which he intermittently invokes in the novel to put the post-1947 past in perspective. This distinguishes his interpretation of India's history from other writers and historians. Saleem's anxiety that he should finish his account before he crumbles under its weight and that it should add up to mean something is also Rushdie's anxiety. This is important for us, because it clarifies that for both of them history has meaning and value. This is where Rushdie departs from the extremist postmodern and poststructural positions, which deny both.[5] At one point, though, *Midnight's Children* does dramatize this extremist position.

In the role of a historian, Saleem, like the traditional historians, aspires to produce some kind of a totalization of the past, in which he can provide continuities and missing links. He wants to write a complete and coherent account: "Most of what matters in our lives takes place in our absence: but I seem to have found somewhere the trick of filling in the gaps in my knowledge, so that everything is in my head, down to the last detail..." (20). He elaborates it with a metaphor from the domain of private histories. In the name of propriety, such histories tended to suppress details which their writers considered unpleasant, unmentionable, or derogatory to the people who figured in them. This would make them partial and distorted. Saleem states that he would eschew the temptation of resorting to such deliberate, selective representation of events in his account:

> Family history, of course, has its proper dietary laws. One is supposed to swallow and digest only the permitted parts of it, the halal portions of the past, drained of their redness, their blood. Unfortunately, this makes the stories less juicy; so I am about to become the first and only member of my family to flout the laws of halal. Letting no blood escape from the body of the tale, I arrive at the unspeakable part; and, undaunted, press on (59).

Pitted against this desire to produce a coherent and total picture of the past is man's inherent incapacity to see things in their wholeness. Contending John Fowles' assertion that novelists are gifted with "whole sight," Rushdie writes in one of his essays that "Human beings do not perceive things whole; we are not gods but wounded creatures, cracked lenses, capable only of fractured perceptions" (Rushdie 1991, 12). This limitation is at the very centre of the novel, and suggested through the metaphor of the perforated sheet, because of which Saleem's grandfather could look at his future wife only in bits and parts; his mother too could love her husband only in fragments. These references to his ancestors are meant to suggest that in spite of Saleem's intention to write a total and complete account of his family, and, by extension, of his country, his lineage made him incapable of doing so. That is why Saleem admits that his perception and understanding of things could be no more than fragmentary: "...and above all the ghostly essence of that perforated sheet, which doomed my mother to learn to love a man in segments, and which condemned me to see my own life—its meanings, its structures—in fragments also..." (106-7).

The tone of this sentence suggests that our incapacity to see things in their wholeness is something to which we are condemned; we just cannot write a full and total account of anything. Rushdie wants to emphasize this and the things that follow from it: that meanings and structures within which we make sense of our lives are no more than fragmentary. In this realization lies the crux of the whole enterprise of history-writing: that all accounts are bound to be incomplete, no matter what claims we might make for their completeness. This makes historical knowledge provisional and relative. This, however, does not imply that history has no value; it only suggests that we should be fully alive to the limitations within which it has to be comprehended.

Rushdie illustrates the fragmentary nature of the historian's recreation of the past by expounding the idea of history reclaimed through memory. It is well known that from Herodotus onwards, memory has been used by the historians as a source of information about the past. Carl Becker went to the extent of saying that "history is the memory of things said and done" (quoted in Ketchum 143). It is equally well known that memory can be inaccurate, unreliable, and extravagant. Saleem states that his only link with the past is through memory: "I have become, it seems to me, the apex of an isoceles triangle, supported equally by twin deities, the wild god of memory and the lotus-goddess of the present." Rushdie could not have chosen a better metaphor than memory for conveying the incompleteness and also the partial reliability of historical recreations. Saleem's reliance on memory as a source of truth about the past is stated in its completeness, when he says:

> 'I told you the truth,' I say yet again, 'Memory's truth, because memory has its own special kind. It selects, eliminates, alters, exaggerates, minimizes, glorifies, and vilifies also; but in the end it creates its own reality, its heterogeneous but usually coherent version of events; and no sane human being ever trusts someone else's version more than his own' (207).

Though the passage comments specifically on the version of history which is based on memory, what it states is true of all historical representations. For the processes of selection, alteration, exaggeration, and elimination come into play in the writing of all histories. Their extent may vary because of differences in the understanding that people have of the past about which they are writing and the kind of coherence they are aiming at. This has partly been clarified in Saleem's description of the halal view of the past, in which facts are wilfully suppressed or modified to produce a desired view of a properly-acceptable past. At another place in the novel, Saleem cuts up bits and parts of newspaper headlines to prepare a note of warning for Commander Sabarmati: "In the secrecy of a bathroom, I glued my complete note—my first attempt at rearranging history—on to a sheet of paper..." (253). That such arrangements can be the result of conscious intention is illustrated through another example. Writing about his friend Shiva, Saleem says: "I pieced the story together from Parvati's accounts, which I got from her after our marriage." But he admits that "I have already been overgenerous to Major Shiva—in this, my personal version of history, I have allowed his account too much of space..." (396). This confirms that we can diminish or enlarge the significance of events in any account by controlling the distribution of space among them.

The fragmentary character of historical reconstructions is related by Saleem to another significant detail. In his eagerness to complete his account before his fissured body cracks up, he is forced to work overtime. This increases the possibilities of mistakes and errors. These mistakes, which may lead to overstatements, exaggerations, and even omissions are different in character from the ones which result from the conscious intention of the historian, as, for example, in the halal view of the past. The risk of unreliability which results from working in a rush is elaborated by Saleem in the following words:

> Because I am rushing at breakneck speed, errors are possible, and overstatements, and jarring alterations in tone; I'm racing the cracks, but I remain conscious that errors have been made, and that, as my decay accelerates...the risk of unreliability grows.... I am learning...what actually happened is less important than what the author can manage to persuade his audience to believe...(263).

The first three lines are a modest admission of the limitations within which we are all forced to work; these make mistakes and exaggerations almost inevitable. But towards the end, we get a statement, which is both arrogant and mischievous: that what happened actually is less important than what the author is able to persuade his audience to believe. This is a pointed reference to the role of rhetoric in the writing of history. It suggests that cohesiveness in historical accounts is more a function of how things are put than the truth of the things themselves. This is where historical truth, no matter how elusive, becomes a casualty.

Rushdie offers another variation on this, when Saleem calls the process of preserving the past through memory the chutnification of history. As a suggestive metaphor, it draws attention to the distortions that become unavoidable in such a process of preservation. Implicit in this is also the possibility that reclamations of the past might virtually turn into fiction. Saleem describes this process thus: "...in words and pickles, I have immortalized my memories, although distortions are inevitable in both methods. We must live, I'm afraid, with the shadows of imperfection" (442). Saleem admits that on one occasion he converted a downright lie into something that had happened: "... for the first time, I fell victim to the temptation of every autobiographer, to the illusion that since the past exists only in one's memories and the words which strive vainly to encapsulate them, it is possible to create past events simply by saying they occurred" (427). This statement recalls the poststructuralist thinking on history, which denies the very possibility of its being. But because he refers to it only once, and is not in conformity with the general tenor of what he has otherwise stated, it can only be taken as an illustration of the extremist position within the gamut of historical reconstructions.

Since Saleem concentrates on the imperfections of accounts which result either from methodological inadequacies or other contingent reasons, he pleads for their revision, so that the mistakes are corrected, or at least minimized. But the task of revising is frustrating, exasperating, and time-consuming. Precisely because of this he writes about it with the same mixture of humility and arrogance, as he did with respect to the unreliability of a historian:

> The process of revision should be constant and endless; don't think I'm satisfied with what I've done.... Sometimes...Saleem appears to have known too little; at other times, too much...yes, I should revise and revise, improve and improve; but there is neither the time nor the energy. I am obliged to offer no more than this stubborn sentence: It happened that way because that's how it happened (443).

The same stubbornness makes Saleem say that even after he found that he had made a mistake about Gandhi's death, he did not feel like correcting it; it would have meant redoing the account, and producing an entirely new rendering of things. Instead, he chose to make it an indicator of the uniqueness of his construction: "in my India, Gandhi will continue to die at the wrong time" (164). This is a metaphoric way of suggesting that the uniqueness of all accounts lies in their novelty of presentation or interpretation. Rushdie's comment on Saleem's error is meant to drive home the truth that reconstructions of reality are "built on our prejudices, misconceptions and ignorance as well as on our perceptiveness and knowledge. The reading of Saleem's unreliable narration might be, I believed, a useful analogy for the way in which we all, every day, attempt to 'read' the world" (Rushdie 1984, 100).

Although Saleem is acutely conscious of his imperfections and the mistakes he might have committed in producing his account, he leaves it to the judgment of his readers to determine its usefulness. He however insists that he has to finish it, no matter how imperfect it might turn out to be. The passage that states his views on this is, once again, a paradoxical mixture of humility and authority. In fact, this is a feature of all the three passages that I have quoted; it is meant to reinforce Saleem's view that the two are inextricably woven. Historical recreations are the result of our knowledge and ignorance; carefulness and carelessness; and finally, of our modesty and arrogance:

> Does one error invalidate the entire fabric? Am I so far gone, in my desperate need for meaning, that I'm prepared to distort everything—to re-write the whole history of my times purely in order to place myself in a central role? Today, in my confusion, I can't judge. I'll have to leave it to others. For me, there can be no going back; I must finish what I've started, even if, inevitably, what I finish turns out not to be what I began...(164).

Another aspect of historiography, which has prompted novelist's intervention into history through the historiographic metafictional mode, and illustrated in *Midnight's Children*, is the opposition between the official and non-official views of the past. It could even be the opposition the writers perceive between how they understand the past and how it has been represented by the historical establishment. It is now widely known that both in the developed and less developed countries of the world, one of the dominant impulses which led the novelists to history-writing through fiction was their dissatisfaction with the attitude of the historians towards power-brokers. They had written accounts of the past that favoured political establishments. Because of this and also because Rushdie felt that history was being used as a source of power by the state "by altering the past to fit its present needs," he chose to use the novel of memory as a weapon to combat the forgetfulness that the exercise of such power induces. He explains it by stating that "Writers and politicians are natural rivals. Both groups try to make the world in their own images; they fight for the same territory. And the novel is one way of denying the official, politicians' version of truth" (Rushdie 1991, 14).

In *Midnight's Children*, Rushdie deals with this issue by referring to contradictions in the accounts of India and Pakistan, especially in their accounts of war. Saleem records their conflicting versions of happenings in the Rann of Kutch, and comments on the untruth of the newspaper reports which appeared in Pakistan:

"Hidden behind newspaper reports— DASTARDLY INDIAN INVASION REPELLED BY OUR GALLANT BOYS—the truth about General Zulfikar became, in the papers, INNOCENT SOLDIERS MASSACRED BY INDIAN FAUJ." Saleem also writes that, in spite of his best efforts, he could not say what really happened during the Indo-Pak war of 1965:

> Important to concentrate on good hard facts. But what facts? One week before my eighteenth birthday, on August 8th, did Pakistani troops in civilian clothing cross the cease-fire line in Kashmir and infiltrate the Indian sector, or did they not? In Delhi, Prime Minister Shastri announced 'massive infiltration...to subvert the state'; but here is Zulfikar Ali Bhutto, Pakistan's Foreign Minister, with his riposte: 'We categorically deny any involvement in the rising against tyranny by the indigenous people of Kashmir' (328).

Within India, Rushdie illustrates his viewpoint with reference to Mrs Gandhi's emergency rule, when history became synonymous with official handouts. The dichotomous versions of the known and suppressed history which the times engendered are suggested metaphorically through the parting of Mrs Gandhi's hair, which was part white and part black. The white represented the one made visible by the official media: "public, visible, documented, a matter for historians." That is why Saleem says that the black part "being secret macabre untold, must be a matter for us" (406). Here Rushdie also implies that revisions of history are not necessitated by methodological inadequacies and imperfections alone, but also by the distortions of those manipulators who use history as a source of power.

I have already stated that there is a specific angle to Rushdie's involvement with the history of India, because of which he sees a particular shape in its thirty-year period. That this shape is dependent upon the kind of meaning he gives to it, is also suggested by Saleem inside the novel: "...at the end of 1947, life in Bombay was as teeming, as manifold, as multitudinously shapeless as ever... except that I had arrived; I was already beginning to take my place at the centre of the universe; and by the time I had finished, I would give meaning to it all" (126). Meanings, as I have been arguing, rest on presuppositions, which we need to uncover. Rushdie's meaning is grounded in several assumptions, whose implications we need to grasp. The first, and a major one, is that India as a nation was born in 1947; this makes it an invented country, which was possible through a massive collective dream. Rushdie's understanding of the problems after its birth is intimately connected with this, and has been expressed in the novel in a passage of remarkable power; it provides vital clues about the telos that informs Rushdie's formulations:

> ...there was an extra festival on the calendar, a new myth to celebrate, because a nation which had never previously existed was about to win its freedom, catapulting us into a world which, although it had five thousand years of history, although it had invented the game of chess and traded with Middle Kingdom Egypt, was nevertheless quite imaginary; into a mythical land, a country which would never exist except by the efforts of a phenomenal collective will—except in a dream we all agreed to dream; it was a mass fantasy shared in varying degrees by Bengali and Punjabi, Madrasi and Jat, and would periodically need the sanctification and renewal which can only be provided by rituals of blood. India, the new myth —a collective fiction in which everything was possible, a fable rivalled only by two other mighty fantasies: money and God (111).

Read along with Rushdie's statement that all reclamations of past are inventions, the passage makes it clear that he is putting a new interpretation on the very entity called India. Since he thinks that it came into existence only in 1947, its five thousand years of history are inconsequential. This can also be regarded Rushdie's massive act of interpretation, which appears both arbitrary and untenable. Five thousand years of history cannot simply be wished away and wiped off by a stroke of one's pen. The new country, in his view, takes on a mythical character, because it is the result of a collective dream of a large number of people, representing its different communities and regions. Rushdie is also suggesting implicitly that the myth and the dream are somewhat fragile, because these would need to be sanctified by periodic rituals of blood. He also states that by its very nature—because it was a collective fiction—there was a danger that it might collapse.

The passage is somewhat paradoxical. Through Saleem, Rushdie ignores India's past before 1947, because he thinks that it was mythical and imaginary. But to counter this, he invents another

India, which is also imaginary. There is a difference between the two, though. The second one is a country of hope and promise; in it "anything was possible." As against this, the first one is so bad that it had better be forgotten. Although Rushdie's view might sound like the well-covered thesis that the British really made us into a nation, it is much more than that. For his India is a wished-for country; he invests it with a new character, so that it could provide a contrast to the old one, which was unhealthy and undesirable.

For grasping the ramifications of Rushdie' view of India's past, we need to examine the things he associates with the new nation. This is where the midnight's children play a crucial part in Rushdie's schema. He invests them with extraordinary significance and loads them with metaphoric meanings. They are special, because, more than anything else, they are the products of history: "...children were being born who were only partially the offspring of their parents—the children of midnight were also the children *of the time*; fathered by...history" (117). In this respect, they truly represent the promise of a new future: "...history, arriving at a point of the highest significance and promise, had chosen to sow, in that instant, the seeds of a future which would genuinely differ from anything the world had seen up to that time" (193). Spelling it out more concretely, he writes that the children suggested the new direction the country was supposed to take, which becomes the basis of Rushdie's view of India's past:

> Midnight's children can be made to represent many things, according to your point of view: they can be seen as the last throw of everything antiquated and retrogressive in our myth-ridden nation, whose defeat was entirely desirable in the context of a modernizing, twentieth-century economy; or as the true hope of freedom, which is now forever extinguished; but what they must not become is the bizarre creation of a rambling, diseased mind (197).

The passage suggestively implies that Rushdie understands the post-1947 past of India from the perspective of the late 1970s, when he saw the strong possibility of the floundering of the new dream-like mythical country. Two significant clues about the hoped-for nature of his new India are: one, it has to be a real, new country, free from the traces of its retrogressive past. This in itself assumes that India's past before 1947 was so unhealthy that it needed to be lopped off through a chronological incision. Second, it was to be a country free not merely from foreign control, which it would be in any case, but also from repressive practices and tyrannical tradition. That is why his insistence that it should be "the true hope of freedom." It is quite obvious that Rushdie wants his invented India to be clothed in modernity: this, he feels, can be done only by denying the country its pre-independence past. Thus Rushdie's construction of its post-independence past is intimately connected with its pre-independence one. Implicitly, he also passes a severe judgment on it; it is so harsh that even the staunchest of imperialist historians pale into insignificance; for they did not propound such a wholesale rejection of the country's past.

If we pursue the inquiry a little further, we find that Rushdie, in effect, projects the view that India has two kinds of past: the old past and the post-independence one, which are qualitatively polar opposites. The thrust of the narrative in the novel is to make us perceive that the problems which faced the post-independence India and threatened its new-found modernist fabric, the very reason of its existence, are because it occasionally lapsed into the myth-ridden undesirable past of the pre-independence days, where time operated at a different scale and the values of secular polity, associated with the new one, were messed up completely. That is why he does not want the children of promise to turn into "the bizarre creation of a rambling, diseased mind." They have to stand for the new qualities, though the task is risky and hazardous. This is made clear in another passage:

> ...history, in my version, entered a new phase on August 15th, 1947—but in another version, that inescapable date is no more than one fleeting instant in the Age of Darkness, Kali-Yuga, in which the cow of mortality has been reduced to standing, teeteringly, on a single leg! Kali-Yuga—the losing throw in our national dice game; the worst of everything; the age when property gives a man rank, when wealth is equated with virtue, when passion becomes the sole bond between men and women, when falsehood brings success...began on Friday, February 18th, 3102 B.C.; and will last a mere 432,000 years! Already feeling somewhat dwarfed, I should add nevertheless that the Age of Darkness is only the fourth phase of the present Maha-Yuga cycle which

> is, in total, ten times as long; and when you consider that it takes a thousand Maha-Yugas to make just one Day of Brahma, you'll see what I mean about proportion (191).

Saleem states that in a country like India, there are alternate ways for understanding the movement of events, because of different notions of time. Saleem's version follows the Western mode of horological, naturalistic time; the other mode is mythical and related to ancient India. The imagery used for characterizing the second mode suggests that it is not even Indian in the sense in which Rushdie understands India, but the Hindu mode. By extension, the two kinds of time lead to two ways of understanding the past: one is based on reason and a secular ideal; the other is shaded by myth and legend and grounded in superstition. The point that Saleem, and through him Rushdie, wants to make is that in 1947, India got a chance to come out from the shadows of myth and legend, to embrace the notion of modernity by accepting the democratic, secular ideal and thus turn into a land of promise and new dreams. But the danger of the remote past overtaking the present, which has already turned into a more recent past, was always there. The opposition between these two modes of time is further clarified when Mary talks to Saleem about the unhealthy tendency among the people of new India to revive past heroes and heroines in the new, myth-free, post-1947 times:

> ...I remain, today, half-convinced that in that time of accelerated events and diseased hours the past of India rose up to confound her present; the new-born, secular state was being given an awesome reminder of its fabulous antiquity, in which democracy and votes for women were irrelevant...so that people were seized by atavistic longings, and forgetting the new myth of freedom reverted to their old ways, their old regionalist loyalties and prejudices, and the body politic began to crack (239).

Mary's concern elaborates in very concrete terms the qualitative difference between the older and post-independence pasts. While the latter is associated with new hopes and promises, the older one is sick and diseased. Since it does not provide for change, it denies the possibility of visualizing a new future. This static past is retrogressive, because it is anti-democratic and anti-women. Although the passage makes references to regionalist loyalties and prejudices, the confusion in the new times is traced mainly to the "fabulous antiquity" of Hindu India. That is why Saleem connects the slide in India's democratic structure during the times of Mrs Gandhi with changes in the functioning of her government, which is tainted by these old elements; it has relapsed into the fabulous past by "falling increasingly beneath the twin spells of power and astrology." At another place, Saleem writes that "Benarsi seers help to shape the history of India" because the "Indira Sarkar, like her father's administration, consults daily with purveyors of occult lore" (379).[6] Since Mrs Gandhi's time was the time of emergency, Rushdie suggests that the biggest threat to Indian democracy was the intrusion of Hindu thinking into its politics and history.

The implications of this intrusion are further elaborated in the contrast Saleem builds between the modes of understanding through memory and Maya, in which the latter is associated with the Hindu view of history. He tells Padma:

> [Maya] 'may be defined as all that is illusory; as trickery, artifice and deceit. Apparitions, phantasms, mirages, sleight-of-hand, the seeming form of things: all these are parts of Maya. If I say that certain things took place which you, lost in Brahma's dream, find hard to believe, then which of us is right'(207)?

Maya implies a virtual denial of history, which, in Rushdie's view, has been the bane of the fabulous past of India. This, as I have pointed out earlier, is related to the notion of mythical time, in which time is held in a kind of stasis. Because of this society perpetuates itself through a regularity of fixity, and there is no hope of controlling the future.

Thus we see that Rushdie's problematization of historical discourse in the novel is rooted in the methodological problems in history-writing, which are largely in evidence in the West. But it also takes cognizance of the very special problems of India, where he visualizes a polarity of pasts, which result from different notions of time and history. These, in his view, have serious implications for the democratic, secular future of India.

Like *Midnight's Children*, *Shame* too problematizes history, along with commenting elaborately on specific historical events of Pakistan. But the novels differ in the relative importance Rushdie attaches to the two components. *Shame* deals more with the history of Pakistan than with the problematization of the historical discourse. Largely because of this, Rushdie made changes in its narrative strategy and introduced a new type of hero in it, who differs from Saleem in many ways.

In *Shame*, Rushdie narrates events and happenings through a conventional, third-person, author-narrator, and not through its protagonist. This shift is significant. It provided him with a greater degree of closeness with his readers. This, I think, he needed for establishing his credibility with them: for clarifying his intention and the nature of his writing and also for defending his involvement with the affairs of Pakistan. This strategy is also suggestive of his sense of urgency in dealing with the social, political, and cultural issues of the country which are at the centre of the novel, and on which he makes elaborate comments. These and other intrusions, which Rushdie makes to clarify his novelistic practice, may look like the intrusions of the novelists of an earlier era, but are not. Rushdie's sitting presence in the novel is different from the authorial presence in the past. It is radical in its orientation, and characterizes the novel with a high degree of self-reflexivity and self-consciousness.[7]

In the beginning, the author-narrator of *Shame* puts on the assumed manner of a traditional story-teller, who believes in a linear order of narration, with a beginning, middle, and end. For, when he anticipates the end of his hero right in the beginning of his account, he considers it a deviation from the normal order, and switches back to his normal mode, but not before he makes this comment:

> ...ends must not be permitted to precede beginnings and middles, even if recent scientific experiments have shown us that within certain types of closed system, under intense pressure, time can be persuaded to run backwards, so that effects precede their causes. This is precisely the sort of unhelpful advance of which storytellers must take no notice whatsoever; that way madness lies (22).

It might appear from this that the narrator is against all violations of old, staid narrative conventions, especially the ones in which the narrative is chopped into fragments to disrupt chronology. The interesting thing is that it is meant to do exactly the opposite: to alert us to the recurrence of such things, and, therefore, to disabuse us of whatever faith we might still have in the conventionality of fiction.

Unlike the traditional narrators, who interrupted their narratives either to expound the characteristic features of the genre or to provide helpful clues and comments on people and events who figured in them, Rushdie's interruptions help us understand his projected design and arrangement of his narrative, because of which it deviates from traditional narratives; he even gives the reasons for doing so. Through these clarificatory statements, he accounts for the very existence of his novel and the shape it would acquire in his hands. Since his involvement with the history of Pakistan leads him to make unsavoury comments on its social and political structures, he even anticipates the objections he would need to answer. He did not need to do so for dealing with the history and politics of India, but the situation in Pakistan was different. Political regimes there were not for writing of histories, especially of and by people who would or could not open their mouths for fear of incurring their wrath or those who did not survive to tell their stories.

The possible questions/objections and the clarifications of the author figure in the narrative as dramatic intrusions:

> *Outsider! Trespasser! You have no right to this subject!*...I know: nobody ever arrested me.... *Poacher! Pirate! We reject your authority. We know you, with your foreign language wrapped around you like a flag: speaking about us in your forked tongue, what can you tell but lies?* I reply with more questions: is history to be considered the property of participants solely? In what courts are such claims staked, what boundary commissions map out the territories (28)?

The passage makes for an interesting scene. The objections to author-narrator's history-writing, which are, in effect, the objections of the establishment, have been put in the mouth of people about whom he feels concerned. That is why he is told that nothing untoward has happened to them; as such, all that he would write would only be concocted and false. This is Rushdie's way of presenting the viewpoint of vested interests, who use the victims to vouch for their tormentors, to prove that all is well with their world. To lend dramatic tempo to their clash, Rushdie makes the author-narrator answer with rhetorical questions, staking the claim of any person, insider or outsider, to write the history of any place or people. But this belligerent tone softens, when he makes a more explicit statement on his involvement. He confirms that the country about which he is writing is a part of the world to which he belonged and with which he still felt connected.

Rushdie comments on another connection he sees between him and Pakistan: both are migrants. The condition of being a migrant can have advantages and disadvantages, for countries as well as individuals. Countries can make a fresh start towards building a hopeful and healthy future; but they can also be plagued by a feeling of emptiness. It is because migration means getting unstuck from one's moorings: of floating "upwards from history, from memory, from Time" (87). This has serious consequences for history-writing, because the new countries have to write their histories afresh. After getting separated from India, Pakistanese had to rewrite their past, which they could not manage successfully, because they could not wipe out the centuries of their Indian past which lay under it; hence the confusion in their thinking. As an individual migrant, Rushdie too had to contend with the problem of history for reclaiming his past. This provides him with a context for theorising on his involvement with historical reconstructions, which have implications for his craft. He writes: "As for me: I too, like all migrants, am a fantasist. I build imaginary countries and try to impose them on the ones that exist. I, too, face the problem of history: what to retain, what to dump, how to hold on to what memory insists on relinquishing, how to deal with change" (87-88). This is how Rushdie draws attention to the decision of the historian to retain and reject details for writing one's version of the past. It is not merely a matter of one's choice; we are also constricted by nature to envision the wholeness of anything: "How hard to pin down the truth, especially when one is obliged to see the world in slices; snapshots conceal as much as they make plain" (116).

Rushdie connects the fact of his incapacity to see things whole with another aspect of his writing: of his decision to abandon the mode of the realistic novel and make use of fantasy. A realistic novel presupposes authorial omniscience, which he could not claim, because he could perceive things only in fragments. That is why he states that even if he had chosen to write about his sister in the realistic mode, he could not have presented a complete picture of her. Extending it to the task of writing about the past, he says: "I think what I'm confessing is that, however I choose to write about over-there, I am forced to reflect that world in fragments of broken mirrors.... I must reconcile myself to the inevitability of the missing bits" (69).

Rushdie further states that even if it were possible for him to write a realistic novel, he could not have written one about Pakistan. Given the grim situation there, realistic details about the country would have made his account transparent and vulnerable. It may or may not have gained in depth, it would certainly have invited official wrath: "The book would have been banned, dumped in the rubbish bin, burned" (70). That is why his laconic, lamentable observation: "Realism can break a writers's heart." Considering that the main thrust of the novel is satiric,[8] Rushdie's comment about the inappropriateness of the realistic mode is similar in spirit to the rejection of this mode by the satirists, who cover up their objects of derision in a cloak of fantasy to save themselves from libel suits. But Rushdie's concern is wider: he wanted the book to speak for the people of Pakistan, and also to ensure that it reached them. It is ironic that in spite of his precautions, it was banned there.

Keeping in view the considerations that made Rushdie to use fantasy in the novel, he calls it a "sort of modern fairy-tale," which has both a general and a specific character:

> The country in this story is not Pakistan, or not quite. There are two countries, real and fictional, occupying the same space. My story, my fictional country, exists, like myself, at a slight angle to reality. I have found this off-centring to be necessary.... My view is that I am not writing only about Pakistan (29).

When Rushdie chooses not to use realism, which could ideally have been an appropriate mode for writing the history of any country, and states that both he and the country he is writing about exist "at a slight angle to reality," he is taking a specific attitude towards reality itself: that he is not interested in all that has been or is happening there, but only in some of its special aspects. This fits in with his twin ideas of the fragmentary nature of our perceptions and the principle of selection and rejection in any representation of reality. Together, the three constitute the main thrust of the problematizing of history.

Through his novel, Rushdie not only comments on the historical reality in Pakistan, but also suggests that it resonates the condition of other countries as well. After all, civil and military dictatorships, which constitute the central core of the novel, are found outside Pakistan also. I have already pointed out how Rushdie's selective representation of events and happenings in India in *Midnight's Children* was governed by his special understanding of the post-1947 developments in the country; in the case of Pakistan, his selection of details is governed by his understanding of what Pakistan meant to him, which is suggestively implied in the very title of the novel, shame, which functions as the controlling metaphor in the narrative (Hollington 403-7). By relating the story of Pakistan from this specific point of view, Rushdie is conscious of having imposed a consctrictive frame on the reality there, which would obviously leave out its several aspects. This is unavoidable, particularly when one aims at some kind of interpretation. That is why he admits that "every story one chooses to tell is a kind of censorship, it prevents the telling of other tales..."(71). This is not merely a literary strategy; it is true of the historian's craft as well. Thus the entire burden of problematizing history, which was undertaken in *Midnight's Children* by Saleem, is handled in *Shame* by the narrator-author.

By putting the author-narrator at the centre of the novel, Rushdie has also experimented with a different kind of hero. Though Omar Shakil shares some qualities with Saleem, he is unlike him in one major way: he is not central to the meaning of the novel. He is not even charged with the responsibility of carrying out tasks for his creator. Rushdie has an interesting detail about the choice of such a hero in one of his interviews. He tells us that by handing over the narrative to Saleem in *Midnight's Children*, he got several advantages, but he had also to reckon with several problems. The most disconcerting was the one to one correspondence the readers had built between Saleem and him; they had gone to the extent of attributing his mistakes to him. To prevent the readers from such distractions and also from considering his novels disguised autobiographies, he chose a hero totally different from him and yet useful for the design of the novel: "...I thought this time I would like to talk about a character who was marginal, a very peripheral figure [like] people who are mostly shaped by things that happen around them, not by the things they do themselves, people who are kind of spectators in their own fates" (Rushdie 1985, 3). That is why the narrator calls Omar a peripheral hero, a bystander of sorts.

Omar is so acutely conscious of his peripheral status that he speaks of it again and again. The narrator too refers to it several times. Right in the beginning, we learn that because of Omar's unusual birth and upbringing, he was afflicted "from his earliest days, by a sense of inversion, of a world turned upside-down. And by something worse: the fear that he was living at the edge of the world, so close that he might fall off at any moment" (21). He confesses to Isky that he was a "fellow who is not even the hero of his own life; a man born and raised in the condition of being out of things" (24). At one point, the narrator sums him up rather sharply: "Dizzy, peripheral, inverted, infatuated, insomniac, stargazing, fat: what manner of hero is this" (25)? The repeated emphasis on the peripheral status of Omar makes him a puzzling character. If he is so marginal to the action, then what he is meant for? A major clue about this is provided by him almost at the end of the novel, when he says about himself:

> I am a peripheral man. Other persons have been the principal actors in my life-story. Hyder and Harappa, my leading men. Immigrant and native, Godly and profane, military and civilian. And several leading ladies. I watched from the wings, not knowing how to act. I confess to social climbing, to only-doing-my-job, to being cornerman in other people's wrestling matches (283).

It is a terse and compact statement about his function in the novel: to provide the main structural and thematic linkages. Though a product of a mysterious and cloistered pregnancy, he soon gets involved with the leading men in the novel, Isky and Hyder. He becomes former's boon companion in his debaucheries and "highly charged sex" with white women during his pre-reformed period. He is linked with the latter through his work as a doctor and subsequently through his marriage with his daughter Sufiya. Through them, he also gets linked with the native and migrant population of Pakistan. Since Isky and Hyder also represent the civil and military rule in Pakistan, he also links civil and military power in the country. And because Hyder's rule has strong links with religion, which was used by him to legitimise his power, Omar also links politics and religion. These linkages notwithstanding, most of the time Omar is a mere watcher, and totally ineffective. This is where he offers a strong contrast to Saleem, who thinks of himself as a person who is manipulated by others, but is also alive to his unique position from where he lends meaning to the world around him. Saleem is both master and slave; victim of history as well as its maker. Omar is only a victim. Though he has evil traits, they are not stressed adequately. If he has to die in the final unleashing of demonic violence in the land, it is because he is thickly involved with people who contributed to it and had to pay with their lives. Since Omar gets involved with women, too, which culminates in his marriage with Sufiya, he also provides a link between the male and female plots in the novel. To sum up: Omar's birth and death frame the narrative and his several involvements with men and women join the male and female plots of the novel.

Apart from providing linkages between the principal characters and plots of the novel, Omar also provides the main thematic link which joins them. At the time of leaving his sheltered existence for the world outside, Omar's mothers tell him not to get involved with shame, which they define elaborately to emphasize that in their country it stood for things "for which English has no counterparts" (39). In a large measure, shame, the main symbol of the social and political degradation of Pakistan, is concretized through his association with people who embody it.

There are two other interesting features to the character of Omar. One, that he is neither a total victim-figure, like Candide and Lemuel Pitkin, nor a totally evil one. As a victim-figure, he could have functioned as an effective satiric persona in the novel, but that would have necessitated investing him with naivety and innocence and also making him an embodiment of positive qualities, to radiate the norms of the writer. Rushdie has not done so. It can only mean that in his estimation the degraded aspects of the society he condemns are so patently obvious that no norms need be invoked to understand their rottenness. Besides, the ones he does invoke at one point are invoked through the agency of the narrator. In fact, in order to show the pervasiveness of the rot that has set in the system, even the peripheral hero has to be contaminated by it.

Even as a contaminated character, Omar could have been used as a satiric agent, as a "tainted satirist" (Kernan 1959, 116): a person who enables the readers to see the perversities of the society and the system which the writer holds up to ridicule, even though he himself is not free from them. This would have required that Omar be provided with an awareness of his role of exposing others; but this he does not have. Rushdie is so full of outrage that he undertakes to expose everything on his own, without any technical props. This further confirms his passionate involvement with a country which had all the promise of developing into an ideal one because it had been provided by history with a rare opportunity of having been rid from the encumbrances of the past, but failed to realize it because the people who got control of it were not just unimaginative, but downright evil.

II

Apart from problematizing history, Rushdie critiques the history of India and Pakistan, through a selective representation of events from their past. In *Midnight's Children*, the narrative is dotted with dates and events, which are linked with the life of Saleem. Since his personal account includes his prenatal past, in which he provides details about his parents and grandparents, some aspects of the pre-partition past of the country also figure in the novel. Following his qualitative distinction between the country's pre- and post-independence pasts, one would have expected that Rushdie's pre-1947 details would include examples of India's retrogressive past, but we do not find any. This is perhaps because the older past he refers to goes too far back in time and, therefore, outside the chronological frame of the novel. The details of pre-1947 past in the novel relate to the repression of Indians by the British and their fight for establishing a democratic and secular system.

Since Saleem's understanding of India and Pakistan is based on his principle of ethical soundness, his norm for judging people and situations in a somewhat rough and ready form is 'Bombayness': his name for religious tolerance and accommodation for each other's views. That is why "Saleem was forever tainted with Bombayness, his head was full of all sorts of religions apart from Allah's...and his body was to show a marked preference for the impure" (301). Its violation by people makes him dislike the march of events in Pakistan, to which there are many references in the novel. For this reason, he includes only positive details from India's pre-1947 past; but from its post-1947 past it concentrates only on unhealthy events and happenings, which represent deviations from the hoped-for nature of the new country. This builds a strong satirical strain in the novel. Rushdie's selection of details is also guided by a rigorous standard of morality, which is explained by Saleem in his concept of nasal ethics:

> Because soon I understood that my work must, if it was to have any value, acquire a moral dimension; that the only important divisions were the infinitely subtle gradations of good and evil smells. Having realized the crucial nature of morality, having sniffed out that smells could be sacred or profane, I invented, in the isolation of my scooter-trips, the science of nasal ethics (308).

The historical specifics described and commented upon by Saleem are apprehended by him through his nose. Even when this is done by other people, the nose is the discriminating instrument. Saleem considers it crucial for the value of his work, which implies that Rushdie's choice of historical specifics is governed by an ethical standpoint, which has implications for the future of the two countries. In this respect, Rushdie is totally different from the postmodernists of the West, in whose work there is no scope for norms of any kind.

Since *Midnight's Children* traces Saleem's ancestry from Kashmir, Rushdie provides interesting details about its people. Through Tai, who is almost ageless and therefore a reliable voice of its people, Rushdie not only suggests that before 1947 times Kashmir was not a part of British India, but also underlines a fundamental difference between the character of Kashmiris and Indians: "Kashmiris are different. Cowards, for instance.... We are not like Indians, always making battles" (34). During the war between India and Pakistan in 1947, he raises the slogan of "Kashmir for Kashmiris," and gets killed. This perception is further reinforced in the words of Salim's grandfather Aziz when he tells his wife: "'Forget about being a good Kashmiri girl. Start thinking about being a modern Indian woman'" (35). Though there has been a change in the distinguishing traits that Rushdie emphasizes in the Kashmiri character, Tai's thinking has surfaced much too often during the past several years.

From among the pre-partition times, Rushdie isolates two details, which had a bearing on the future of India. In 1913, Aziz smelt that "something was not right" in Jallinawallah Bagh. His efforts to keep himself on his feet got mixed up with gun-fire and the cries of people. Through a cool and efficient description of the massacre, which is ironical, Rushdie suggests the callousness of the British towards the Indians:

> Brigadier Dyer's fifty men put down their machine-guns and got away. They have fired a total of one thousand six hundred and fifty rounds into the unarmed crowd. Of these, one thousand five hundred and sixteen have found their mark, killing or wounding some person. 'Good shooting,' Dyer tells his men, 'We have done a jolly good thing'(36).

The second incident relates to the British policy of divide and rule, which worked through interference in the religious affairs of Hindus and Muslims, for creating bad blood between them. When Aziz quarrels with his wife because the maulvi they had engaged to teach their children tells them to "hate Hindus and Buddhists and Jains and Sikhs and who knows what other vegetarians" (43), he actually fights the politics of the Muslim League. Their policies were contested politically by Mian Abdullah, who was attacked by the British, because he worked against their interests.

Rushdie does not make any elaborate reference to the partition of the country and the riots that followed in its wake. He is critical of Jinnah, for his determination "to see Pakistan formed in his lifetime, and would have done anything to ensure it." The violence and disillusionment that followed the ghastly event is sniffed by Joseph D'Costa in Bombay; he tells Mary: "The independence is for the rich only; the poor are being made to kill each other like flies. In Punjab, in Bengal. Riots, riots, poor against poor" (104).

From the post-partition times, Rushdie isolates some events and happenings for elaborate comment; the rest he weaves into happenings in Saleem's life, to give the narrative a semblance of a linear motion. The logic of selection and the distribution of space between events is dictated by the downward slant he perceives in India's march towards the building of a secular democracy. For example, he comes down heavily on the bifurcation of provinces in India on the basis of language, by associating it with their dreams, produced by heat and characterized by "fantasy; unreason; lust." The language marchers of Bombay are in effect its victims:

> Language marchers demanded the partition of the state of Bombay along linguistic boundaries—the dream of Maharashtra was at the head of some processions, the mirage of Gujarat led the others forward. Heat, gnawing at the mind's divisions between fantasy and reality, made anything seem possible; the half-waking chaos of afternoon siestas fogged men's brains, and the air was filled with the stickiness of aroused desires (165).

Rushdie condemns the regional hatred that this division unleashed, by showing how the midnight's children of promise also started taking after the adults. This hatred led to other hatreds, based on religion and class.

> The rich children turned up their noses at being in such lowly company; Brahmins began to feel uneasy at permitting even their thoughts to touch the thoughts of untouchables; while, among the low-born, the pressures of poverty and Communism were becoming evident...and, on top of all this, there were clashes of personality, and the hundred squalling rows which are unavoidable in a parliament composed entirely of half-grown brats (248).

Rushdie's account censures events, policies, and even the mood of the nation, including that of Pakistan. He characterizes the shortlived Indian mood at the time of Chinese invasion as the "disease of optimism," though it was labelled variously by others as an era of industrial peace, of emotional integration, and as one which strengthened people's faith in their government. He blames people for this false sense of euphoria and for not seeing the country's drift towards disaster. Right around this time, Pakistan was promoting unhealthy practices through its experiment of Basic Democracy, for the 420 (the number itself has a strong cultural resonance of cheating) "Basic Democrats included mullahs, roadsweepers, the Nawab's chauffeur, numerous men who sharecropped hashish on the Nawab's estate, and other loyal citizens"

(311). Rushdie makes it clear that India was better than Pakistan, because of its superior political system. In Pakistan, truth was manufactured to distort reality. Saleem has a devastating comment on the victory of Democrats over the Combined Opposition Party:

> ...in a country where the truth is what it is instructed to be, reality quite literally ceases to exist, so that everything becomes possible except what we are told is the case; and maybe this was the difference between my Indian childhood and Pakistani adolescence—that in the first I was beset by an infinity of alternative realities, while in the second I was adrift, disoriented, amid an equally infinite number of falsenesses, unrealities and lies (315).

The repressive nature of this lie-making machinery is illustrated by the efforts of Yahya Khan and Bhutto to crush the Bengali people in East Pakistan by the brutal Pakistani army and the dismantling of the democratic processes in both wings of the country.

In conformity with his overall design, Rushdie provides proportionately large space to emergency which, in his view, signalled the collapse of the dream of new India. In narrating the events leading to this catastrophic situation, which released dictatorial and fanatically communal tendencies in the body-politic, Rushdie is conscious of the problem of perspective, of writing about events and happenings near our time. He realizes that one may not see the shape of things clearly, and therefore fail to offer a balanced assessment, but because the event is important for him, he cannot help writing about it in detail. In fact, as I have been arguing, it is at the very centre of his understanding and interpretation of India's post-and pre-1947 past. That is why he writes:

> ...as to the question of guilt, I refuse absolutely to take the larger view; we are too close to what-is-happening, perspective is impossible, later perhaps analysts will say why and wherefore, will adduce underlying economic trends and political developments, but right now we're too close to the cinema-screen, the picture is breaking up into dots, only subjective judgments are possible. Subjectively, then, I hang my head in shame (419).

The novel includes all the significant details connected with it: from the time the Allahabad High Court found Mrs Gandhi guilty to the point the emergency was actually declared by her. By banning dissent of any and every kind, it brought the democratic process to a grinding halt and led to the arrest of a large number of people.[9] With trenchant irony, we are told that the arrested people included "schoolteachers lawyers poets newspapermen trade-unionists, in fact anyone who had ever made the mistake of sneezing during the Madam's speeches..." (404).

Taking recourse to the method of metaphoric connections between private and public history, the birth of Saleem's son is equated with the birth of Mrs Gandhi's emergency; his sickness symbolizes the sickness of the entire nation: "I suspected, from the first, something darkly metaphorical in this illness— believing that, in those midnight months when the age of my connection-to-history overlapped with his, our private emergency was not unconnected with the larger, macrocosmic disease, under whose influence the sun had become as pallid and diseased as our son" (408). In consonance with the principle of nasal ethics, Saleem smells the evils of emergency and the unhealthy practices it promoted, which are linked with the country's diseased past:

> When the Constitution was altered to give the Prime Minister well-nigh-absolute powers, I smelled the ghosts of ancient empires in the air...in that city which was littered with the phantoms of Slave Kings and Mughals, of Aurangzeb the merciless and the last, pink conquerors, I inhaled once again the sharp aroma of despotism. It smelled like burning oily rags (409).

The true import of emergency is suggested through the popularization of the new slogan of India is Indira and Indira is India. This new dictatorial style, which was shamelessly legitimised through a seemingly constitutional process, is censured by Rushdie by equating it with the most despicable parts of India's past, which were dominated by cruel despots, who had no regard for the country and its people. Rushdie also links these developments with the undoing of the hopes and promises symbolized by the children who were born along with the new nation: "...the truest, deepest motive behind the declaration of a State of Emergency was the smashing, the pulverizing, the irreversible discombobulation of the children of midnight" (412).

The novel provides elaborate descriptions of the programmes of slum clearance and family planning to bring out the element of coercion behind such schemes, and dramatizes the pain and suffering they caused to thousands of innocent people. As one of the sufferers in the new regime, in the custody of the Widow, Saleem understood that Mrs Gandhi had elevated herself to the status of a devi, because she feared the potential deities in the midnight's children. That is why in her new incarnation she represents to him the most fearful aspect of a dictatorial ruler, who exploited religion to mythify her personal rule:

> ...we, the magical children of midnight, were hated feared destroyed by the Widow, who was not only Prime Minister of India but also aspired to be Devi, the Mother-goddess in her most terrible aspect, possessor of the shakti of the gods, a multi-limbed divinity with a centre-parting and schizophrenic hair.... And that was how I learnt my meaning in the crumbling palace of the bruised- breasted women (422).

Thus we see that Saleem's main objective in the novel has been to concentrate on showing how from 1947 onwards, the promise that the country held at the time of its birth was gradually destroyed because the people in general and the politicians in particular could not stop their present from getting tainted by the shadows of its abhorrent past. This is the main lesson of the narrative, Rushdie's lesson of history for us.

In comparison with *Midnight's Children*, *Shame* has a larger historical core, which provides for a more exhaustive critique of Pakistan's social and political history. I have already pointed out how Rushdie admits that his picture of Pakistan is a partial one. The slicy bits he chooses are patterned in a manner that shame becomes both the informing principle and the controlling metaphor.[10] This makes the novel an effective work of satire as well. In the main, the shameful aspects of the social, political, and cultural scene are crystallized in the lives and activities of its two prominent leaders, representing civilian and military authority in the country and its coercive political structure. The narrative is linked through the agency of its hero Omar. It also focuses on other men and women, mostly victims of the despotic machinery of its leaders. The victims include a person like the narrator's friend, a poet, who had to spend "many months in jail, for social reasons." Though he refused to speak to him about his experiences, the narrator learnt from others that "he was in bad shape for a long time after he got out. They said that he had been hung upside-down by the ankles and beaten, as if he were a new-born baby whose lungs had to be coerced into action so that he could squeal" (28).

Rushdie emphasizes two details about the nature of shame in Pakistan. One, that shame did not just mean shame as it was understood in English; it meant *sharam*, with its "encyclopaedias of nuances," suggested in its elaboration by Omar's mothers (39). Two, that in Pakistan, shame has become a part of the ethos of the country, and indistinguishable from civilized living: "…live with it for long enough and it becomes part of the furniture. In 'Defence,' you can find shame in every house, burning in an ashtray, hanging framed upon a wall, covering a bed. But nobody notices it any more. And everyone is civilized" (28). In short, by becoming a part of the social and cultural life of the country, it has become invisible.

Rushdie traces the seeds of Pakistan's shamelessness to its birth. He thinks that the very idea of Pakistan was a mistake, for it was the result of a moth-eaten partition of the subcontinent, in which it got a "few insect-nibbled slices of it, some dusty western acres and jungly eastern swamps that the ungodly were happy to do without (Al-Lah's new country: two chunks of land a thousand miles apart. A country so improbable that it could almost exist)" (61). The disadvantages of its birth were compounded by the fact that its immediate control passed into the hands of people who had come from outside. They failed to give it any meaningful direction: "The newness of those days felt pretty unstable; it was a dislocated rootless sort of thing." This resulted in lawlessness and wholesale cheating, in which people

> —not only Prime Ministers—got shot from time to time, throats got themselves slit in gullies, bandits became billionaires …there were a few voices saying, if this is the country we dedicated to our God, what kind of God is it that permits — but these voices were silenced before they had finished their questions, kicked on the shins under tables…(82).

The conditions, in fact, had turned so bad that the people who controlled it held that certain things "cannot be permitted to be true." In Rushdie's estimation, both Bhutto and Zia represent the worst period in Pakistan's history, for they grew bigger and uglier as the country started "growing fast, but in a stupid way." The major part of the shameful history of Pakistan, therefore, gets connected with their rise to power, for which the base had been laid by their irresponsible and corrupt predecessors.[11] Rushdie also connects the shame of the country as a whole with another kind of shame, which he locates in family structures, governed by the tyrannical patriarchy in the main.

Rushdie's exposure of the exploitative political structure of Pakistan is realized through an interesting mix of a pinch of the real with a heavy dose of the fantastic. Although he pleads that he was forced to adopt the mode of a fairy tale for his novel, he intersperses the account with short and compact descriptions and comments, which make pointed references to the objects of his condemnation. One such example is the passage which describes the very idea of Pakistan being a mistake, which is at the basis of its unstable polity, which has been riddled with senseless violence and repression.

Of the two political leaders who constitute the staple of the male plot of the novel and have been severely castigated by him, Isky stands for Bhutto. He has been presented in his twin incarnations in history and myth. As a historical figure, he has two profiles. Before taking to politics, he was a playboy, a rake, a debauchee, who dissipated his energies by indulging in all kinds of excesses. However, when he realized that for joining politics, he needed to cast himself in a new role, he embarked upon a massive transformational programme; he gave up "stud poker, chemin de fer, private roulette evenings, horse-race fixing, French food, opium and sleeping pills...his habit of seeking out beneath ...tables the excited ankles and compliant knees of society beauties, and stopped visiting the whores" (124). To put it in a sentence: "He stifled forever the high-pitched giggle of his unreliable playboy self and substituted a rich, full-throated, statesmanlike guffaw" (125).

The entire description of Bhutto's transmutation from a playboy into a saint is permeated with fine irony. The final, sarcastic blow is delivered in this mock-encomium: "Did any man ever sacrifice more for his people? He gave up cock-fights, bear-fights, snake-and-mongoose duels; plus disco dancing, and his monthly evenings at the home of the chief film censor, where he had watched special compilations of the juiciest bits excised from incoming foreign films" (25). Consistently, Rushdie also suggests that in spite of the transformation that Isky undertook to launch himself into politics, he was essentially the same person. He had only put on a face to dupe people. It is primarily for this reason that from the time he assumed power to the time he was arrested by Zia and hanged, he has been presented through his daughter Arjumand, who covers up his past to make him into a mythical figure of gigantic proportions. After his death, she devotes herself solely to the task of deifying him, so that he could be restored to history in his new incarnation. She is so passionately involved in this enterprise that she "empties herself of everything to make room for the memories. They fill her up, her bowels, her lungs, her nostrils…" (178). Through them, she allows her "remembering mind to transmute the preserved fragments of the past into the gold of myth" (181).

In order to make us perceive that the mythical and historical versions of Bhutto are at variance, the narrator constantly punctures Arjumand's account to tell us what had actually happened. For this, he chooses a style, which comes very near the mock-epic manner. This is how the balloon of his electoral victory is pricked:

> O confusion of people who have lived too long under military rule, who have forgotten the simplest things about democracy! Large numbers of men and women were swept away by the oceans of bewilderment, unable to locate ballot-boxes or even ballots, and failed to cast their votes. Others, stronger swimmers in those seas, succeeding in expressing their preferences twelve or thirteen times (178).

When the eastern wing of the country turned tables on him, Isky made the president of the country despatch "an enormous Army to restore a sense of proportion in the East." In Arjumand's version it is a perfectly justified measure, because the people there were no more than "savages, breeding endlessly, jungle-bunnies good for nothing but growing jute and rice, knifing each other, cultivating traitors in their paddies" (179). The strife that ensues and which led to the dismemberment of the country is for her no more than India's intrusion in the affairs of Pakistan. In the narrator's version, it is a story of their exploitation by the western wing. The humiliating defeat of the army in the eastern wing, which led to the arrest of the president, was exploited by Isky for his self-promotion, forgetting that he had been instrumental in starting the trouble there. He demonstrated his trumped-up anguish before the people of his amputated country with a theatrical flourish: ripped his shirt before them to show his wounded chest.

Throughout his political career, Isky disregarded his wife and made his daughter his permanent ally. She paid back this trust by transmuting his actual life into a mythical one, as an offering to the people of the country. Her impulse is similar to that of Omar's mothers, who transformed the death of their second son Babar from a rebel into an angel, because they thought they "have the right to present him with a good death, a death which the living can live" (132). Since Arjumand's version of Isky veers towards myth, Rushdie not merely deflates it by providing a short version of what actually happened, but also pits it against the account of her mother, who knew the real Isky and his tyrannical ways. She tells her daughter: "... Your father, whom I always loved, was world champion of shamelessness; he was international rogue and bastard number one. You see, daughter. I remember...Isky...before he became a saint" (108). It is not that Isky was shameless before he joined politics; he remained so even after that, though he maintained a facade of saintliness. The real character of Isky is preserved by his wife in the eighteen shawls she knitted during the time she lived in utter loneliness. They provide the most telling account of his shameful deeds: his philandering after women, his authoritarian manner, his torture of his opponents, the death blows he gave to democratic structures, his use of police force to oppress people, the genocide of the Pathans, and his election manoeuvrings. He would constantly hurl foul oaths and imprecations at people and even get them murdered. The shawls are a miniature portrait of the historical Bhutto, which is meant to be a foil to his mythical representation by his daughter. The imagery of the shawls points to the severity of Rushdie's disapproval of Isky as a person and leader.

If Bhutto represents a politician who exploited the people of Pakistan by invoking the codes of civil liberty and democratic spirit, Raza Hyder, who stands for Zia, represents the greedy military generals of Pakistan, who always tried to compete with their civilian brethren to take control of the country, and have their share in the spoils of power. In his early stint in the Needle Valley, where he was meant to quell the rebellious tribals, he teaches political lessons to the Prime Minister and advocates the use of force to suppress dissent: "Sir, you must place the law in my hands. Carte Blanche. At certain moments civil law must bend before military necessity" (101). When the Prime Minister refuses his advice and help, he threatens him: "'Army is watching these days.... All over the country the eyes of honest soldiers see what they see, and we are not pleased, no sir. The people stir, sir. And if they look away from politicians, where will they turn for purity'" (102)? The most interesting feature of the army rule in Pakistan has been that the generals legitimised it by linking it with religion.

When Hyder put Isky to death and consolidated his power over the state, he let it be known that his main purpose for doing so was to put the country on a firm foundation of faith, which had been the very reason of its existence. This is suggested through a telling image:

> On the morning after the coup Raza Hyder appeared on national television. He was kneeling on a prayer-mat, holding his ears and reciting Quranic verses; then he rose from his devotions to address the nation. This was the speech in which the famous term 'Operation Umpire' was first heard by the people. 'Understand,' Raza said briskly, 'the Army seeks to be no more than an honest ref or ump' (223).

The main thrust of Rushdie's censure of the regime of Zia is that he used religion to perpetuate himself in power and revived medieval barbaric laws and practices. He justified measures like flogging and cutting of limbs as injunctions of God. To a team of foreign journalists, he says: "...these are not laws...which we have plucked out of the wind. These are the holy words of God, as revealed in sacred texts. Now if they are holy words of God, they cannot also be barbaric. It is not possible. They must be some other thing" (245).

Shame also details several measures which Raza introduced to Islamize Pakistan. These included the banning of booze, promoting religion through the media, even incarcerating beggars, because "God and socialism were incompatible." In the name of God he invoked the principle of stability for the country, only to put

"Generals everywhere, so that the Army got its fingers deeper into things than it had ever done before" (249). It is not that Rushdie is against the organization and working of states on Islamic principles; he even suggests that such principles could have provided the basis for a possible unity of what had been left of the country after it got split into two; but he does not approve of the manner in which it was done by Zia, who imposed religion on people, not because it was good for them or for the country, but because it provided him with a convenient and dependable exploitative ideology to maintain the *status quo*, which people found difficult to oppose. That is why the narrator makes a comment, which is both general and specific:

> Autocratic regimes find it useful to espouse the rhetoric of faith, because people respect that language, are reluctant to oppose it. This is how religions shore up dictators; by encircling them with words of power, words which the people are reluctant to see discredited, disenfranchised, mocked (251).

Thus we see that the main purpose of Rushdie's engagement with history in Pakistan is to show that the country's decline began right from the time it was born; it touched its lowest ebb during the times of Bhutto and Zia, when democratic rule and secular polity suffered irreparable damage.

If oppression characterizes the male plot of Bhutto and Zia, it turns into a dominant feature of the female plot too. The narrator records how at one point women virtually take over the narrative, to stress that they too are victims of the unhealthy cultural practices in Pakistan:

> [Women] marched in from the peripheries of the story to demand the inclusion of their own tragedies, histories and comedies ...their stories explain and even subsume, the men's. Repression is a seamless garment; a society which is authoritarian in its social and sexual codes, which crushes its women beneath the intolerable burdens of honour and propriety, breeds repressions of other kinds as well. Contrariwise: dictators are always—or at least in public, on other people's behalf—puritanical. So it turns out that my 'male' and 'female' plots are the same story, after all (173).

The novel builds an interesting parallel between Pakistan and its women: both are wrong miracles. Pakistan was a "failure of the dreaming mind," because it could not acquire a coherent shape. It was and remained a "picture full of irreconcilable elements, midriffbaring immigrant saris versus demure, indigenous Sindi shilwar-kurtas, Urdu versus Punjabi, now versus then: a miracle that went wrong" (87). Sufiya, who, as a symbol of the women of Pakistan, is central to the conception of the novel, is, like her country, a wrong miracle, because she failed to come up to the dreams of her parents: she was not born a male. The narrator explicitly builds the connection between the country and Sufiya by stating that "This is a novel about Sufiya Zinobia," or more accurately "that Sufiya Zinobia is about this novel" (59).

Rushdie's concern for women in the novel stems from his understanding of their wronged social status, characterized by two features. First, women have a very low social acceptability, because the society is governed largely by feudal codes of honour and respectability; it is a male-dominated world in which women do not count. This is reflected in Raza's noise and bluster at the time of Sufiya's birth, when he constantly draws attention to her sex. She had defeated his expectations, because he had all the time been dreaming of a male child. When he is forced to reckon with the fact of her birth, he suffers a kind of paralysis. His defeated aspiration and the resultant frustration are sufficiently indicative of the kind of future she would have in his house; she has to live with neglect and later with humiliation and oppression. Through a well-conceived piece of anticipation, Rushdie suggests the cage-like life of women in the very opening scene of the novel. Omar's mothers have to lead a cloistered existence because their father raises them in strict conformity with "an iron morality that was mostly Muslim" (13). Consequently, they remained uneducated, in a state of interminable captivity, imprisoned in the zenana. The last part of the sentence draws our attention to the intrusion of Islamic codes in the lives of women, which distinguished the plight of Pakistani women from women in other repressive societies. The demands of faith put additional burdens on them; the constricting chains of patriarchy grow longer there than in other places. This diminishes their role and place in society.

The shame in the situation of women in Pakistan is encompassed in the fate of Sufiya. Representing its wronged women, she becomes the girl who was murdered by her father in London because of her alleged affair with a white boy. The father took it as an affront, a violation of his code of honour. Rushdie adds many more names to the ever-growing list of female sufferers. Sufiya has to suffer for all of them, because the society, dominated by its menfolk, has to meet its cultural obligations. This makes Sufiya into a perfect victim-figure, and also explains why she has to be made into an idiot. Rushdie uses her idiocy to highlight another fact: to make her pure, so that she could contrast with the impurity around her: "Sufiya Zinobia has grown, her mind more slowly than her body, and owing to this slowness she remains, for me, somehow clean (pak) in the midst of a dirty world" (120-21).

The contrast between Sufiya and the world around her is also connected by Rushdie with the all-enveloping shame in society. She blushes quite often for people who act shamelessly. It is because through her brain-fever she could absorb a host of unfelt feelings of shame. Thus the secret of Sufiya's blushes was that it felt shame where it ought to have been felt, but was not. This is meant to imply that in Pakistan shame is felt for wrong things, while the really shameful things are done without any compunction. It also confirms that people have linked it to wrong notions of evil; where it really exists, it is overlooked and even indulged. Sufiya could not have performed all these functions, if she had been cast in the mould of a normal person, for no normal being in the novel feels and reacts the way she does. It is because they are governed by norms and codes of behaviour which they think ought to be observed, though these have been exposed by the novelist as unjust and unfair.

That shame pervades the thinking of people and that women are conscious of the hostile attitude of the society towards them is established in the novel beyond any doubt. I give three random examples:

i) Isky tells his daughter Arjumand in very clear words that she should forget that she is a woman: "'It's a man's world, Arjumand. Rise above your gender as you grow. This is no place to be a woman in'" (126).

ii) When Sufiya's sister refuses to marry Haroun because she is in love with Talvar, Hyder and his relatives think that it is a matter of shame and no less than a scandal. Hyder agrees to her marriage with Talvar not because he has any respect for her wishes, but because he believes that his daughter had behaved no better than a whore, and "A whore with a home is better than a whore in the gutter" (167).

iii) Although Talvar is in love with Naveed, he considers her no more than a child-bearing machine. The result is that after producing a very large brood, she gets sick and tired and commits suicide.

Rushdie also suggests that *sharam* inevitably leads to violence. After taking in too much of shame, her own and that of others, Sufiya bursts into fitful acts of violence. When she destroys the turkeys of Pinkie Aurangzeb by removing their heads and taking out their guts, the narrator remarks:

> What seems certain is that Sufiya Zinobia, for so long burdened with being a miracle-gone-wrong, a family's shame made flesh, had discovered in the labyrinths of her unconscious self the hidden path that links *sharam* to violence; and that, awakening, she was as surprised as anyone by the force of what had been unleashed (139).

By linking the beauty and the beast, Rushdie drives home two points. One, that such beasts are the products of a civilized society in the "heart of the respectable world." Two, that the beauty turned into a beast and became ferocious day after day because she remained unattended for a long time. If only people had tried to understand her, then their sense of themselves would have been shattered; they would have been made pure. Since this did not happen, Sufiya's adventures into ferocity multiplied to create a sense of panic among people and their rulers. The narrator emphasizes that her tendency towards violence intensifies with fall in the ethical and political norms of the country. Later, even her husband found it difficult to control her. When Hyder became thoroughly evil and God and devil created two "conflicting soliloquies inside his skull, marching leftright," Omar felt that it was time for God to step forward and take charge of events. The novel ends in one final orgy of violence in which Hyder and his dead wife are torn to bits and Omar is consumed by Sufiya in her violent embrace, giving an apocalyptic ending to the novel.

It is true that *Shame* is a grim novel, but it is not wholly bleak and hopeless. If the images of perversion, cruelty and waste dominate the narrative, it is because the reality of Pakistan is unpleasant, repressive, and exploitative. But the narrator's impulse for writing it is not just to dramatize his disgust at the repulsive aspects of the political and cultural life of Pakistan; it is also actuated by hope, that someday people would be drawn to the old myth of liberty, equality, and fraternity. This would bring shameful things to end. With regard to women, too, the narrator concedes that "women are much more impressive than men," although in the novel most of them are in chains. This, however, does not negate the hope of their freedom.

Notes

1 Viney Kirpal (xiii). In a special issue of *Seminar* on New writing in English, Rukun Advani writes in the same vein. Rushdie's novel marks a watershed "with an aesthetic force that seems stupendous and unlikely to be matched—as also a cultural and literary break.... Rushdie is the Colossus who strides across and fuses diverse words and worlds, most specifically the Anglo-Saxon and the Indian, deploying a vocabulary and syntax that draw from both. Irreverence, iconoclasm, and witty forms of subversion in relation to institutionalized, fossilized and dominant forms of thought and power characterize his fiction" (16).

2 The essays on Rushdie are constantly on the increase. In an annotated piece on critical response to Rushdie's fiction between 1982 and 1991, M D Fletcher comments on their main concerns: "One involves Rushdie's use of language and particularly his 'Indianization' of English. The second is his intermingling of the personal with the public for political comment. The third combines the two, emphasising the politics of (post-colonial) language" (6-23).

3 This is a commonplace observation of many Western critics. See, in particular, Patricia Merivale (5-21) and Linda Hutcheon (1986, 80-82). For more details on this, see also C Kanaganayakam (86-87) and Linda Hutcheon (1989, 62-71). The most compact statement on Rushdie's postmodernism figures in Amin Malek (176 and 182). In spite of his affinity with postmodern writers, Rushdie's fiction has a

basic core of meaning which arises from his serious interplay with historical specifics and his awareness of the historiographic contest, which is unique to India. Reservations about approaching Rushdie's work from a totally postmodernist perspective have been voiced by critics, but in a different context, especially because of the fear that this could lead to the trivializing of the Third World. See especially, Aruna Srivastava (62) and Arun Mukherjee (2).

4 Part of the discussion on Saleem draws on my earlier essay (1985, 16-23).

5 Brenda K Marshall states it clearly when she writes that "Postmodern fictions suggest that every position should remind us of its own critique.... The counter-memories of historiographic metafiction problematize history and subvert meaning, but they deny neither" (178).

6 Pupul Jayakar admits that during the last phase of Mrs Gandhi's Prime Ministership, that is during the post-emergency times, "it was astonishing to see the hold orthodox religion had gained on her" (421). But no such thing has been said about Nehru.

7 In this respect, Rushdie is like Kundera. See David Lodge (105-21).

8 M D Fletcher has discussed it as a satire (99-111). Fletcher states that in *Shame* satire is complemented by fantasy, which makes it different from a work like *Catch-22*. This sounds inappropriate. If we look at the whole range of satiric tradition, from the Greeks to the present, fantasy has invariably been a part of satire. Peter Briggs's argument that Rushdie uses fantasy in the novel to suggest that history makes no sense in Pakistan underplays the use of fantasy as a satiric device (130).

9 The drift of the narrative in *Midnight's Children* is similar to the import of one of his essays in which he states that India has been plagued by communalism, particularly of the Hindu kind (1991, 26-33).

10 Rushdie's concentrated attention on the repulsive aspects of Pakistan's political and cultural life is not necessarily because of his love for postmodernist technique; this kind of concentrated focus on selected aspects of societies and their history is a known feature of satiric works. Criticism of Rushdie on this count, as in Aijaz Ahmad, is unfair (1461-71). He attributes the bleak and cage-like quality of the novel to Rushdie's class origin, because of which he shuts himself to "innumerable heroisms of the ordinary and extraordinary kinds." In fairness to Rushdie, it could be argued that if a writer chooses to concentrate on exposing the shameful aspects of a society, heroisms of any kind would spoil the design and power of satire.

11 Helen Watson-Williams remarks that there is some confusion about uncovering the historical core of the novel, but accepts that "the basic struggle for dominance and power between Bhutto and Zia shapes the fictional plot" (37-38). I think she says so because she reads the narrative like an allegory, and looks for extended parallels between the fictional and the actual, against which Rushdie has consistently warned the readers. If we accept that there is a strong streak of satire in it, then we have to permit Rushdie the freedom to exaggerate, about which he has himself written that "What I hoped for is that one would make figures in the book who were somehow bigger than the particular instances of them that history had offered us" (1985, 18). One could think of them like the satirical portraits of Dryden, though for him the portraiture of the political figures of his time stressed their personal traits. The difference between Rushdie and Dryden is that the former sees them as part of a larger historical reality, in which they have a considerable effect on the lives of ordinary people.

Chapter VI

Entering History through the Backdoor with Tharoor and Vijayan

In the third and fourth chapters I discussed how the novels of Anand and Sahgal incorporate their distinct understanding of the country's old and more recent past, through the realistic mode. Their involvement with history is direct, even though Sahgal covers it up by using the strategy of disguise. This chapter is meant to illustrate that a writer can use history, by which I mean that he can recreate, reinterpret, critique, and problematize it indirectly, through narrative procedures which are non-mimetic and strategies which operate through contrived mechanisms and schemas. The reason for discussing them under a separate category is not only to illustrate the variety in the novelist's use of history, but also to reaffirm the role of fantasy in incursions into reality, which have largely been overlooked because of the mimesis-oriented assumptions of literature, in which it is assumed that the use of fantasy in a fictional work makes it remote from actual experience and from history. It has increasingly been recognized that the impulse towards fantasy is as significant as the mimetic impulse (Hume xii). It has also been cogently demonstrated that fantasy may not always lead to escapism, but may be an effective technique for "approaching and evaluating the real world"; it could even be "imbued with a moral purpose" (Swinfen 230). The reason for emphasizing this is to reaffirm that even when fantasy may provide fictional works with a playful exterior, they could still promote a serious understanding about the real world. It took critics a great deal of time to realize that Swift's *Gulliver's Travels* is seriously involved with the history of England. I have already pointed out how Rushdie too uses fantasy very effectively in his fiction, because of which his involvement with history becomes distinguishable from that of Anand and Sahgal, though he does it without using any schemas. The texts discussed in this chapter deal with history indirectly. Tharoor uses the mode of allegory, in which the *Mahabharata* becomes a structuring device to create his version of India's past and its understanding; he uses this frame quite profitably to critique events and important leaders and to problematize the discourse itself. Vijayan uses the well-known satiric codes to make a scathing criticism of several aspects of India's social and political culture. Vijayan does it in a manner that his work also resonates the problems of post-colonial societies in general.

History through the Allegorical Frame: Tharoor's *The Great Indian Novel*

In one of his lecture/interviews, Rushdie referred somewhat disparagingly to the Indian tendency of reading allegories in creative works as a kind of sickness (1985, 3). Whether this is really so and more conspicuous in Indians than in the people of other cultures could be a debatable issue. It certainly does not diminish the truthfulness of a common tendency among people (including Indians) to make sense of things through correspondences: by relating experiences and phenomena to the ones already known. This is at the root of impulse towards allegory. It has been exploited by writers all over the world from earliest times, by casting works in a mould of correspondences with narrative schemas and systems of beliefs and thoughts of already-known works. Literary historians testify that the practice has proved useful and rewarding; the new works gained in suggestive power and liveliness of interest by ensuring imaginative participation of their readers, which was not always possible in straightforward representations of reality. A writer can exploit the tension between two contrary impulses which are always at work in allegorical representations: that of closing as far as possible, the gap between his work and the one he is using as a base or model, and for providing divergences between the two, especially in their meaning.[1] In more recent times, allegory has shot up in estimation. It is considered a unique mode of the times; in fact, "the ultimate discourse itself, so that all writing is deemed to be allegorical, and all reading allegorical misreading" (Selmon

157). In spite of its new prestige and its differing implications for the Eurocentric and post-colonial worlds, it is generally agreed that the conception of allegory is rooted in the principle of "correspondence of text to the old, authoritative text," which "encourages the reader to look for a *tertium quid*, a principle of interpretation to which the correspondence points" (Barney 16-17).[2]

Shashi Tharoor's *The Great Indian Novel* is principally in the allegorical mould, though the novelist does not say so specifically in or outside the novel. He does, however, provide some hints. The novel's title, he tells us, is linked to the great epic *Mahabharata*, his "primary source of inspiration" (6). In the 'Afterword' to the novel, he expands on this: "Many of the characters, incidents and issues in this novel are based on people and events described in the great epic…a work which remains a perennial source of delight and inspiration to millions in India" (419). A more explicit statement occurs in one of his essays, in which he states that the novel is "an attempt to retell the political history of 20th century India through a fictional recasting of events, episodes and characters from the *Mahabharata*" (Tharoor 1991, 30). This is closest to saying that the shape and sequential drift of the novel is dictated by a text already known to his readers, and confirming that it is a rational construct predetermined by another work.

Though allegorical representations can be trying and exasperating for writers, because they have to strive consistently for working out varying levels of similitude with the chosen model, which puts arbitrary checks on their inventive faculty, they also provide them numerous advantages in the bargain. In Tharoor's case, the advantages were more than usual, because of the special features of his master-text. One does not need to overemphasize that the *Mahabharata* is both a grand, founding text of Indian literature and a part of its living tradition.[3] Any work based on it would be assured of general acceptability and a liveliness of interest among its readers. The epic provided Tharoor with two additional gains. Though a part of the ancient Hindu tradition of *asa-puranas*, it scores over other texts of this kind, because of its known historical value. Compared, for example, with the *yana*, which is considered more of a *kavya*, it is more of *itihasa*, with a firm overarching historical core, which embraces virtually all aspects of human living: "The *Mahabharata* is not merely a great narrative poem; it is our *itihasa*, the fundamental source of knowledge for our literature, dance, painting, sculpture, theology, statecraft, sociology, ecology—in short, our *history* in all its detail and density" (Barucha 230). This makes it a suitable model for any fictional reconstruction of history. The *Mahabharata* is also an appropriate text for writing any account which centres around themes and concerns which are at the heart of Tharoor's rendition of the history of India: power, politics, schisms, personality-clashes, institutional structures, individual and social dharma, etc.

Since the *Mahabharata* does not have a fixed text, because of having gone through various versions from the time it was first conceived, it provides a great deal of flexibility to a writer who wants to use it as a model. Considering that the epic was rewritten from time to time, Tharoor had the freedom to write, as it were, his own version of the epic, which he partially does. In spite of this, the novel conforms to its most known, recognized and accepted core. However, because of Tharoor's special problem of fitting the actual historical personages and events into the narrative design and cast of characters of the epic, he had to make changes and adjustments of various kinds:

> ...the yoking of myth to history restricted some of my fictional options: as the novel progressed, I was obliged to abandon novelistic conventions and develop characters who were merely walking metaphors. Draupadi, thus, became emblematic of Indian democracy, her attempted disrobing a symbol of what was sought to be done to democracy not so long ago (Tharoor 1990, 19).[4]

One could add on to these details. Except Yudhistir, Pandavas too have been conceived as embodiments of various institutions, meant to keep democracy in good health. Because of changes in the character of dramatis personae, Tharoor had to make adjustments in the distribution of narrative space among people and events. Some deviations from the original also became inevitable. For example, there are no one hundred Kauravas; Priya Duryodhani has to represent them all with a changed sex. The parentage of the Pandavas in the narrative mismatches with the original. Adjustments in time-scheme and the sequential ordering of events also became necessary. Relating the epic to the actualities of history also produced awkward incongruities. For example, in

Tharoor's version, Yudhistir has to share power for some time with Duryodhani, which is unimaginable in the original. Gangaji has to die before he witnesses the disrobing of Draupadi. In spite of these changes in Tharoor's rendering of *Mahabharata* and the actual historical personages and events through them, Tharoor has worked out a reasonable degree of semblance between the mythical and the historical.

By casting actual people in history in the mold of characters from the epic, Tharoor aimed at writing a version of the history of India which would be "laden with resonance"; he also wanted the actual people and events to gain through the "mythic charge." Here too Tharoor stood to gain through his model. The resonance and charge in the narrative is not realized merely by Tharoor's contextualizing actual people and events in a suggestive frame, but also by the model on its own, which offers perspective on the present in terms of the past. It has rightly been pointed out by Iravati Karve that apart from its eternally-relevant core, the epic has a surprising element of perennial contemporaneity, which has accounted for its popularity and relevance in every age,[5] which has been admitted by the novelist himself.

The variegated nature of the epic, with its loose, episodic structure, due to its multiple levels of accretion, provided Tharoor with another freedom: to try and use a wide range of stylistic variations in his narrative, which he has exploited cleverly for critiquing historical personages and events. If Rushdie found that the history of Pakistan in *Shame* could be represented only through tragedy and farce, Tharoor felt that the history of India could be refracted only through the vein of satire: "to throw certain trends and issues into sharper relief than history makes possible" (Tharoor 1991, 31). For this, he chose several forms of irreverent style—puns, wordplay, light verse, irony, sarcasm, jokes, playful stories and witty digressions. Through this, he also wanted to approximate another feature of the original: "The story of India, like that of *Mahabharata*, had to come across as a tale of many tellers, even if it is ascribed only to one."[6] But underneath the irreverent surface of Tharoor's narrative lies his serious involvement with history.

In *Midnight's Children*, Rushdie employed the oral tradition of narrative of our country to invest Saleem Sinai's story with a definite cultural character. In the case of Tharoor, the requirement of the model necessitated it. The entire narrative is dictated by the participant-narrator VV to Ganapathi. However, like Saleem, VV not only narrates his version of the history of India, he also comments on the nature of the historical discourse, building into it a strong element of self-consciousness. He calls his account a selective recall of the past with the help of his memory, which approximates Saleem's version of memory's truth; but unlike Saleem, he is more explicit in stating that his account has been prompted by his need to have lessons for the future. That is why, in spite of its overall tone of playfulness and irreverence, he wants it to be taken seriously and not as a "piddling Western thriller" (18). The account is also grounded in VV's awareness of the historiographic contest, which has been a marked feature of the recreations of India's past. This is true of history proper as well as of its representations in fiction. VV's account implicitly contests the imperialist-colonial historiography and some forms of nationalist historiography as well.

The overall spirit of the narrative is suggested by the words of Gunter Grass, which constitute one of the three epigraphs of the novel: "Writers experience another view of history, what's going on, another understanding of 'progress'....Literature must refresh memory" (7). This is a significant statement on the novelist's active involvement with history, which reflects an influential trend in history-fiction interface in the West and the Third World. It not only provides space for fictional recreations of history, but also underlines their need. Grass concedes that writers provide a view of history which is different from that of the historians; he also regards their writings as vehicles for renewing people's memory of their past. The word 'progress' in his formulation also subtly suggests that writers could provide alternative renderings of what happened in the past to counter the versions of official groups and establishments. On all these counts, the cultural importance of the efforts of the novelists cannot be underestimated. By being more accessible and readable than serious, academic histories, novels can influence public opinion and political practice. The connection of Tharoor's novel with *Mahabharata* furthers its chances of readability and impact on popular imagination.

For a proper focus on Tharoor's involvement with history in general and the history of India in particular, I shall concentrate on three things: i) the shape of the novel's coherent and understandable narrative, which is dictated by the drift of the master narrative; ii) the bases and assumptions underlying the account, which provide Tharoor the required space for problematizing the discourse itself; iii) and the assessment of people and events who figure in the account, which include his comments on the Indian character and the institutional structure of its polity.

In conformity with the narrative design of the *Mahabharata*, Tharoor begins his account from the time of the birth of the narrator, VV, and then moves on to the loves of King Shantanu, his affair with Satyavati, the appearance of Bhishma on the scene, and the birth of Dhritarashtra, Pandu, and Vidur. The birth of the five Pandavas is also described according to the original, though Tharoor spices the narration with humour and witty comment. The wives of Pandu, who have to have their children from other beings, speak in modern idiom, and even with a bit of levity. This gives the account an occasional parodic tinge, but there is no evidence to show that Tharoor's intention is to mock the originals. He is only attempting to visualize his characters in a modern setting; this deviation in itself makes the account diverting. The narrative also makes room for a large number of incidents in the epic, which are not necessary for its historical design. These include the adventures of Pandavas during the course of their exile, their misadventure in the Lakshagraha, Bhim's affair with Hidimba, Arjun's banishment for a year, in which he combines business with pleasure, his love for Subhadra and his humiliation at the hands of Kameshwari. To overcome the problem of fitting some key events from the epic into the chronological frame of the historical account, Tharoor shifts them into a dream-world in which contemporary characters are "transported incongruously through time to their oneiric mythological settings" (355). This he chooses for dramatizing the scene of disrobing of Draupadi and the ascent of Yudhistir to heaven. The inclusion of all these scenes gives Tharoor's narrative the magnitude, solidity, and digressive quality of the original. In a sense, he provides his version of the present-day *Mahabharata*, without its serious tone. This is because he is not interested in the epic in itself; he uses it only as a frame for accommodating another narrative, for which it provides a suggestive cover of inference and detail.

Tharoor's version of the historical account begins roughly from the time when Gandhi entered into Indian politics till the time Mrs Gandhi returned to power after the fall of the Janata government. VV's claim for his account as a definitive memoir of his life and times is meant to characterize the historical account as well. Gandhi is represented through Bhishma, also called Ganga Datta to bring him nearer our times. Since like Bhishma he gave up claim to power and governance of the country, it leaves two main contenders from the later progeny: Dhritarashtra and Pandu, who stand for Nehru and Subhash. The narrative suggests that Nehru gained influence in the party hierarchy and succeeded in controlling the reins of power in post-independence India, because of the blessings of Gandhi. This is suggestively reinforced by Bhishma's continuance in the court of Dhritarashtra, even after he knew of the falsity of the Kauravas. Another contender for power is a member of the same clan, but the circumstances of his birth prevent him from coming to the forefront. He is Karna, who stands for Jinnah. He succeeds in taking away a chunk of territory from the country to set up the state of Karnistan, which stands for Pakistan; this particular detail is a deviation from the original. In India, except for a brief period, Nehru is succeeded by Duryodhani, who stands for Mrs Gandhi. The fact that she equals the whole of the Kaurava clan is meant to suggest what one political commentator once remarked about her cabinet, that she was the only man there. She tries her best to keep the Pandavas away from the seat of power and devises stratagems even to finish them off. In making Pandavas into an assorted group, Tharoor could be held guilty of a confusion of categories: for mixing human beings with institutions, but that would be unfair, because he had to observe similitude with the original. If Yudhistir is Morarji Desai, Arjun, Bhim, Nakul, and Sahadev represent institutions of the press, army, bureaucracy, and foreign service. They are meant to protect democracy, represented through Draupadi. Since Nehru and Mrs Gandhi dominated the political scene in post-independence India, they dominate the narrative as well. Most of the time, Pandavas are away from the corridors of power and very appropriately spend their time with their guru Drona, who stands for Jayaprakash Narayan. Though Tharoor manages to fit the main events and personalities of pre- and post-independence India within the plot-outline of the main narrative, there is no special place for Krishna in the account. A friend of Arjun, he is just a small-town MLA and even performs the ritual of giving a short spiritual discourse to him. It is quite likely that Tharoor took cover under the convenient fact that in earlier versions of the epic, Krishna was not as godly a figure as he became in later versions.

Through the balancing of the two-way process of adapting historical reality to fit the requirements of the original and by incorporating into the narrative most of its diverting incidents, Tharoor works out a delightful mix of the real and the fantastic as in *Midnight's Children*; he, of course, does not make use of the grotesque the way Rushdie did. Tharoor also succeeds in providing his narrative a tonality of romance of the original; simultaneously, he prepares the reader for alternating between the literal and the emblematic modes. Some characters and happenings are to be understood the way they have been represented, others for the things they represent. The reader's responsibility in Tharoor is to work conceivable parallels between the historical and the mythical and to grasp their implications for understanding his version of India's past.

Since VV dictates the narrative to his amanuensis Ganapathi in several short and long spells, in which he digresses to address issues relating to historical discourse and the nature of the historical process, this provides Tharoor with space for articulating his own views through him. VV distinguishes between past as a flux of events in time and past as an intelligible and readable account produced by the historian. He accepts that the past is a collective entity, the result of the efforts of hundreds and thousands of people—nameless, faceless, unrecognized—but when it is shaped into a written, historical account, several of them get left out. This is a problem inherent in the very process of composing history. VV illustrates this with reference to the independence of India:

> Independence was not won by a series of isolated events but by the constant, unremitting actions of thousands...of men and women across the land. We tend, Ganapathi, to look back on history as if it were a stage play, with scene building upon scene, our hero moving from one action to the next in his remorseless stride to the climax. Yet life is never like that. If life were a play the noises offstage, and for that matter the sounds of the audience,

> would drown out the lines of principal actors. That, of course, would make for a rather poor tale; and so the recounting of history is only the order we artificially impose upon life to permit its lessons to be more clearly understood (109).

The idea of history as an ordered composition hints at two things. One, that we have to pay attention to the role of rhetoric in its creation; two, that the ordering may not necessarily be prompted by the historian's disinterested obligation. By accommodating only some events, happenings, and people into their ordered versions, the historians exercise choice, which also suggests a lurking pattern or design. The happenings and events which get left out in any ordered narrative may not be of lesser significance than the ones which get included. As part of what VV describes "unrecalled past," the things that get left out provide scope for other narratives, which can be equally interesting and valuable. VV's version is based on his memory—the faltering memory of an old man; other versions could have other sources. All this implies that in historical accounts the mode and purpose of recording the past are of utmost importance. When VV tells Ganapathi that "History marched on, leaving only a few footprints on our pages. Of its deep imprints on other sands, you do not know because I do not choose to wash in the waters that have swept them away" (110), Tharoor draws attention to the selectivity of his version. It is significant that soon after he finishes his account, he feels dissatisfied with it, because he has told his story "from a completely mistaken perspective," and would like to retell it.

At another place, VV refers more specifically to the role of rhetoric in historical narratives. He tells Ganapathi that the flux of life is like a continuous, interminable wave; to capture it for posterity, we have to shape it, by visualizing it with a beginning and an end. The necessity for closure, which is "an arbitrary invention of the teller," in particular, separates life from art. This arbitrariness is essential if we want the account to yield knowledge, even though that may not always help shape the course of future history. He knows that knowledge is not wisdom, because it "suffers from the crippling defect of ephemerality. All knowledge is transient, linked to the world around it and subject to change as the world changes.... It is the fate of the wise to understand the process of history and yet never to shape it" (163). This partially accounts for the rewriting of history, so that it can become relevant to the times in which one lives. VV modestly claims that he is neither a wise man nor a philosopher; he is only a "chronicler and a participant in the events I describe" (163). But he insists on its truth-value, even though he knows that it is only a selective account, which is also suggested in a series of metaphors, which figure in a short poem about it: "...a slender filament,/A rubbing from a colossal monument"; full of "... colour and cast/A snip from a canvas impossibly vast"; "... recalled, words plucked from the crush" (164).

VV's final, clinching statement which ties up these different observations matches the boldness and spirit of Rushdie's views on the problematics of historical reconstructions:

> ...for every tale I have told you, every perception I have conveyed, there are a hundred equally valid alternatives I have omitted and of which you are unaware. I make no apologies for this. This is my story of India I know, with its biases, selections, omissions, distortions all mine.... Every Indian must for ever carry with him, in his head and heart, his own history of India (373).

This forceful statement captures the essence of the postmodernist thinking on the nature of historical discourse. It admits that history is provisional and plural, and provides for the validity of different versions of the past. It also points to the limitations of the historians, which come in the way of their producing full and total accounts, and closely resembles Rushdie's idea of the fragmentary nature of our perceptions. Interestingly, Tharoor, like Rushdie, also refers to the possibility of historical reconstructions touching the extreme slide into non-history: "How much may one select, interpret and arrange the facts of living past before truth is jeopardized by inaccuracy" (164)? However, this is only an extremist position; it does not inform the spirit of Tharoor's account of India's past. In fact, in spite of the awareness that Tharoor and Rushdie have of the problems of reconstructing the past and the provisional nature of the discourse itself, both are keen on giving their versions. These are the ones they know. They also have faith in the value of history.

That the tone and tenor of Tharoor's version of India's history is shaped by his consciousness of the historiographic contest is borne by the fact that it makes reference to earlier accounts, hagiographies as he calls them (1990, 16), which are indiscriminately laudatory in their evaluation of particular individuals, who had a part in India's struggle for freedom and its post-independence politics. His main complaint is against the ones which give too much importance to the role of Nehru. He is particularly unhappy with versions made current after Nehru's death by the Congress party, particularly by Mrs Gandhi. In the same vein, the narrative disapproves of the flattering estimates of Jayaprakash Narayan's abilities and his role during the emergency. However, the dissatisfaction with older accounts does not lead to any radical shift in his methodological apparatus or his historiographic stance, which could be considered a weakness of his version, too. He does not, for example, approach the story of India's freedom struggle through classes or groups which played a significant part in the national movement, but were overshadowed by leaders of higher stature. Like the accounts he censures, Tharoor's account is dominated by the leading lights of the day and is elitist in its approach.[7] This is confirmed by the choice of the model for writing his version; the *Mahabharata* too sidelines ordinary beings for heroic figures. It is difficult to say whether Tharoor's allegorical mode foreclosed his option or whether the choice of the model reflects his understanding of the essence of what happened in India's freedom struggle. Given what we have, all that we can say is that Tharoor's account is no more than an alternative version of the extant elitist versions. He implicitly criticizes them, because he thinks that they need to be redressed, to be cured of tilts and imbalances. However, though Tharoor recognizes the role of heroes in history, he neither romanticizes them, nor is he unduly deferential towards them: "...this is one memoir which will not conceal the crassness of its heroes. No more than it will be embarrassed by their greatness" (333).

Another interesting feature of Tharoor's pluralistic historiography is that he does not consider it a Western concept, though one can see that it bears close resemblance to what obtains there. He thinks that it is an offshoot of a peculiarly Indian phenomenon, which is both a source of strength and weakness of its people:

"How easily we Indians see the several sides to every question!" We give too much importance to discourse and relativism, and have an "instinctive awareness of the subjectivity of truth" (373).

Tharoor's account is also informed with a specific understanding of history, which could partially explain his preference for concentrating on key figures in India's past. He considers history a process of births and rebirths, caused by sudden changes, projecting thereby a kind of catastrophic view of history; for the "flowing dance of creation and evolution" is visualized by him not as a "tranquilizing wave of smoothly predictable occurrences," but as a series of "sudden events, unexpected happenings, dramas, crises, accidents, emergencies" (245). He explains this cataclysmic view with the help of a familiar metaphor: "This constant rebirth is never a simple matter of the future slipping bodily from the open womb of history. Instead there is rape, and violence, and a struggle to emerge or to remain, until circumstances bloodily push tomorrow through the parted, heaving legs of today" (245). Tharoor thinks that it is universally true and it holds the key to our learning about what is right and proper:

> This is as true of you or me as of Hastinapur, of India, of the world, of the cosmos. We are all in a state of continual disturbance, all stumbling and tripping and running and floating along from crisis to crisis. And in the process, we are all making something of ourselves, building a life, a character, a tradition that emerges from and sustains us in each succeeding crisis. This is our dharma (245).

Tharoor's historical account begins around the time when Gandhi established his presence on the Indian political scene. This was when colonialism had consolidated into a tyrannical system. In a short comment the narrator lays bare the inhumanity of the colonial ethics and the hollowness of the claims made for it by British historians and writers:

> [By] the simple logic of colonialism...the rules of humanity applied only to the rulers, for the rulers were people and the people were objects. Objects to be controlled, disciplined, kept in their place and taught lessons like so many animals: yes, the civilizing mission upon which Rudyard and his tribe were embarked made savages of all of us, and all of them (80).

The Jallianwallah Bagh massacre, which Tharoor calls the Bibigarh massacre to spite at the likes of Paul Scott, is described with cool irony, which matches the spirit of its description in *Midnight's Children*: "They loaded and fired their rifles coldly, clinically, without haste or passion or sweat or anger.... [The result was] a frozen tableau from a silent film, black and white and mute, an Indian *Guernica*" (80-81). The exploitative aspects of the British presence in India and its harmful effect on the economy has also been stressed: "...the British killed the Indian artisan, they created the Indian 'landless labourer,' they exported our full-employment and they invented our poverty" (95).

The Indian resistance against the British is seen mostly through the efforts of Gandhi. The narrative provides his compact and well-rounded portrait, with the intention of reviving his memory among the public. For Tharoor states that although Gandhi left behind a thoroughly documented life, almost like an open book, contemporary Indians have consigned him to the "mists and myths of historical legend"; with sarcastic wit, he remarks: "he might as well have been a character from *Mahabharata*" (47). He believes that Indians have failed to relate him to their lives, not merely because of the "bastard educational institutions the British sired on us," but also because the political system of the country promoted its own favourites by pinning the ones it did not like, including Gandhi, to concrete slabs. Through this ingenious mechanism, Gandhi was erased from the realm of cultural influence.

Gandhi is commemded for awakening public consciousness against the British by perfecting a system of non-violent struggle against their unjust exercise of power. As solid examples of Gandhi's triumph, he documents his charisma in Motihari, where he pushed the British to the defensive and forced them to see his point of view. The uniqueness and efficiency of his concept of truth, which entailed taking punishment willingly for the strength of one's convictions is thoroughly approved: "No dictionary imbues the word with the depth of meaning Gangaji gave it. His truth emerged from his convictions: it meant not only what was accurate, but what was just and therefore right. Truth could not be obtained by 'untruthful' or unjust, or violent means" (48). Gandhi's concept of non-violent struggle is praised not only for being worthy in itself, but also as a timely and effective method for fighting the British: "When sporadic terrorism and moderate constitutionalism had both proved ineffective, Ganga took the issue of freedom to the people as one of simple right and wrong—law versus conscience—and gave them a method to which the British had no response" (55). One of the significant aspects of Gandhi's campaign was that it brought ordinary men and women into the mainstream of the freedom struggle. With this mass base, the poor and the middle classes got "their place in the sun" and the concept of nationalism acquired a new orientation. The account also emphasizes that in spite of piquancies in Gandhi's style of functioning, he was a master strategist; though there was a great deal of drama and theatricality to his campaigns, which has been used to great comic effect, he gave the movement much-needed publicity in and outside India. The people, whom he made into a strong force, were convinced that "they were not led by a saint with his head in the clouds, but by a master tactician with his feet on the ground" (122).

Though the narrative praises Gandhi's role in India's struggle towards freedom, singling out in particular his honesty and steadfastness of purpose, it does not overlook the amusing aspects of this personality and thinking. Repeated attention is drawn to his numerous fads and his baggage from the past: enemas, sanitary preoccupations, fasts, love for the cow, etc. On account of the bewildering diversity of his reading—Vedas, Manu, Tolstoy, Ruskin, Bible, Gita—his dividing line between matters temporal and spiritual often became somewhat fuzzy: "His manner had grown increasingly other-worldly while his conversational obligations remained entirely mundane, and he would often startle his audiences with pronouncements which led them to wonder in which century he was living at any given moment" (26).

This aspect of Gandhi's thinking, in which he would lapse into the nebulosity of timelessness, has been severely censured by Anand, for being inimical to changes which were necessary for shaking Indians out of their fatalistic moorings. Tharoor's narrative draws attention to its other serious implications. Because of his deep-rooted grounding in the Hindu tradition, Gandhi consistently exploited Hindu symbols for galvanizing people against the British; this made the leaders of other communities conscious of the dangers of the rising tide of Hindu influence to their identity. It is true that at no place does the narrative suggest that Gandhi caused disaffection among the minorities, but makes it amply clear that it led to the alienation of political leaders like Jinnah. This eventually sharpened the sources of conflict between the Hindus and Muslims which led to the division of the country. Since several historians have expressed their uneasiness over this aspect of Gandhi's thinking and practice,[8] it is interesting to note how Tharoor couches the disapproval of Jinnah for Gandhi:

> Karna was not much of a Muslim but he found Gangaji too much of a Hindu. The Mahaguru's traditional attire, his spiritualism, his spouting of the ancient texts, his ashram, his constant harking back to an idealized pre-British past that Karna did not believe in ...all this made the young man mistrustful of the Great Teacher.... And Gangaji's mass politics were, to Karna, based on an appeal to the wrong instincts; they embodied an atavism that in his view would never take the country forward. A Kaurava Party of prayer-meetings and unselective eclecticism was not a party he would have cared to lead, let alone to remain a member of (142).

Jinnah's dislike of Gandhi's ways and thinking is quite well-known and has been widely documented. It is somewhat ironical that a person who fought all his life for Hindu-Muslim unity has to be made responsible for encouraging Muslim separatism, but this is implicit in Tharoor's understanding of Gandhi and of several historians too.

Tharoor's narrative unequivocally criticizes Gandhi for slackening his grip over the Congress party around the time of India's independence, when it was needed most. He thinks that Gandhi was wrong in letting the question of partition be decided by his lieutenants. That is why the scene of Gandhi's death in Tharoor's account is important; here the mythic charge is at its strongest. He lets Gandhi's murderer Shikhandin berate him for his dereliction of duty and also for neglecting the issue of leadership of the party. His words openly declare him a failure: "'You make me sick, Bhishma. Your life has been a waste, unproductive, barren. You are nothing but an impotent old walrus sucking other reptiles' eggs, an infertile old fool...a man who is less than a woman. The tragedy of this country springs from you..." (232). These are harsh words and cannot be taken lightly. Their import is reinforced by the words

Tharoor puts in the mouth of the dying leader. Instead of uttering "Hey Ram," as is commonly believed, he says: "I...have...failed."

The narrative picks actual words of various world leaders and famous people who spoke on the occasion of Gandhi's death. The narrator's comment suggests several causes for his death, in which both he and the people of the country are implicated. The overall tone confirms that he died a defeated and disillusioned man:

> I will not ask whether Amba/Shikhandin was truly responsible for the Mahaguru's death, or whether it was not India collectively that ended Gangaji's life by tearing itself apart. Nor will I ask you, Ganapathi, to reflect on whether Ganga Datta might in fact have been the victim of an overwhelming death-wish, a desire to end a life that he saw starkly as having served no purpose, a desire buried deep in the urge that led him, all those years earlier, to create and nurture his own executioner (234).

As a possible contender for the leadership of the Congress party, the narrative dwells on the vicissitudes of Subhash's career vis-a-vis his relationship with Gandhi. It praises his efforts in the cause of India's freedom, but also explains how he perished because of his quixotic dreams. Nevertheless, it is made clear that he lost the race for the leadership of the Congress party because Gandhi preferred Nehru over him. Tharoor's extremely negative estimate of Nehru's abilities and his role in the politics of pre- and post-independence India is suggested in the allegorical frame itself. As Dhritarashtra, he is made into Gandhi's "blind and visionary son," with a vaulting ambition and monumental ego. His English education comes in for special attack: it gave him only "a formidable vocabulary and the vaguely abstracted manner of the over-educated" (41). His blindness is used to a trenchant metaphoric effect: "...the blind man's gift of seeing the world not as it was, but as he wanted it to be" (85), made him completely out of tune with the reality around him. Even though he was absent from some of the most momentous events in Gandhi's struggle against the British, he succeeded in gaining importance when the fate of the country was about to be decided. The account also implicates him in the hasty deal of the partition of the country, by colluding with Mountbatten and his charming wife Edwina. It makes no secret of his amatory laison with her, and charges him with having failed to see that she was used by her husband as his "secret weapon" (215).

Tharoor holds that after taking charge of the affairs of independent India, Nehru bungled the Kashmir issue and showed extreme shortsightedness in taking it to the United Nations. He is also charged with having mastered the "technique of self-perpetuation" by issuing periodic threats of resignation (261). His major policies also come in for attack. Nehru's emphasis on setting up big and heavy industries in the country was ill conceived, because it ignored the unpleasant reality that eighty percent people were without basic amenities of life, such as drinking water, shelter, and electricity; it was wrong to concentrate too much on building institutions of higher learning, because they only turned out products for the international market, and ignored the huge forests of illiteracy which covered vast regions of the country. The setting up of the huge centralised and cumbersome machinery of parliamentary democracy proved ineffective because "parliament passed laws that a few implemented and many ignored." Considering that we have already begun to doubt the efficacy of the Nehruvian model of economic development and that the authority of the state in redressing social and economic imbalances has proved ineffective, there is a great deal of truth in Tharoor's attack on Nehruvian policy and performance.

Tharoor's main complaint against Nehru is that at the cost of neglecting the needs of his country, he directed his energies towards gaining recognition in international fora. He worked for promoting non-alignment without estimating whether the country was strong and powerful enough to give it any meaningful credibility. In a sarcastic tone, the narrator states that he and his friend Menon "developed into a fine art the skill of speaking for the higher conscience of mankind," though "neither could control the convictions or even the conduct of those who were to implement their policies" (295). This is reflected most conspicuously in his failure on the foreign front, when the country had to suffer military humiliation at the hands of China. This broke his heart and hastened his death.

I have already pointed out that Tharoor's version of the political history of India is the result of his dissatisfaction with earlier versions, especially the ones with laudatory evaluations of Nehru. By concentrating solely on deficiencies in Nehru's person and policies, his version touches the other extreme and lacks the balance one finds in his portrait of Gandhi. If the earlier estimates of Nehru were fired by excesses of one kind, Tharoor's is characterized by excesses of another kind. It is one of complete selective condemnation. The only credit Nehru gets is that he was not guilty of meanness or villiany. When he is advised by his ministers to deal with his political adversaries according to the tenets of Kautilya's *Arthasastra*, he does not accept it.

In Tharoor's allegorical design, Indian democracy, represented in the person of Draupadi, has a mixed parentage: she is the product of the illicit union of Nehru and Edwina, which is meant to suggest that India came into being because of their unholy alliance. Through her marriage to Arjun, Draupadi is shared by his other brothers, who personify "the hopes and the limitations of each of the national institutions they served" (319). During Nehru's tenure, her health remained stable, but started deteriorating after his death, especially during the time of Mrs Gandhi. The narrative records how after the short spell of Shishu Pal's tenure in office, the elders chose Mrs Gandhi to lead the party, mainly because they thought her pliable. But very soon she turned into a menacingly arrogant person, and threatened the very fabric of the democratic structure of the country.

Tharoor prepares the readers for a negative portrait of Mrs Gandhi through a piece of well-conceived anticipation, in which he uses animal imagery to suggest the brutality and oppression of her times:

> [Her birth-cry] is a rare, sharp, high-pitched cry like that of a donkey in heat, and as it echoed around the house a sound started up outside as if in response, a weird, animal moan, and then the sounds grew, as donkeys brayed in the distance, mares neighed in their pens, jackals howled in the forests, and through the cacophony we heard the beatings of wings at the windows, the caw-caw-cawing of a cackle of crows, and penetrating through the shadows, the piercing shriek of the hooded vultures circling above the palace of Hastinapur (73).

At first, Mrs Gandhi tried to entrench herself by carrying out a series of populist measures, such as the abolition of privy purses and the nationalisation of banks, which made hardly any difference to the people in general. Later, she promoted the culture of slogans, which replaced policies. Tharoor blames the left and progressive forces in the country, including recognized political parties, for being taken in by her rhetoric and bluster. In her own party, she reduced even cabinet ministers into non-entities. Her return to power made her more arrogant and dictatorial in her style of functioning. She succeeded in arrogating to herself the power to "prohibit, proscribe, profane, prolate, prosecute or prostitute all the freedoms the national movement had brought to attain..." (357). Events took on a dizzy turn when, after the Allahabad High Court judgment, she declared a state of emergency in the country, which proved the most disastrous part of her tenure. It is interesting as well as significant that the emergency has been considered by the Indian English novelists as the most traumatic event of post-independence India. Sahgal devotes a whole novel to the emergency to dramatize its effect on the general ethos of the country. In Rushdie, it becomes the focal point of the degradation in the political and secular character of the country, which leads him to postulate two different kinds of India's past. In Tharoor's account, it is a part of the deteriorating democratic culture of the country, because of which the blame on Mrs Gandhi is not as pronounced as in the other two.

Tharoor understands the emergency in its very immediate context, when it was declared by Mrs Gandhi. He is critical of her decision, but also blames the people whose attacks pushed her into taking the extreme step, especially Jayaprakash Narayan, who launched a full-scale movement against her. Though he concedes that arrests and censorship and other repressive measures taken by her were "primarily cynical and self-serving," he adds that "I still believed that the political chaos in the country, fuelled by Drona's idealistic but confused uprising which a variety of political opportunists had joined and exploited, could have led the country nowhere but to anarchy" (369).[9] In this, Tharoor's thinking is different from that of Sahgal and Rushdie. In fact, his scepticism about the worth of the people who combined against her is reflected in his comment on their coming to power: "The Indian people gave themselves the privilege of replacing a determined, collected tyrant with an indeterminate collection of tyros" (402).

Tharoor's views on the emergency and the people who fought against Mrs Gandhi stem from his estimate of the character and abilities of Jayaprakash Narayan. The narrative gives him his due by documenting in detail how he was far away from the taint of power and made strenuous efforts for raising the consciousness of the people by educating them about their rights and duties; he provided moral support to the protecting pillars of Indian democracy, but his complicated thinking proved his undoing.

In spite of the praise showered on him after his death, in which he was compared with Gandhi, the narrator makes a mixed comment:

> ...he was a flawed Mahaguru, a man whose goodness was not balanced by the shrewdness of the original. He had stood above his peers, a secular saint whose commitment to truth and justice was beyond question. But though his loyalty to the ideals of a democratic and egalitarian India could not be challenged, Drona's abhorrence of power had him unfit to wield it. He had offered inspiration but not involvement, charisma but not change, hope but no harness. Having abandoned politics when he seemed the likely heir-apparent to Dhritarashtra, he tried to stay above it all after the fall of Dhritarashtra's daughter, and so let the revolution he had wrought fall into the hands of lesser men who were unworthy of his ideals (409).

With the coming to power of Mrs Gandhi, the narrative brings to an end the story of India's political vicissitudes. Its thrust is to suggest Tharoor's disillusionment with the country's declining political culture. Its institutional structures, such as the press, bureaucracy, and party system have not done much in promoting any meaningful change in the country. Tharoor makes us believe that the Indian people in general have perfected the art of living with whatever they get, strengthening their vestiges of fatalism. He visualizes a bleak future for the country. This partially explains why people have become obsessive about their past. For some it is a source of power; for others a comfortable retreat.

The Eunuch Voice of History: Vijayan's *The Saga of Dharmapuri*

In his analysis of the historical works of the nineteenth-century Europe, Hayden White plots a position in his schematic chart where the representation of history moves from "processionary, or diachronic history to structural or synchronic history," by which he means that "the element of theme tends to override the element of plot, at least insofar as plot may be conceived to be a strategy by which an unfolding is articulated" (1975, 230). This is best represented by Burckhardt, in whose accounts

> things did not develop [but], coalesced to form a fabric of greater or lesser brilliance and intensity, greater or lesser freedom or oppression, more or less movement...there was no progressive evolution in artistic sensibility, and in the end nothing but oppression stemmed from political and religious impulses. The truths taught by history were melancholy ones. They led neither to hope nor to action (1975, 230).

Historical representations of this kind, White writes, are informed by irony and satire. When we accept the possibility of historical accounts being structured on the mythoi of irony and satire, one of the four major structures in Frye's schema of plots, then it is not difficult to visualize that novelists too can deal with history through the satirical mode. Though there is a strong streak of satire in Tharoor's recreation of the history of 20th-century India in *The Great Indian Novel*, it lacks most of the essential formal features of satirical works. Vijayan's *The Saga of Dharmapuri* has them in full measure, which makes it a better example of a writer's intervention into history through the mode of satire.

Since White uses Frye's theory of mythoi for explaining and understanding the satirical mode of historical representations, it is appropriate that we begin with Frye to delineate the formal features of satirical compositions. Satire, in his view, can be best approached as a parody of the mode of romance. A romance is structured around a protagonist, who is cast generally in heroic proportions (Frye 187). His major and minor adventures, in which he fights human and superhuman beings for upholding cherished values and ideals, constitute its main action. In the process, he may live or die; in both cases, he affirms a positive vision of society. Satire is a parody of this process. The protagonist in satire can either be a cruel or tyrannical person, whose oddities and perversities are exposed by the satirist, or a victim, whose sufferings at the hands of the cruel forces of society make these exposures possible.

The satirist may also employ other kinds of sophisticated personae for his plan of exposures.[10] Because the primary objective in satire is to expose and ridicule, it projects a world which is characterized by ugliness, cruelty, and oppression, and is peopled mostly by embodiments of reprehensible qualities. Even when the protagonists in it go through minor and major adventures, there may not be any linear progression in them. The scenes and episodes connected with them only fill out the picture of a society which the writer finds degraded and perverted. Focussing on an individual or a group, a tendency or a situation, or a crisis-point in a nation's history, which he considers a deviation from what is normal or desirable, a satirist chooses any mixture of the modes of realism and fantasy to attack and expose them. He makes use of time-tried techniques of satire, such as exaggeration in detail, caricature in the presentation of characters, different shades of grotesquery, and militant humour and irony. Used singly or together, they cause dislocations in the customary logic of the narrative. The satirist also uses a special kind of language and imagery, which Frye calls "demonic," for sharpening his sense of disapproval of the things he castigates. When a writer's understanding of the past, represented through people, situations, or tendencies is realized through the mediation of the satiric codes, in contrast with the mimetic codes, we get a satirical representation of the past. He may also use wild fancy to create extraordinary beings and beasts, as Swift does in *Gulliver's Travels* or Anatole France in *The Penguin Island*.[11] Vijayan's mode of representation does not touch such fanciful heights, though there are strong Swiftian elements in his work.

When a writer refracts history through the satiric lense to express his disapproval of or dissatisfaction with a particular moment, tendency, or period from the past, he lets his narrative shrink to its minimal core, to provide for a corresponding expanded thematic core, to deal with his subject in its wholeness and complexity. Whatever semblance of narrative progression there is, does not lead to any significant movement forward, for the scenes and episodes which constitute the plot of satire, which is generally disjointed, are in effect repetitive in their essence; they only help dramatize the patterns of grossness the satirist wants to attack. Since his primary object is to produce the desired emotional response of disgust and anger and promote a specific kind of understanding among the readers, satire is the most rhetorical of art forms.

As a satirist, Vijayan is concerned mainly with aspects of our social and political past which are characterized by oppression and the institutional forms that support it, such as the dictatorial leanings of *de jure* and *de facto* power-elites. In *The Great Indian Novel*, Tharoor demonstrated that the social and political reality in India can spawn dictators even within supposedly democratic structures. The frightful aspects of such possibilities have been concretely dramatized by Vijayan in "The Foetus," one of the four stories in a group called "Allegories of Power." The foetus symbolizes the "new sovereign," who works out a new pattern of relationship with his people, which is different from what obtained in the past. When it moves out of the precincts of his palace, it turns into dirty slime whatever comes into its contact. For its continued survival, it destroys all possibilities of new life by blocking every conceivable source of renewal and regeneration. With its coercive apparatus, it moulds people into submissive automatons. All this is described in a language charged with menace:

> With misshapen hands the foetuses [grown from the big foetus] now began to massage the men's temples and foreheads, as though rubbing in a lethal unction. *Submit*, said an unspoken and monstrous command, *We vamparize your Revolution, we vamparize your historical memory*. The captives winced in pain. The insistent message went on, *We want your Revolution's fullblooded wenches whom we shall deflower for the New Order* (Vijayan 1989, 36).

The New Order is a tyrannical order. For its very existence, it needs to finish off all traces of possible alternative orders and the historical memory of the people. Together they spell the death of a nation. The monstrous features of this new order, which quells everything that comes in its way, and its fearsome consequences have been dealt with in detail in *The Saga*, within the framework of a concrete historical situation from our recent past.

The motive force for the happenings in *The Saga* comes from a number of tendencies in the body-politic of India, which reached their nadir during the times of Mrs Gandhi, when she declared a state of emergency in 1975. It is somewhat ironic that degradation in the social and political fabric of the country should have touched an all-time low during her time, because she was the one who should have understood best the disastrous import of her actions. In one of his letters to her from his prison during the 1930s, Nehru had written to her that the most cherished moments in the history of a nation are those when ordinary people stir out of their shells and cocoons to take part in larger social action, giving it a new direction and character (Nehru iii-iv). This had happened in India in 1920s and 30s, when there was national awakening among people on a massive scale, and history was at its processionary best. Vijayan thinks that the emergency turned into a moment which was the very opposite of this. It made people withdraw into their shells; every household turned into an island; the voice of love and reason turned mute; and slogans supplanted the spontaneous depths of response. For this reason, Vijayan calls it the "Eunuch voice of history." If the first voice, articulated by Nehru, is one of joy and celebration, because people have overcome one of their greatest enemies in fear, the second is of sadness and sorrow, because they submit to what is repressive and unhealthy. The first foregrounds courage and bravery; the second cowardice and servility. *The Saga* is a dramatization of this voice in history, which is both horrifying and depressing, and, therefore, condemnable. Although the moment is crystallized in the emergency, its roots go back into time. Vijayan catches the moment at its worst, lays bare its repulsive aspects, and invites his readers to share his hatred of this dismal experience. The implicit point here is that in a society where people live in a state of dread and bondage and their exploitation at the hands of the state touches abysmal depths, we cannot have history, as it should be, we can only hear its eunuch voice.

For understanding this moment in its fullness, Vijayan locates it in the larger framework of a post-colonial society, suggesting thereby that this possibility is latent in all such societies. In this respect, the kingdom of Samarkhand, the other post-colonial society invoked in the book, and Dharmapuri are alike, for they derive their existence from the same colonial past. Vijayan also suggests that this voice has been heard even outside these societies, in other parts of the world, though there its character has been different. But its effect has been the same everywhere. When this voice is in the ascendant, oppression, destruction, and devastation are justified in the name of reason; sometimes, even values like patriotism are invoked to legitimise them. Vijayan believes that it was this voice which created Auschwitz and Warsaw ghettos, helped the rise of Hitler, and led to the "flaming orgasm of the apocalypse" in Hiroshima and Nagasaki. It has been heard "Time after time, in country after country...is repeated, and the old man with the toothless whimper pleads in vain, the child from the far depths of the city cries out in vain."[12] When Rushdie stated in *Shame* that his novel had both a specific and general character, he meant to suggest that civil and military dictators were not unique to Pakistan; they could be found anywhere. The same could be said about *The Saga.* Although it treats of a significant period in Indian history, it could apply to any post-colonial society, and to other societies, too. Through these layers of expanded contexts, Vijayan treats it as a recurrent historical tendency, which lets loose the forces of unreason and lust, and causes pain and suffering to the common people.

The title of the novel clarifies that its central focus is on Dharmapuri— its subjects and its political structure headed by the President. With its traces in folklore and a rich tradition of ethical correctness, it may have an air of antiquity about it, but within its specific historical location, which is established right in the beginning, it is actually a deviation from that. Contrary to what its rulers claim, Dharmapuri is neither rooted in its indigenous past, nor is it actuated by anything like ethical correctness. Its very description disproves its assumed character: "Feringhee Empire's freed colony" (15). Though it has the semblance of a free country, it is in effect a colony. Through its institutional structures, it continues to be controlled by outside powers. Even after becoming free, it chose to retain the entire coercive apparatus of its colonial masters,[13] though for fulfilling the "need to improvise selfhood and historical antecedents," it gave these institutions new respectable names. Vijayan's militant irony condemns this spurious game of renaming. It not merely indicates that freedom has led only to trivial surface changes, which are inconsequential, but also confirms that the authoritarian tendencies which erupted in their ugliest form during the emergency were a natural consequence of the political framework the country chose to retain after it became free. The description of these changes is full of satiric humour:

> ...armies changed overnight into Congregations of Persuaders, and the murderous encounters with neighbouring countries, which took place ever so often, were designated the Sorrows of Dharmapuri. Rabble-rousers and storm troopers, who, during the days of Empire, had done the state small-time violence, now called themselves Partisans and banded into the Convention of the Holy Spirit and took over the governance of the new republic (15).

Through the same exercise, "bark [like khadi] became a fetish of patriotism" and the ideology of the state, in line with its "spiritual predication" [non-alignment and peaceful co-existence] was represented by the celestial birds, after the famous legend of Shakuntala, who had been fed by the shakuntas in the forest. Vijayan is implying that the state is a victim of empty formalism.

Dharmapuri's state of servitude is suggested both by its retention of the oppressive colonial baggage and by the close watch of two super-powers: the Red Tartar Republic ruled by the Communard party and The White Confederacy, a loose capitalist world of the West. Their spies, who have their secret places in the President's court, surface only when the country does not follow the direction set by them; their newspapers monitor developments in Dharmapuri to ensure that their political and economic interests do not suffer.

Dharmapuri is also completely dependent on the two superpowers for arms supplies and economic aid. At the time of leaving the country, the colonizers had left behind "costume kits and obsolete weapons," which it accepted with pride. Its armouries "were replenished regularly by the White Confederacy." With trenchant irony, Vijayan states that because of its "spiritual predication" Dharmapuri had no military budget, only a budget for Sorrowing and Persuading" which made it "the most pacific nation on earth." The economy of Dharmapuri is also manipulated indirectly by "confederate trading houses." As signposts of neo-colonialism, they flourish because of their proximity to power-elites of such countries. That is why the business houses are headed by people close to the family of the President. Since Vijayan disapproves of these neo-imperialist manipulations, he describes the visit of the President's progeny to one of the power-centres in the most repulsive, excremental imagery:

> ...in defiance of the hypocrisies of protocol, [they] waylaid the stewards even before the banquet had formally begun, and seized the food with whoops of delight.... As the chase for food got under way, one of the presidential offspring shat in the excitement of pursuit and circled the banquet table with a trail of slime. Then another shat, and yet another; soon the whole brood followed suit. Their indulgent grandsire, meanwhile, fed avidly on a steak, until unable to hold it inside him, he opened his sluices as well; presently he was sitting on a sumptuous cushion of excrement...(20-21).

Vijyan makes a consistent use of scatology as a satiric device. At one time, when the President, who is arrogant and authoritarian and changes his ministers with the same rapidity with which he changes his concubines, shamelessly falls at the feet of a newspaper reporter from one of the superpowers, pleading with him not to send dispatches which might threaten his position, Vijayan denounces his abject surrender by connecting it with excrement. Prostrating before the reporter "threw his [President's] behind into relief. The sight of that behind, with its scab of excrement, terrified the Imperialist" (116).

The President of Dharmapuri, in a way, typifies the servile soul of the new nation. Vijayan associates some of the most unpleasant qualities with him, so that his depravities are thrown into bold relief. There is concentrated focus on his main activities, which consist of eating, defecating, and sleeping with his concubines. The functioning of the state is tied to the punctuality of his bowel-movement and the satisfactory working of his genitals. This is suggested most repulsively by puffing up his act of daily defecation into a national ritual, which is covered with ceremony. On it depends the health and activity of the people. It is also linked with the "rhythm of sovereign nationhood" because it activates the "broadcasting network" and the "national anthem." What the President throws out becomes the seismograph of the nation, and is commented upon elaborately by the national and international press. For the people of Dharmapuri, it is "sovereign excrement," partaken gladly by young and old. People evolve elaborate strategies to procure it and the press usually carries pictures of the fortunate few "excrement-venerators."

The extensive focus on President's genitals and his fornications with concubines, from kitchen-maids to the wives of his ministers, is significant because Vijayan uses sex as a metaphor for domination and subjugation. The details of President's promiscuous sex with men and women are meant to project their loveless aspect. Vijayan also uses them to symbolize his dictatorial yearnings. His excessive indulgence also suggests that it is a perversity. The important point here is that the pleasures of the body, such as eating, drinking, and sex, which stand for freedom and liberation in folk traditions, to which Dharmapuri claims to aspire, are made by Vijayan into symptoms of oppression and perversion. Indulgence in *The Saga* does not indicate freedom and joy, as it does in the Carnivalesque celebrations in Rabelais, but cruelty and subjugation.

Another aspect to it is that though the President of Dharmapuri and the Prime Minister of Samarkhand subjugate others, they, in turn, are subjugated by the powers on whom they depend. If the two political heads sleep with the wives of other people, their wives too have to sleep with the White Confederates. One of the concubines of the Prime Minister of Samarkhand has a true vision of her country, and this, as I have already suggested, is true of Dharmapuri too: "The vision of her nation as a pimp, its armed legions and its flying machines and flotillas, its spies and prosecutors and judges, its convocations, protocols and glittering ceremony, all the many arms of a pimp-god, made the concubine sad" (69). This suggests effectively that the newly-freed colonies continue to be in a state of bondage, their decorous trappings of freedom hiding their deep servility.

After establishing the true character of Dharmapuri and its sovereign head, Vijayan puts the main action of the book within a specific historical context by stating that the President has been disturbed by "distant stellar presences," because of which he is "gripped by colic." This is an indirect reference to the confusion in government circles in India soon after Mrs Gandhi's election was questioned by the Allahabad High Court. To get over it, the President, on the advice of his ministers, makes a proclamation, which Vijayan describes in repulsive imagery: "The President bent forward and crowed, and out came a turd as big as a sewer rat; and with that was promulgated what came to be known as the State of

Crisis" (22). The state of crisis is in actuality the state of emergency declared by Mrs Gandhi in June 1975, when she told the people that forces inside and outside the country were working to destabilise it. Vijayan's description captures the essence of the reasons given by the government at that time:

> The news was broadcast that the country was besieged by the Enemy, and that neither sea nor mountain were defence enough.... 'My beloved people,' the President said in a midnight broadcast, 'give me your freedoms, henceforth let them be hidden inside me, because it is to rob you of these that the insidious enemy has penetrated us' (23).

Vijayan records that the decision of the President, like that of Mrs Gandhi, was endorsed by the official organ of the Communard Republic, Prava: "'Dharmapuri has done away with the last obstacle which Imperialism had left in the way of liberation, the Law of Habeas Corpus. Now Dharmapuri joins those who march in the grand parade of human progress.'" Inside the country, it was supported by the Communists, who "welcomed these abridgements of rights with a fervour...the Communards recalled the Great Tartar Purges and rejoiced in the comparison."[14]

Vijayan exposes the President and his cohorts by building into the narrative a dichotomy between the real and stated motives for declaring the state of crisis. Although the President justified his action by telling the people that the country was threatened, Vijayan clarifies that the real reason was his dread that the sins of his past actions would recoil on him, the "past with its shame of pimping and vagrancy, demagogy and terrorism, and the frenetic pursuit of food" (22). All this made him fear for his safety. In this short description, Vijayan hints at the diseased political structure of the times of Mrs Gandhi, characterized by extra-constitutional authoritarianism, rabble-rousing techniques of manipulating public opinion, and a shameful lust for power.

Within the framework of a country which is sovereign only in name and has been plunged into a state of crisis, which has given its ruling clique more powers than they would normally enjoy, Vijayan builds in *The Saga* a series of scenes, some of them bordering on the surreal, to dramatize the cruelty and oppression implicit in the new order. These are scenes of bondage, pain, suffering, exploitation, and callous misuse of power. The implicit point made is that in such times the history of a nation ceases to be normal: the voice of the people is neither effective nor meaningful. That is why he calls it the eunuch voice of history. In order to ensure unequivocal condemnation of the sordid reality that these scenes suggest, they have been rendered in a frightfully exaggerated mode.

Dharmapuri is in a state of pain because its political structure has been instrumental in causing a large scale disruption in the lives of its people. This is suggested by the fact that all the able-bodied men have been posted on hills and mountains to lie in wait for the enemies of the country. Vijayan's point here is that militarisation in post-colonial societies is not a national necessity, but a political compulsion, which is intimately connected with their character. It serves the interests of their masters, the superpowers, by providing them markets for their hardware; for the local power-groups it is an effective strategy for containing possible forces of dissent and confrontation. Because of this, wars between post-colonial societies do not figure in regular military manuals. In the words of the Prime Minister of Samarkhand, these are the "war[s] of togetherness." "'If we launch this war,'" he tells one of his concubines, "'the ensuing tide of patriotism in both the countries will greatly strengthen the respective regimes'" (69). In such wars, both the warring countries are winners: "'In Samarkhand I win, and in Dharmapuri, its President'"; the losers are the soldiers who die on both sides and the people who have to face the resultant hardships. That is why the womenfolk live in a state of perpetual gloom. Whenever ruling regimes feel insecure, they make efforts to "tap the reservoirs of patriotism." Public opinion is manipulated so skilfully and propaganda keyed to such an effective level that even the perpetually-suffering people are taken in by official versions. When the President of Dharmapuri declares war against its neighbour for his own survival, he arranges "garish exhibitions" of "Persuaders' corpses, embalmed and resplendent with medals. On gilded platforms sat the live exhibits: heroic orphans, naked and jewelled widows." On seeing them, "the people looked on and lusted for war"; women "lusted for widowhood"; men "lusted about their wives whoring in the cages." And thus "in the mystique of the State, men and women chanted, they clapped and sang and danced around the exhibits, living and dead" (150).

Apart from this potential threat of war, the general condition of Dharmapuri, which has been aggravated by the state of crisis, is such that the life of an average citizen has become vulnerable and risky. Individual liberty is under perpetual threat and law-enforcing agencies have turned into machines for exploiting people. These are best illustrated in the travails of Laavanya and her son Sunanda. She loses her husband to the mountains and her own self to the defence minister of the country who, interestingly, shares several striking similarities with Krishna Menon. Like him, the former had a long sojourn in Feringheeland, had delivered a seven-hour long speech in the Assembly of Nations, and had pronounced communist leanings. When she learns one day that her husband had come to see her in her absence, and had been arrested and put in prison, she leaves her home to look for him along with her son. The moment they are on the road, they are besieged by spies, arrested, and taken for interrogation. Since the officers, like their President, exercise their authority over people by laying claim over their bodies, they attempt to rape her. Her resistance is interpreted as treason, because her actions have frustrated the servants of the state. Finding no way of escape from her situation, she speaks to her son in words charged with irony: "'Whatever your mother is doing is for the country, and countries make demands that are often inscrutable to their citizens'" (38).

When Laavanya mentions to the officer her connection with the minister, there is a dramatic transformation in his ways. He apologises for his behaviour and lets her go. But the traps in her way are so many that even the ministerial connection cannot save her from harm. When she goes to the House of Healing to get medicine for her sick son, she is caught by the police and made to prove her innocence by disrobing herself. Because she expresses anger against this treatment, she is raped in public by the custodians of law; the crowd participates in the act through gasps and by cheering the rapists. Her son connects the shame of the moment with the suffering people of the past: "He was blotting out the sight of aggregation and violence, the relentless repetition of which has made the history of man" (60).

The journey of Laavanya and her son inside the tunnel is like a journey into the hellish underworld. It includes several nightmarish scenes, which dramatize exploitative acts of the most bizarre kind. For the political bosses and its corrupt administrative machinery, the tunnel provides a safe cover for processing "preserved cadaver" which is exported to the white confederate countries for earning foreign exchange; this is used for paying the medical bills of ministers and soldiers who get themselves treated abroad. The cadavers are generally of the poor and the lowly, who either die for want of proper medical aid or are forced to sell off their bodies because they find it difficult to support them. Since Vijayan implicates the government and its communist friends for promoting such trade, he censures the practice by offering an ingeniously perverse interpretation of the concept of surplus value: "This brilliant harnessing of gains for eventual use in the struggle of the people is called Surplus Value" (64). Later, the government uses cadavers for manufacturing new appetizing foods for export and for secret use in the Presidential palace. Since people who come to the tunnel for medical help generally end up as cadavers, Laavanya and her son see men, women, and children "drawn in calisthenics of despair, and the ululation of primordial sorrow" (62-63). They also witness another fearful sight, in which the concept of class war takes on a vicious and dehumanizing aspect, when an attendant mounts the inert body of a beautiful woman only because she had been the daughter of a merchant. This makes the "menacing dusk of the tunnel [grow] dense with funereal lust" (62).

A number of scenes in the book condemn the methods of the dictator for quelling popular discontent, particularly after the state of crisis. They are a clear exposure of the situation in India during the emergency. The President has reduced the ministers to abject servitude; their appointments and dismissals are linked with the changing whims of his concubines. To suggest how spineless they are, the minister of sorrowing has the "grotesque coyness of a whore" (124). When the media interprets changes in ministerial portfolios by the president as calculated and sagacious moves, Vijayan describes "the elaborate and learned commentaries on the event" sarcastically as "printed excresence" (80). Besides, in the charged atmosphere of the post-crisis era, the President adds to the columns of secret agents, who always report to him not what was happening, but what they felt he wanted to hear. This too is reminiscent of the role of the secret agencies in the times of Mrs Gandhi. "'My Lord,'" says one of the Agents to the President: "'the people revel in their prosperity, and the Birds minister to the destitutes....'"[15] The media and the press are silenced and official propaganda is strengthened to justify the gains of the new dispensation and hide the infirmities of the President.[16] The worm inside him, which symbolizes these infirmities, is covered up by his wily minister of figures, Shakuni, whose very name resonates treachery and deceit. He assures the President that adequate measures would be taken to let the official view prevail: "'There will be no street gossip, our police will take care of that; no newspapers will write about it. And you can, meanwhile, get the scribes to produce volumes of commemoration, hide-bound and gilded, and cast your likeness in bronze; behind all that historical rubble your worm will find refuge'" (133).

Through several other sights of pain and suffering, which are meant to contrast with the ones projected by the establishment, Vijayan suggests the sordid picture of living in Dharmapuri. These include scenes of destitution in which a young boy is forced to sell newspapers because of indigence and need. The same need pushes another person into selling his parents and children. Dharmapuri is also full of waifs and stragglers, who invite the attention of the White press. When its reporters write about them, the so-called patriotic forces in the country come together to demonstrate against them. One of the most frightful scenes in the book is about a young boy who is declared a traitor and a spy of imperialism by a furious mob. The impact of the mob-fury is so strong that even the parents, brothers and sisters of the boy ask for his blood. The judges who should ordinarily have investigated the charges against him, only confirm the "wisdom" of the crazy crowd and pronounce him guilty. The cry for his death is so strong and powerful that even when a "primordial cry rose within the mother, My son! My son!...its syllables, chiselled by the pervasive evil, came out as the chant of slogans" (110). Vijayan exposes the inhumanity of this new culture of slogans, and its baneful effect of destroying all conceivable possibilities of sensible discourse on anything.

I have already discussed how Vijayan attacks the communists for supporting the government in Dharmapuri during the state of crisis and exposes the perversities in their theoretical apparatus and their cherished concepts, such as the class war and surplus value. In one particular episode, he exposes their aspirations, too. This is when they seek to establish a more purposeful relationship with the Red Tartar Republic (the former Soviet Union) with whom they "practised the ancient regimen of historical and dialectical sorcery" (51). In their bid to play the game of oneupmanship they take a delegation to Tartarland to show their solidarity with their comrades-in-arms. But all that they get from them are truncheon-blows, because the white communards looked upon them as a batch of parasites who "had come to lay hands on the Revolution's white bread and pork chops" (53). They are made to flee, give up their delusory dreams, and ordered to demonstrate their solidarity with the government in Dharmapuri by partaking of the presidential excrement. This started a "new era of Eucharistic togetherness...between the Communards and the Presidency" (54). It is both a confirmation and a criticism of the role of the Russians and communists during the emergency.

In order to emphasize the strength and power of the oppressive system, Vijayan includes in the book two episodes of rebellion against the political set up of the state, which end disastrously. They have no apparent basis in actuality, but function as metaphors to confirm what was true: that the forces of resistance in the country had been rendered weak and ineffective. The first episode, though meant to suggest the possibility that in the "slow cycles of endurance there comes now and again an unexpected pinnacle of imperious power"(89), which may hold promise of change, is actually ironical, because it is far from hopeful. It has the trappings of a miraculous dream, which ends in tragedy. Even a dream cannot yield anything meaningful, when the forces of evil are in command. Inventing "the Night of the Bondsman," when actions and instruments of the class in power go dead, Vijayan provides an opportunity for the people to do whatever they liked, but this does not bear any fruit.

In this miraculous night, Vaatsena breaks himself free from his prison walls. But he finds that there are many more prisons outside, which he could never have imagined. This is no metaphysical intimation, only historical knowledge. For these were "prisons of free men," which did not need guards and soldiers. Some people were in prisons of servitude, and some in prisons of authority. He sees the wielders and victims of power in a state of bondage, though, in actuality, there is a difference in their relative condition. Since Vaatsena considers the wielders of power the cause of the prisons of servitude, he decides to destroy them. He hurls imprecations against the President who is always found on "his pile of dung"; he curses his dead father for pursuing policies which reeked of his lust for power and for neglecting the poor: "...while you postured and preened, my class, deprived of nutrients for their bodies, begat blind progeny" (91). Condemning him in the strongest possible terms, he addresses his statue: "...had you a living body, I would have shorn your genitals from it and destroyed your seed, because those that exercise power over their fellow-creatures have no right to procreate, nor do they deserve a requiem when they are gone" (91). His anger and rage turn his mind back to the suffering of his people, epitomized in the recurring image of the blind girl Kanchanmala. She stands for all those children of the state who were born blind because their mothers could not get enough to eat.

When Kanchanmala meets Vaatsena, she urges him to meet the Mendicant and free him from his prison, as a possible hope for fighting repression in the state. The Mendicant had fought the Feringhees with his unique weapon of non-violence, but had been imprisoned by his own people. This is a clear reference to Gandhi who organized people to fight the British. His imprisonment is meant to suggest that he had steadily gone out of the sphere of influence in the governance of the country. Later, when we are told that he has been killed, it implies that the possibility of his making a comeback in the political and cultural domain of the state has been lost forever.

Vaatsena's search for the Mendicant gets slowed down because he runs into another young girl, a victim of the brutality of the police and the proletariat. She had ben removed from a hermitage along with some hermits and her companions. The hermits had been imprisoned and the companions taken away by the police. She had been raped, even though she knew no lust, and was now hiding for her life. After soothing her, Vaatsena heads towards the prison of the Mendicant, but by that time the miraculous night has worn off. His bruised and cold body is found outside the prison gate in the early hours of the morning. The officials pick it up and examine it clinically; not finding it fit for export, they despatch it to the nearest soap factory. The scene is meant to reinforce the pervasiveness of the gloom that characterizes the world of suffering. Even though armed with will and purpose to fight the enemy, all that Vaatsena can do is to rant ineffectively against the tokens of tyranny. His aspiration to move towards liberation is thwarted at every step. What he finally gets for his efforts is an early death.

Another incident, though somewhat different in character, relates to the minister of defence of Dharmapuri who resolves to shake off his servitude and work for freeing the people from their tyrant master by organizing a rebellion against him. He succeeds in persuading people and soldiers to join him for spreading the new wave of awareness, which had already been initiated by Siddhaartha, who had come into the country from outside to make the people see the evil they were living with. He even arrests the defence minister who had replaced him and forces him to order his soldiers to leave their positions in the hills and stop fighting for the President. But his efforts do not yield any tangible result because the President uses to good effect the old technique of rallying the people in support of the state by declaring a new war. Since this works like a potent drug, the efforts of the minister end in vain. To his deep distress, he saw that "The soldiers whom he had freed were coming back to battle. For the President! They had left their women and children behind; war called them back to the trenches like a regressive and obscene vice. They found shelter in the trenches, and the ant and the worm waited once again in the marts of death" (146).

Thus we see that the scenes of nightmare and bondage in which people are victims and scapegoats are contrasted with the possibilities that are never allowed to take seed. Through this mechanism, Vijayan comments elaborately on the sorry situation that has come to stay, and the implications it has for people. Since he uses the conventions of literary satire, he also pays attention to the satiric norm, which makes the book complex and controversial. Normally, in a satirical work in which the images of exploitation and brutality and callous abuse of power are too pervasive, a satirist may not invoke any norms to make his satire credible and understandable. But because of the specific ambience in which Vijayan locates his work, he does implicitly weave norms in the texture of his book. These may take us in the realm of controversy, if we associate them with any kind of purposive action against the existing evils. It is important, therefore, that the function of norms be understood purely in literary terms, which is to heighten the satirical thrust, and not be construed as programmes of viable alternatives, as was the practice in the eighteenth century. In fact, the norms in the book are not reposed in any single person; they lie scattered. The reason for locating them within the texture of the book is to provide for a clearer understanding of the basis of Vijayan's attack.

Some norms, which have a direct bearing on the historical moment which Vijayan has satirized in the book are brought out in the series of contrasts worked into the movement of its plot. Vijayan constantly reminds us of the differences between what Dharmapuri aspired to be and what it actually became. For example, it aspired to be peaceful, and chose the celestial birds as its national symbol, but it was always prone to declaring and fighting wars for stabilising its corrupt power structures, as it did during the time of crisis. By spending its resources on war-preparations, it let poverty grow. This had grievous results, which are symbolized in the birth of blind children. Dharmapuri aspired to provide for its young ones all possible facilities for their development, but it actually promoted policies which benefited only a few. That is why we find that when "winter came, within the warm classrooms the children of the wealthy were taught the lore of the Celestial Birds, while the waifs froze on the sidewalks" (16). This is brought out in the trade of cadavers too: the poor and deprived people of the society have to part with their lives to provide money for the upkeep of the bureaucracy, the politicians, and the army personnel. Dharmapuri, in short, is a place distinguishable by the contrast between what it aspired to be and what it actually became.

Besides the norms implicit in these contrasts, which have significant political implications, norms are also radiated through two characters. The first one is the Mendicant, who is easily identifiable as Gandhi, whose presence has serious political and cultural importance. The first major reference to him occurs in Laavanya's conversation with Siddhaartha, in which she talks to him about the "lore of Dharmapuri" and its abiding traditions. For her the Mendicant was the "Father of our Nation" who had already died. It was widely believed that he would come back some day, even though it was treason to say so. Siddhaartha tells her that he had not died, but was in prison. When her husband Vaatsena goes to look for him there, he finds the Mendicant in penance for "the misspent freedoms of men" and later draws his attention to the "vast servitude sorround[ing]" his prison. For Vijayan, he embodies the ideal mode of fighting repression, which he used effectively against the British, and laments that he has been rendered useless by the corrupt system, when he should have been an inspiration for the people to fight the new oppression. If the ruling elite makes people forget him, it is because they fear the power of his message and methods.

The most complex figure in the book, however, is Siddhaartha. He looms large in the background of its action, as a voice of sanity and reason, to contrast with the oppression and inhumanity that is dramatized in the foregrounded action. When we see him right in the opening sections of the book, he has lucent locks and gentleness of manner. His questioning of the existing practices in Dharmapuri is Socratic in character, for he makes people see deficiencies in their thinking and practice. His spontaneous laughter of freedom is the most striking part of his personality. When it sinks into Paraashara, the first defence minister of Dharmapuri, he is awakened to the knowledge of his servitude, and gives up his position to be his own self. Siddhaartha brings cheer and peace to the oppressed people by keeping alive the possibilities of hope. During his journeys in Dharmapuri, he works relentlessly for spreading his message. When he is with Laavanya and her son Sunanda, he saves them from lapsing into a state of despondency. However, when Vijayan gives him magical powers and mystical knowledge, it creates complications. In the tunnel with Laavanya and her son, he stills a guardsman, because he was trying to create trouble for them. He also provides for the Night of the Bondsman. But once we accept that miraculous powers can be accommodated within the conventions of satire, then things fall into their place. For he functions like a prism through which we see the happenings in Dharampuri in their true colours. He stirs suppressed feelings of freedom in people and motivates them to move ahead in search of "cleansing waters," in which men, women, and children can experience love. It is because of Siddhaartha that several other possibilities which could have come into their own, but were not allowed to grow, actually flower. Kashyapa the tradesman is made to see the destructive potential of his trade, the devastation he had been causing by his wanton felling of trees, and the exploitative character of the mushrooming workhouses. Risking official wrath, he pleads with his workers to stop their operations. Like Kashyapa, Vedavrata too tells his workers not to do anything which would endanger free breeze and fruit trees and women's capacity to make love "long and deep." These are all suggestive of the renewal of good sense, which would result in peace and joy in Dharmapuri. It is true that at the end of the book, Siddhaartha is in some kind of despair, but he has done his job. To Paraashara, who has failed in his rebellion against the President, he offers love and compassion; for the rest, he keeps alive the hopes of renewal. He also provides a sane perspective on the conditions in Dharmapuri. He condemns what is undesirable, because it is anti-people, and thus makes us perceive, in all its pervasiveness, the horror of the eunuch voice of history.

Notes

1 For details on the various ways in which allegory provides for compositional and interpretive strains, see Jon Whitman (1-9).

2 Stephen Barney (16-17). This has also been clarified by Todorov: "We must insist on the fact that we cannot speak of allegory unless we find explicit indications of it within the text. Otherwise, we shift to what is no more than a reader's interpretation; and at this point every literary text would be allegorical, for it is the characteristic factor of literature to be endlessly interpreted and reinterpreted by its readers" (73-74).

3 Vijay Mishra goes to the extent of saying that "There is something so dreadfully imperialistic about this text that, in a moment of wilful generalization or enthusiasm, we may indeed claim that all Indian literary, filmic, and theatrical texts endlessly rewrite *The Mahabharata*" (334).

4 Prema Nandakumar has stated that the image of India as Draupadi, like a mother in chains, was used by Subramaniam Bharati (19).

5 Iravati Karve writes: "Besides giving a glimpse into that which is eternally human, old literature of this type makes one aware of cultural

alternatives in human choice, and also of the surprising fact that some of the newest literary and philosophical trends are but a new form of an old nagging" (19).

6 For an explication of the variety of techniques used by him, see Shyamala A Narayan (35-44).

7 Elitist historiography is not something special to Tharoor. Many historical accounts of the freedom struggle in India have an elitist bias. In fact, this has been the main complaint of the subalterns against virtually all accounts on the subject. Nevertheless, we cannot say that Tharoor does not make his points squarely. P K Rajan, with his pronounced Marxist bias, is somewhat unfair to Tharoor, when he writes that "The ruling concept of history in the novel seems to be basically flawed as it sees history as a gorgeous spectacle, a dexterous chess-play of heroic personages, a splendid pantomime in which men and women move about theatrically in their make-believe world...history becomes a splendid frame without much substance in it, a body without a soul" (28). To this one could say that a version of history which reassesses the role of leaders like Gandhi, Nehru, Jinnah, Jayaprakash Narayan, and Indira Gandhi cannot be dismissed as one without much substance.

Almost like Rajan, E V Ramakrishnan writes that "By equating Nathuram Godse with Shikhandin or Jaya Prakash Narayan with Drona no particular insight into the nature of Indian society is provided" (63). To this one could say that in a large allegorical frame, it is unfair to pick on one or two comparisons to denounce a writer. Besides, Tharoor certainly uses the Shikhandin episode to a telling effect: for exposing the weaknesses of Gandhi. Tharoor also has his own understanding of the character of Jayaprakash Narayan.

8 Hector Bolitho points out that Jinnah's dream of seeing India as one nation was destroyed by the rise of Gandhi's influence. He considered Gandhi a "Hindu revivalist," and a leader meant only for the Hindus, whose "power over them went deeper than politics—into subconscious instincts that were fused with their mysticism and their worship of many deities" (81-84). In his essay on the age of Gandhi, Ainslee T Embree makes a similar comment on Gandhi's use of Hindu vocabulary, etc, but in a slightly different manner: "...Muslim separatists, including Jinnah himself, did not denounce Gandhi for his use of religious vocabulary. On the contrary, they applauded him for his honesty in demonstrating that the Congress was a Hindu organization" (171).

9 In his book on the emergency, Sachchinanda Sinha writes about Jayaprakash Narayan somewhat slightingly, which comes very close to the view of Tharoor, that he "had no mass organisation nor had he any concrete programme beyond a proclamation of noble intentions. The chief support of his movement came from the educated youth. There was no doubt about their enthusiasm. But lacking any perception of the problems the nation faced and their solution, the youth movement could prove merely froth on the surface." (48).

10 For examples of sophisticated personae, see Alvin Kernan (1959, 116), Leonard Feinberg (239), and Robert C Elliott (188).

11 This brief discussion of the features of satire is based, besides Frye, on the work of Leonard Feinberg, Alvin Kernan and Ronald Paulson.

12 (Vijayan 1988, 99). The book is a translation by the author from the Malayalam version, first published in 1985.

13 We have already seen how like several historians and analysts Sahgal too holds this responsible for the ills of the country. In his essay on "The Emergency as a Signpost of India's Future," Ainslee Embree puts it clearly, when he states that "Indian nationalists had rejected the British rulers, but had not rejected the institutions the British had created in India before 1947. They had struggled for participation in those institutions, not their destruction" (179). This is the burden of Sinhas's book on the emergencycy. He points out that for enforcing her harsh measures, Mrs Gandhi did not need to create a special organisation, as Hitler had to do, because the administrative apparatus, both civil and police, was already there. The "seed of dictatorship was always there in the old apparatus"(87).

14 In her biography of Indira Gandhi, Pupul Jayakar writes that Jayaprakash thought that the emergency was the Soviet plot to replace the existing democracy by a totalitarian plan and later to replace Indira "by a Soviet stooge" (284).

15 Pupul Jayakar confirms that this was true in the case of Indira Gandhi. She did not hear anybody because "her advisers and the Intelligence agencies were sending her reports based on what they thought she would like to hear. They were afraid to speak the truth" (296).

16 Embree's contention is that ancillary institutions in India, such as the press, judiciary, and the universities have invariably acted as the creatures of the ruling power (176-77).

Select Bibliography

Aaron, Daniel. "Fictionalizing the Past." *Partisan Review* 47 (1980): 231-41.

Advani, Rukun. "Novelists in Residence." *Seminar 384* (August 1991): 13-16.

Adiswarananda, Swami. "Philosophy of History, the Hindu View" *Contemporary Indian Philosophy of History*. Ed. T M P Mahadevan and Grace E Cairns. Calcutta: The World Press, 1977: 21-58.

Ahmad, Aijaz. "Rushdie's *Shame*: Postmodernism, Migrancy and Representation of Women." *Economic and Political Weekly* 15 June 1991: 1461-71.

Anand, Mulk Raj. *Across the Black Waters*. 1940. Delhi: Orient Books, 1980.

———. *Apology for Heroism*. 1946. Arnold-Heinemann, 1986.

———. *The Big Heart*. 1945. New Delhi: Arnold Publishers, 1980.

———. *The Bubble: A Novel*. New Delhi: Arnold-Heinemann, 1984.

———. *Confessions of a Lover*. New Delhi: Arnold-Heinemann, 1976.

———. *Coolie*. 1936. New Delhi: Arnold Publishers, 1981.

———. *Gauri*. New Delhi: Arnold-Heinemann, 1981.

———. *Homage to Tagore*. Lahore: Sangam Publishers, 1946.

———. *Is There a Contemporary Indian Civilisation?* Bombay: Asia Publishing House, 1963.

———. *Morning Face*. Bombay: Kutub Popular, 1968.

———. "A Note on Modern Indian Fiction." *Indian Literature* 8.1 (1965): 44-57.

———. "Old Myth New Myth, Recital Versus Novel." In *Indian Literature of the Last Fifty Years: 1917-1967*. Ed. C D Narasimhaiah. Mysore: Univ of Mysore, 1970.

———. *The Private Life of an Indian Prince*. 1953. New Delhi: Arnold-Heinemann, 1983.

———. *Seven Summers: A Novel*. 1951. New Delhi: Arnold-Heinemann, 1987.

———. "The Sources of Protest in My Novels." *Littcrit* 18.4 (1983): 1-12.

———. "The Story of My Experiment with a White Lie." *Indian Literature* 10.3 (1967): 28-43.

———. *The Sword and the Sickle.* 1942. London: Asia Publishing House, 1986.

———. *Two Leaves and a Bud.* 1937. New Delhi: Arnold Publishers, 1981.

———. "An Undeclared War." *Littcrit* 3.1 (1977): 11-24.

———. *Untouchable.* 1935. New Delhi: Arnold Publishers, 1970.

———. *The Village.* Bombay: Kutub Popular, 1960.

Ankersmit, F R. "Historiography and Postmodernism." *History and Theory* 28, 2 (1989): 137-53.

Asthana, Pratima. *The Indian View of History.* Agra: M G Publishers, 1992.

Aurobindo, Sri. *The Foundations of Indian Culture.* Pondicherry: Sri Aurobindo Asharam Trust, 1980.

Bakhtin, M M. *The Dialogic Imagination: Four Essays.* Trans. Caryl Emerson and Michael Holquist. Austin: Univ of Texas Press, 1981.

Bald, Suresht Renjen. *Novelists and Political Consciousness.* Delhi: Chanakya Publications, 1982.

Barnes, Harry Elmer. *A History of Historical Writing.* 2nd rev ed. New York: Dover Publications, 1962.

Barney, Stephen. *Allegories of History, Allegories of Love.* Hamden, Connecticut: Archon Books, 1979.

Barthes, Roland. "Historical Discourse." *Structuralism: A Reader.* Ed. Michael Lane. London: Jonathan Cape, 1970.

Barucha, Rustom. "A View from India." *Peter Brooke and the* Mahabharata*: Critical Perspectives.* Ed. David Williams. London: Routledge, 1991.

Basu, Aparna. "Women's History in India: An Historiographical Survey." *Writing Women's History: International Perspectives.* Ed. Karen Offen *et al.* London: Macmillan, 1991.

Berger, Morroe. *Real and Imagined Worlds: The Novel and Social Science.* Cambridge, Mass.: Harvard Univ Press, 1977.

Bernbaum, Ernest. "The Views of the Great Critics on the Historical Novel." *PMLA* 41 (June 1926): 424-441.

Berry, Margaret. *Mulk Raj Anand: The Man and the Novelist.* Amsterdam: Oriental Press, 1971.

Bhatnagar, M K. *Political Consciousness in Indian English Writing: A Study of Manohar Malgonkar, Nayantara Sahgal and Bhabani Bhattacharya.* New Delhi: Bahri Publications, 1991.

Bhattacharya, Kalidas. "The Meaning and Significance of Social Revolution and the Idea of Progress in Hegelian, Marxian and Indian Philosophies of History." Ed. Mahadevan and Cairns. Calcutta: The World Press, 1971.

Bolitho, Hector. *Jinnah: Creator of Pakistan.* London: John Murray, 1954.

Bourne, Bill *et al* eds. *Voices: Writers and Politics.* Nottingham: Atlantic Highlands, 1987.

Braudy, Leo. *Narrative Form in History and Fiction: Hume, Fielding, and Gibbon.* Princeton, N.J.: Princeton Univ Press, 1970.

Bremner, Robert, ed. *Essays on History and Literature.* Athens, Ohio: Ohio State Univ Press, 1966.

Brigg, Peter. "Salman Rushdie's Novels: The Disorder in Fantastic Order." *World Literature Written in English* 27.1 (Spring 1987): 119-30.

Burke, Peter. *History and Social Theory.* Cambridge: Polity Press, 1992.

Carroll, David. *The Subject in Question: The Languages of Theory and the Strategies of Fiction.* Chicago: The Univ of Chicago Press, 1982.

Cauto, Maria. "Midnight's Children and Parents: The Search for Indo-British Identity." *Encounter* 58.2 (1982): 61-66.

Chandra, Bipan, *et al. India's Struggle for Independence.* New Delhi: Penguin Books, 1988.

Chaudhuri, Nirad. *The Intellectual in India.* New Delhi: Vir Publishing House, 1967.

Chatterjee, Partha. "History and the Nationalization of Hinduism." *Social Research* 59.1 (Spring 1992): 111-49.

Clark, T W, ed. *The Novel in India: Its Birth and Development.* London: George Allen and Unwin, 1970.

Collingwood, R G. *The Idea of History.* 1946. London: Oxford Paperbacks, 1961.

Cowasjee, Saros. "Anand's Literary Creed." *Journal of Indian Writing in English* 1.1 (January 1973): 66-71.

———. *Author to Critic: The Letters of Mulk Raj Anand.* Calcutta: Writers Workshop, 1973.

———. "Mulk Raj Anand: The Fusion of History and Fiction." *Subjects Worthy of Fame*. Ed. A L Mcleod. New Delhi: Sterling Publishers, 1989.

———. *So Many Freedoms: A Study of the Major Fiction of Mulk Raj Anand*. Delhi: Oxford Univ Press, 1977.

Craig, David. "Lukacs' Views on How History Moulds Literature." *Georg Lukacs: The Man, His Work, and His Ideas*. Ed. G H R Parkinson. New York: Vintage Books, 1970.

Crane, Ralph J. *Inventing India: A History of India in English-Language Fiction*. London: Macmillan, 1992.

Crosby, Christina. *The Ends of History*. New York and London: Routledge, 1991.

Deshpande, V.V. "Itihasa and Purana in Hindu Purusartha Vidyas." *Contemporary Indian Philosophies of History*. Ed. T M P Mahadevan and Grace E. Cairns. Calcutta: The World Press, 1977: 137-66.

Devahuti, ed. *Bias in Indian Historiography*. Delhi: D K Publications, 1980.

———, ed. *Problems of Indian Historiography*. Delhi: D K Publications, 1979.

Dewey, John. "Historical Judgments. *The Philosophy of History in Our Time*. Ed. Hans Meyerhoff. Garden City, N.Y.: Doubleday, 1959.

Dhar, T N. "Clio and Contemporary American Fiction." *Indian Journal of English Studies* 26 (1987): 53-61.

———. "Consciousness Raising in a Cultural Frame: The Fiction of Mulk Raj Anand before 1947." *Social Awareness in Modern Indian Literature*. Ed. R K Kaul and Jaidev. Shimla: Indian Institute of Advanced Study, 1993.

———. "Micro-Macro Symbiosis: The Form of Salman Rushdie's *Midnight's Children*." *Journal of Indian Writing in English* 13.1 (January 1985): 16-23.

———. "The Use of the Historical Method by Indian English Critics: An Evaluation." *The Literary Criterion* 25.1 (1990): 71-83.

Dhawan, R K, ed. *Indian Women Novelists*, Set II, Vols IV and V. New Delhi: Prestige Books, 1993.

Elliott, Robert C. *The Power of Satire: Magic, Ritual, Art*. Princeton, N.J.: Princeton Univ Press, 1960.

Embree, Ainslee T. *Imagining India: Essays on Indian History*. Ed. Mark Juergensmay. Delhi: Oxford Univ Press, 1989.

Episto, Joseph. *Transcendence of History: Essays on the Evolution of Historical Consciousness*. Athens, Ohio: Ohio Univ Press, 1984.

Feinberg, Leonard. *Introduction to Satire*. Ames, Iowa: Iowa Univ Press, 1967.

Ferrier, Carole. "Historical Fiction and Fictional History: An Interview with Valerie Miner." *Meanjin* 46.4 (December 1987): 546-56.

Fielding, Henry. *Jonathan Wild and the Journal of a Voyage to Lisbon*. London: J M Dent, 1973.

Fisher, Marlene. *Wisdom of the Heart: Novels of Mulk Raj Anand*. New Delhi: Sterling Publishers, 1985.

Fisher, P P. "Providence, Fate, and the Historical Imagination in Scott's *The Heart of Midlothian*." *Walter Scott*. Ed. D D Delvin. London: Macmillan, 1968.

Fleischer, Helmut. *Marxism and History*. 1969. London: Allen Lane, The Penguin Press, 1973.

Fleishman, Avrom. *The English Historical Novel: Walter Scott to Virginia Woolf*. Baltimore and London: The Johns Hopkins Press, 1971.

Fletcher, M D. "An Annotated Bibliography of Articles about Salman Rushdie's Fiction." *Journal of Indian Writing in English* 20.1-2 (January-July 1992): 6-23.

———. "Rushdie's *Shame*: Political Satire and Fantasy." *Contemporary Political Satire: Narrative Strategies in the Post-Modern Context*. Lanham: Univ Press of America, 1987.

Foote, Shelby. "The Novelist's View of History." *Sewanee Review* 99.3 (Summer 1991): 439-45.

Foucault, Michel. *The Archeology of Knowledge*. Trans. M Sheridan Smith. New York: Pantheon Books, 1972.

Frye, Northrop. *Anatomy of Criticism: Four Essays*. Princeton, N.J.: Princeton Univ Press, 1957.

Gallie, W B. *Philosophy and the Historical Understanding*. London: Chatto and Windus, 1964.

Gandhi, M K. *Hind Swaraj or Indian Home Rule*. Ahmedabad: Navjivan Press, n.d.

———. *The Removal of Untouchability*. Compiled and ed. Bharatan Kumarappa. Ahmedabad: Navjivan Publishing House, 1954.

Gardiner, Juliet, ed. *What is History Today...?* London: Macmillan Education, 1988.

Gasset, Jose Ortega y. *History as a System and Other Essays: Towards a Philosophy of History*. 1941. New York: W W Norton, 1962.

Ghoshal, U N. *Studies in Indian History and Culture*. 2nd rev ed. Calcutta: Orient Longmans, 1965.

Gokhale, B G. "Gandhi and History." *History and Theory* 11.2 (1972): 214-25.

Gramsci, Antonio. *Selections from Political Writings: 1910-1920*. Selected and ed. Quintin Hoare. London: Lawrence and Wishart, 1977.

Green, Anne. *Flaubert and the Historical Novel: 'Salambo' Reassessed*. Cambridge: Cambridge Univ Press, 1982.

Grossman, Lionel. *Between History and Literature*. Cambridge, Mass.: Harvard Univ Press, 1990.

Haldar, M K. *Foundations of Nationalism in India: A Study of Bankim Chandra Chatterjee*. Delhi: Ajanta Publications, 1989.

Hale, J R, ed. *The Evolution of British Historiography*. London: Macmillan, 1967.

Haliwell, Stephen. *The Poetics of Aristotle*. Trans. and commentary. London: Gerald Duckworth, 1987.

Hardy, P. *Historians of Medieval India: Studies in Indo-Muslim Historical Writing*. London: Luzac & Company, 1960.

Hassan, Mohibbul, ed. *Historians of Medieval India*. Meerut: Meenakshi Prakashan, 1968.

Henderson, Harry B. *Versions of the Past: The Historical Imagination in American Fiction*. New York: Oxford Univ Press, 1974.

Hexter, J H. *Reappraisals in History*. London: Longmans, Green, 1961.

Hollington, Michael. "Salman Rushdie's *Shame*." *Meanjin* 43.3 (September 1984): 403-7.

Hume, Kathryn. *Fantasy and Mimesis: Responses to Reality in Western Literature*. New York and London: Methuen, 1984.

Humphreys, R Stephen. *Islamic History: A Framework for Inquiry*. Rev ed. London: I B Tauris, 1991.

Hunt, Lynn. *The New Cultural History*. Berkeley: Univ of California Press, 1989.

Hutcheon, Linda. 'The Pastime of Past time': Fiction, History, Historiographic Metafiction." *Genre* 20 3-4 (Fall-Winter 1987): 285-305.

———. *A Poetics of Postmodernism: History, Theory, Fiction*. New York and London: Routledge, 1988.

———. *The Politics of Postmodernism*. New York: Routledge, 1989.

———. "Subject In/Of/To History and His Story." *Diacritics* 16.1 (Spring 1986): 78.

Iyenger, K R Srinivasa. *Indian Writing in English.* Rev and updated edition. New Delhi: Sterling Publishers, 1985.

Iyer, Raghavan N. "Gandhi's Interpretation of History." *Gandhi Marg* 6.4 (1962): 319-27.

Jain, Jasbir. *Nayantara Sahgal.* New Delhi: Arnold-Heinemann, 1978.

James, Henry. *The Art of Fiction and Other Essays.* New York: Oxford Univ Press, 1974.

Jameson, Fredric. *The Political Unconscious: Narrative as a Socially Symbolic Act.* London: Methuen, 1981.

Jayakar, Pupul. *Indira Gandhi: A Biography.* New Delhi: Penguin Viking India, 1992.

Jayaraju, M A. "A S P Ayyar as the Father of the Indian Historical Novel." *Indian English Literature Since Independence.* Ed. K Ayyappa Paniker. New Delhi: The Indian Association for English Studies, 1991.

Jha, Rama. *Gandhian Thought and Indo-Anglian Novelists.* Delhi: Chanakya Publications, 1983.

———. "Interview with Nayantara Sahgal." *Indian Literary Review* 1.1 (May 1978): 6-14.

Johnston, John. "Postmodern Theory/ Postmodern Fiction." *Clio* 16.2 (Winter 1987): 139-58.

Kanaganayakam C. "Myth and Fabulosity in *Midnight's Children.*" *Dalhousie Review* 67.1 (Spring 1987): 87-98.

Karve, Iravati. *Yuganta.* Poona: Deshmukh Prakashan, 1969.

Keith, A B. *A History of Sanskrit Literature.* London: Oxford Univ Press, 1920.

Kernan, Alvin. *The Cankered Muse: Satire of the English Renaissance.* New Haven: Yale Univ Press, 1959.

———. *The Plot of Satire.* New Haven: Yale Univ Press, 1965.

Ketchum, Richard M. "Memory as History." *American Heritage* (November 1991): 142-48.

Kirpal, Viney, ed. *The New Indian Novel in English: A Study of the 1980s.* New Delhi: Allied Publishers, 1990.

Kramer, Lloyd S. "Literature, Criticism, and Historical Imagination: The Literary Challenge of Hayden White and Dominick LaCapra." *The New Cultural History.* Ed. Lynn Hunt. Berkeley: Univ of California Press, 1989.

Kreiger, Murray. "Fiction, History, and Empirical Reality." *Critical Inquiry* 1.2 (1974).

Kumar, Ravinder. *Essays in the Social History of Modern India*. Delhi: Oxford Univ Press, 1983.

———. *The Making of a Nation: Essays in Indian History and Politics*. New Delhi: Manohar Publications, 1989.

Kundera, Milan. *The Art of the Novel*. Trans. Linda Asher. 1986; London: Faber and Faber, 1988.

LaCapra, Dominick. *History and Criticism*. Ithaca: Cornell Univ Press, 1985.

———. *Rethinking Intellectual History: Texts, Contexts, Language*. Ithaca: Cornell Univ Press, 1983.

Laurence, Margaret. "Ivory Tower or Grassroots?: The Novelist as a Socio-Political Being." *A Political Art: Essays and Images in Honour of George Woodcock*. Ed. William H New. Vancouver: The Univ of British Columbia Press, 1978.

Leclair, Tom and Larry McCaffery, eds. *Anything Can Happen: Interviews with Contemporary American Novelists*. Urbana: Univ of Illinois Press, 1983.

Lehan, Richard. "The Theoretical Limits of the New Historicism." *New Literary History* 21.3 (Spring 1990): 533-53.

Lerner, Laurence. *The Frontiers of Literature*. Oxford: Basil Blackwell, 1988.

Lindsay, Jack. *The Elephant and the Lotus: A Study of the Novels of Mulk Raj Anand*. Rev ed. Bombay: Kutub Popular, 1965.

"Literary Imagination and the Sense of the Past." *Salmagundi* 68- 69 (Fall 1985-Winter 1986): 19-367.

Lodge, David. "Milan Kundera, and the Idea of the Author in Modern Criticism." *Critical Quarterly* 26.1-2 (1984): 105-21.

Lukacs, Georg. *The Historical Novel*. Trans Hannah and Stanley Mitchell. London: Merlin Press, 1962.

Mahadevan, T M P. "History in Ancient India." *Readings in Indian History, Politics and Philosophy*.. Ed. K Satchidananda Murty. London: George Allen and Unwin, 1967.

Majumdar, R C. *Historiography in Modern India*. Bombay: Asia Publishing House, 1970.

Malek, Amin. "Reading the Crisis: The Polemics of Salman Rushdie's *The Satanic Verses*." *Ariel* 20.4 (October 1989): 176-86.

Mandelbaum, Maurice. "A Note on History as Narrative." *History and Theory* 6 (1967): 413-19.

"Mandelbaum on Historical Narrative: A Discussion." *History and Theory* 8 (1969): 275-94.

Manzoni, Allesandro. *On Historical Novel.* Trans Sandra Bernman. Lincoln: Univ of Nebraska Press, 1984.

Marshall, Brenda K. *Teaching the Postmodern: Fiction and Theory.* New York and London: Routledge, 1992.

McLennan, Gregor. *Marxism and the Methodologies of History.* London: Verso, 1981.

Merivale, Patricia. "Saleem Fathered by Oskar: Intertextual Strategies in *Midnight's Children* and *The Tin Drum.*" *Ariel* 21.3 (July 1990): 5-21.

Miller, J Hillis. "Narrative and History." *ELH* 40.3 (1974): 455-73.

Millgate, Jane. *Macaulay.* London: Routledge and Kegan Paul, 1973.

Mink, Louis O. "History and Fiction as Modes of Comprehension." *New Directions in Literary Theory.* Ed. Ralph Cohen. London: Routledge and Kegan Paul, 1974.

Mishra, Vijay. "The Great Indian Epic and Peter Brook." *Meanjin* 47.2 (Winter 1988): 343-52.

Mukerjee, Hiren. *Recalling India's Struggle for Freedom.* Delhi: Seema Publications, 1983.

Mukherjee, Arun. "Whose Post-Colonialism and Whose Postmodernism?" *World Literature Written in English* 30.2 (Autumn 1990): 1-9.

Mukherjee, Meenakshi. *Realism and Reality: The Novel and Society in India.* Delhi: Oxford Univ Press, 1985.

Mukhia, Harbans. *Historians and Historiography during the Reign of Akbar.* New Delhi: Vikas Publishing House, 1976.

Murty, K Satchidananda, ed. *Readings in Indian History, Politics and Philosophy.* London: George Allen and Unwin, 1967.

"My Favorite Historical Novel." *American Heritage* (October 1992): 84-107.

Nair, Rukmini Bhaya. "The Voyeur's View in *Midnight's Children* and *Shame.*" *ACLALS Bulletin*, 7th Series, 1 (1985): 57-75.

Nandakumar, Prema. "Shashi Tharoor's Karna." *Littcrit* 16.1-2 (June-December 1990): 17-26.

Nandy, Ashish. *The Intimate Enemy: Loss and Recovery of Self under Colonialism.* Delhi: Oxford Univ Press, 1983.

Narayan, Shyamala A. "Verbal Pyrotechnics: A Note on *The Great Indian Novel.*" *Littcrit* 16.1-2 (June-December 1990): 35-44.

Nehru, Jawaharlal. *Glimpses of World History.* Vol 1. Allahabad: Kitabistan, 1934.

———. *The Discovery of India.* Calcutta: The Signet Press, 1946.

Newman, Judie. "Bellow's Sixth Sense: The Sense of History." In *Saul Bellow in the 1980s: A Collection of Critical Essays.* Ed. Gloria L Cronin and L H Goldman. 1989. New Delhi: Affiliated East-West Press, 1992.

———. *Saul Bellow and History.* London: The Macmillan Press, 1984.

Ngugi wa Thiong'o. *Homecoming: Essays on African and Caribbean Literature, Culture and Politics.* 1972. New York: Lawrence Hill, 1973.

Nizami, K A. *On History and Historians of Medieval India.* New Delhi: Munshiram Manoharlal, 1983.

Pannikar, Raimundo. "Time and History in the Tradition of India: Kala and Karma." *Cultures and Time.* Paris: The Unesco Press, 1976.

Parameswaran, Uma. "Manohar Malgonkar as a Historical Novelist." *World Literature Written in English,* 14.2 (November 1975): 329-38.

Paranjape, Makarand. "Inside and Outside the Whale: Politics and the New English Novel." *The New Indian Novel in English: A Study of the 1980s.* Ed. Viney Kirpal. New Delhi: Allied Publishers, 1990.

Parekh, Bikhu. *Colonialism, Tradition, and Reform: An Analysis of Gandhi's Political Discourse.* New Delhi: Sage Publications, 1989.

Pattanayak, Chandrabhanu. "Interview with Salman Rushdie." *The Literary Criterion* 18.3 (1983): 19-22.

Paulson, Ronald, ed. *Satire: Modern Essays in Criticism.* Englewood Cliffs, N.J.: Prentice-Hall, 1971.

Pontes, Hilda. *Nayantara Sahgal.* New Delhi: Concept Publishing Co, 1985.

Poster, Mark. "Foucault, the Present and History." *Cultural Critique* 8 (Winter 1987-88).

Rajan, P K. "History and Myth in *The Great Indian Novel.*" *Littcrit* 16.1-2 (June- December 1990): 27-31.

Ramakrishnan, E V. "The Politics of Language and the Language of Politics." *Littcrit* 16.1-2 (June-December 1990): 55-69.

Ramamurti, K S. *Rise of the Indian Novel in English.* New Delhi: Sterling Publishers, 1987.

Rao, A V Krishna. *Nayantara Sahgal: A Study of Her Fiction and Non-Fiction.* Madras: M Seshachalan & Co, 1976.

———. "Nayantara Sahgal's Recent Fictions of History: A Study." *Essays in Criticism on Indian Literature in English.* Ed. M S Nagarajan *et al.* New Delhi: S Chand, 1991.

Riemenschneider, D. *An Ideal of Man in Anand's Novels*. Bombay: I Popular, n.d.

———. "History and Individual in Salman Rushdie's *Midnight's dren* and Anita Desai's *Clear Light of Day*." *Kunapipi* 6.2 (1 53-66.

Ross, Andrew, ed. *Universal Abandon: The Politics of Postmoder* Minneapolis: Univ of Minnesota Press, 1966.

Rushdie, Salman. "'Errata': Unreliable Narration in *Midnight's* (*dren*." *A Sense of Place: Essays in Post-Colonial Literatures*. Ed. B Olinder. Gothenburg: Gothenburg Univ, 1984.

———. *Imaginary Homelands: Essays and Criticism: 1981-1991*. I Delhi: Penguin Viking India, 1991.

———. "Interview with Rushdie." *Kunapipi* 4.2 (1982): 17-26.

———. *Midnight's Children*. London: Jonathan Cape, 1981.

———. "Rushdie's *Midnight's Children* and *Shame*: Lecture/Intervie *Kunapipi* 8.1 (1985): 1-19.

———. *Shame*. London: Jonathan Cape, 1983.

———. *The Jaguar Smile: A Nicaraguan Journey*. 1987. New Yo Penguin Books, 1988.

Sahgal, Nayantara. *A Situation in New Delhi*. 1977. New Delhi: Pengu Books, 1988.

———. *A Time to be Happy*. 1957. New Delhi: Sterling Paperbacl 1975.

———. *A Voice for Freedom*. Delhi: Hind Pocket Books, 1977.

———. *From Fear Set Free*. London: Victor Gollancz, 1962.

———. *Indira Gandhi's Emergence and Style*. New Delhi: Vikas Pul lishing House, 1978.

———. *Indira Gandhi: Her Road to Power*. 1982. London: Macdonal & Co, 1983.

———. *Prison and Chocolate Cake*. 1954. Bombay: Jaico Books.

———. *Rich Like Us*. 1983. Sceptre Books, 1987.

———. *Storm in Chandigarh*. 1969. New Delhi: Penguin Books, 1988.

———. *The Day in Shadow*. 1971. New Delhi: Penguin Books, 1991.

———. *This Time of Morning*. New York: W W Norton, 1965.

Samantarai, Dipak. "A Conversation with Mulk Raj Anand." *Chandrabhaga* 9-10 (Summer-Winter 1983): 113-23.

Sarkar, Sumit. *Modern India: 1885-1947*. Madras: Macmillan India, 1983.

Seamon, Roger. "Narrative Practice and the Theoretical Distinction between History and Fiction." *Genre* 16.3 (Fall 1983): 197-18.

Selmon, Stephen. "Post-Colonial Allegory and the Transformation of History." *Journal of Commonwealth Literature* 23.1 (1988): 157-68.

Sen, S P, ed. *History in Modern Indian Literature*. Calcutta: Institute of Historical Studies, 1975.

Shaw, Harry E. *The Forms of Historical Fiction: Sir Walter Scott and His Successors*. Ithaca and London: Cornell Univ Press, 1983.

Singh, Bhupal. *A Survey of Anglo-Indian Fiction*. 1934. London: Curzon Press, 1974.

Singhal, D P. *Nationalism in India and Other Historical Essays*. New Delhi: Munshiram Manoharlal, 1967.

Sinha, Sachchinanda. *Emergency in Perspective: Reprieve and Challenge*. New Delhi: Heritage, 1977.

Srivastava, Aruna. "'The Empire Writes Back': Language and History in *Shame* and *Midnight's Children*." *Ariel* 29.4 (October 1989): 62-78.

Stanton and Vidal, eds. *Views from a Window: Conversations with Gore Vidal*. Syracuse, N.J.: Lyle Stuart, 1980.

Strout, Cushing. "The Voracious Imagination." *Partisan Review* 50 (1983): 428-43.

Subramanian, N. *Historiography*. Madurai: Koodal Publishers, 1978.

Swann, Joseph. "'East is East and West is West?': Salman Rushdie's *Midnight's Children* as an Indian Novel." *World Literature Written in English* 26.2 (Autumn 1986): 353-62.

Swinfen, Ann. *In Defence of Fantasy*. London: Routledge and Kegan Paul, 1984.

Thackeray, W M. *The History of Henry Esmond*. London: J M Dent, 1963.

Tharoor, Shashi. "Myth, History, and Fiction." *Seminar* 384 (August 1991): 30-31.

———. *The Great Indian Novel*. New Delhi: Penguin Books, 1989.

———. "Yoking of Myth to History." *Littcrit* 16.1-2 (June-December 1990): 5-8.

Tickner, F J, ed. *Modern Historical Fiction*. New Delhi: Deep and Deep Publications, 1990.

Todorov, Tzvetan. *The Fantastic: A Structural Approach to a Literary Genre*. 1973. Ithaca: Cornell Univ Press, 1975.

Toynbee, Arnold J. *A Study of History*. Abridged D C Somervell. London: Oxford Univ Press, 1960.

Trevor-Roper, Hugh. "History and Imagination." *History and Imagination*. Ed. Hugh Lloyd-Jones *et al.* London: Gerald Duckworth, 1981.

Turner, Joseph W. "The Kinds of Historical Fiction: An Essay in Definition and Methodology." *Genre* 12 (Fall 1979): 333-55.

Vijayan, O V. *After the Hanging and Other Stories*. New Delhi: Penguin Books, 1989.

———. *The Saga of Dharmapuri*. New Delhi: Penguin Books, 1988.

Walsh, W H. *An Introduction to Philosophy of History*. London: Hutchinson, 1951.

Warder, A K. *An Introduction to Indian Historiography*. Bombay: Popular Prakashan, 1972.

———. "The Pali Canon and Its Commentaries as an Historical Record." *Historians of India, Pakistan and Ceylon*. Ed. C H Philips. London: Oxford Univ Press, 1961.

Watson-Williams, Helen. "An Antique Land: Salman Rushdie's *Shame*." *Westerly* 29.4 (December 1984): 37-45.

Weinryb, Elazar. "If We Write Novels So, How Shall We Write History?" *Clio* 16.2 (Winter 1987): 139-58.

White, Hayden. *Metahistory: The Historical Imagination in Nineteenth-Century Europe*. 1973. Baltimore and London: The Johns Hopkins Univ Press, 1975.

———. *The Content of Form: Narrative Discourse and Historical Representation*. Baltimore and London: The Johns Hopkins Univ Press, 1987.

———. "The Question of Narrative in Contemporary Historical Theory." *History and Theory* 23 (1984): 1-33.

———. *Tropics of Discourse: Essays in Cultural Criticism*. Baltimore and London: The Johns Hopkins Univ Press, 1982.

Whitman, Jon. *Allegory: The Dynamics of an Ancient and Medieval Technique*. Oxford: Clarendon Press, 1987.

Wilson, Keith. "*Midnight's Children* and Reader Responsibility." *Critical Quarterly* 26.3 (Autumn 1984): 23-37.

Index